GASTRO GRILLING

ALSO BY TED READER

Beerlicious

The Complete Idiot's Guide to Smoking Foods

Napoleon's Everyday Gourmet Grilling

Napoleon's Everyday Gourmet Plank Grilling

Napoleon's Everyday Gourmet Burgers

King of the Q's Blue Plate BBQ

The Art of Plank Grilling

Hot and Sticky BBQ

Hot, Sticky, and on Fire

On Fire in the Kitchen

Sticky Fingers and Tenderloins

GASTRO GRILLING

FIRED-UP RECIPES TO GRILL GREAT EVERYDAY MEALS

TED READER

PINTAIL

PINTAIL
a member of Penguin Group (USA)

Published by the Penguin Group
Penguin Canada Books Inc., 90 Eglinton Avenue East, Suite 700, Toronto, Ontario, Canada M4P 2Y3

Penguin Group (USA) Inc., 375 Hudson Street, New York, New York 10014, U.S.A.
Penguin Books Ltd, 80 Strand, London WC2R 0RL, England
Penguin Ireland, 25 St Stephen's Green, Dublin 2, Ireland (a division of Penguin Books Ltd)
Penguin Group (Australia), 250 Camberwell Road, Camberwell, Victoria 3124, Australia
(a division of Pearson Australia Group Pty Ltd)
Penguin Books India Pvt Ltd, 11 Community Centre, Panchsheel Park, New Delhi – 110 017, India
Penguin Group (NZ), 67 Apollo Drive, Rosedale, Auckland 0632, New Zealand
(a division of Pearson New Zealand Ltd)
Penguin Books (South Africa) (Pty) Ltd, 24 Sturdee Avenue, Rosebank, Johannesburg 2196, South Africa

Penguin Books Ltd, Registered Offices: 80 Strand, London WC2R 0RL, England

First published in Penguin paperback by Penguin Canada, 2013
Published in this edition, 2014

1 2 3 4 5 6 7 8 9 10 (CR)

Copyright © Ted Reader, 2013

Food photographer: Mike McColl
Assistant food photographer: Lee Waddington
Principal food stylist: Mia Bachmaier

Manufactured in the U.S.A.

ISBN: 978-0-14-319004-2

Visit the Penguin US website at **www.penguin.com**

GASTRO GRILLING

FIRED-UP RECIPES TO GRILL GREAT EVERYDAY MEALS

TED READER

PINTAIL

PINTAIL
a member of Penguin Group (USA)

Published by the Penguin Group
Penguin Canada Books Inc., 90 Eglinton Avenue East, Suite 700, Toronto, Ontario, Canada M4P 2Y3

Penguin Group (USA) Inc., 375 Hudson Street, New York, New York 10014, U.S.A.
Penguin Books Ltd, 80 Strand, London WC2R 0RL, England
Penguin Ireland, 25 St Stephen's Green, Dublin 2, Ireland (a division of Penguin Books Ltd)
Penguin Group (Australia), 250 Camberwell Road, Camberwell, Victoria 3124, Australia
(a division of Pearson Australia Group Pty Ltd)
Penguin Books India Pvt Ltd, 11 Community Centre, Panchsheel Park, New Delhi – 110 017, India
Penguin Group (NZ), 67 Apollo Drive, Rosedale, Auckland 0632, New Zealand
(a division of Pearson New Zealand Ltd)
Penguin Books (South Africa) (Pty) Ltd, 24 Sturdee Avenue, Rosebank, Johannesburg 2196, South Africa

Penguin Books Ltd, Registered Offices: 80 Strand, London WC2R 0RL, England

First published in Penguin paperback by Penguin Canada, 2013
Published in this edition, 2014

1 2 3 4 5 6 7 8 9 10 (CR)

Copyright © Ted Reader, 2013

Food photographer: Mike McColl
Assistant food photographer: Lee Waddington
Principal food stylist: Mia Bachmaier

Manufactured in the U.S.A.

ISBN: 978-0-14-319004-2

Visit the Penguin US website at **www.penguin.com**

To the loves of my life, my wife, Pamela,
and my children, Layla and Jordan,
you are my inspiration. Thank you,
my family, for all you do for me.

CONTENTS

INTRODUCTION

WHAT IS GASTRO GRILLING?

The word "gastro" comes from "gastronomy," and most people seem to think that means pretentious. Understandable, given the way the word is thrown around these days. It shouldn't be known this way, but it sort of is. For the last 10 years or so, we have seen the word "gastro" get itself attached to endless other words. Probably best known are the "gastro pubs" still popping up all over the place.

Gastro does not imply pretentious when I'm involved. Gastronomy means "the art and science of good eating." There are other definitions in play, but I like this one. It's simple and the truth and unpretentious, like me and my food. Gastro grilling is aimed at the man or woman who, like me, loves to fire up the grill any time of the year and turn an everyday meal into a gastronomic delight. They fancy themselves gastronomes and consider grilling and cooking over the hot fire a hobby, not a chore.

Food is a thing we nourish ourselves with. We all know at least one person for whom food is a big nuisance. It gets eaten over sinks and in cars and is rarely tasted and appreciated. It's kind of like filling your gas tank. Anyone who knows me or my books knows that that is as far from what I represent as you can get. Food is for fun and savoring and sharing with friends. There is as much pleasure in its preparation as in its eating. The enthusiastic "gastro griller" takes pride in their ingredients, sourcing out the best and freshest ingredients as well as mixing in a bit of grocery convenience. They create delicious feasts for the senses right in their own backyards. The "gastrosexual" is keen to have that deliciousness bring them the spoils of praise, pleasure and possibly even seduction.

I am never happier than when I am in my backyard playing eeny meeny miney mo choosing the grill, or grills, I'll use next. Even happier when I hear the snap, crackle of new wood getting ready for me to start cooking. Happiest of all after I've singed the hair off both arms and burned myself at least twice. I just love to cook. I love to cook best in my own backyard with my family and friends and kids and dogs all around me. I love to cook any old place at all, as long as there's a grill and some smiles and maybe a few beers in a cooler. But my backyard is where I really get my glow on.

The true purpose of the first gastro pubs in the UK was to take typical bar food and raise it to a level that would surprise even the most discerning palate. They used superior ingredients; often a gastro pub has its own garden for fresh produce. They make their own takes on traditional recipes, and add in a few surprises. How often do you expect to see a Caramel Shrimp Banh Mi on a pub menu? The overall idea seemed to be make it really good, make it affordable and make it fun.

I think we all know that I stand for fun. So the more I heard this term, the more I found myself interested in exploring it. But the more pretentious the establishment I might wander into was, the surer I was that fun was getting lost. I'm all about fresh ingredients and twisting things in my own crazy ways. Gastro grilling seemed like something I should, if not invent, at least reinvent. It's about cooking food that I love. In *Gastro Grilling*, you will find recipes for that special gastrosexual in your family, such as Fire-Roasted Oysters with Crawfish Bacon BBQ Butter (page 44) or Grilled Squid with Grilled Prosciutto-Wrapped Radicchio & Caper Balsamic Sauce (page 312) or Grill-Blackened Turkey Tenderloins with Celery Blue Cheese Salad (page 285). Or what about the ever-succulent Stone-Grilled Butter Burgers (page 148) or Hot English Cheese Steak with Pale Ale & Stilton (page 138)? I could go on for days.

In my professional life, there has always been a battle: am I a gourmet or a gourmand? The *Food Lover's Companion* defines a gourmet as "one of discriminating palate; a connoisseur of fine food and drink" — food that is "of the highest quality, perfectly prepared and artfully presented." A gourmand is defined as "one who appreciates fine food . . . often to indiscriminate excess." I would be lying if I didn't admit to the gourmand title, but then gourmet applies too. I appreciate food, and I believe that it is my job to teach people to appreciate it as something more than fuel. Maybe you don't ever sit down and really eat a meal, but that doesn't mean you shouldn't enjoy and appreciate the food you do eat.

For me, "gastro" means wanting you to have as much fun in your backyard as I have in mine. This book is about food that is of the highest quality you can afford, prepared with fun and passion. I'm a fat kid in a candy shop, only the candy shop is a circle of hot smoking and crackling grills and you're along for the ride. I don't care if you have a charcoal grill, a gas grill or even a fire pit in your backyard, I just want you out there in that yard cooking something you love.

All the recipes and inspirations in this book are a part of my real life. What's old is new again and what's new is to be messed with. Pick a starter, pick a side, find a sauce, find a main, and yes even a dessert. A meal is born and we're already having fun. Choose a fancy beer to enjoy and get out there in the great outdoors. Show the neighbors that "gastro" is far from pretentious. In fact, ask them over for dinner and to join in the fun.

Gastro Grilling is intended for folks who are somewhat practiced at the grill. Those people who, a little like me, can "feel" the fire. Who have no fear of taking a risk and trying something new and outside the box. You know who you are. You are the ones who get all tingly looking into the butcher's case to see what's there. You didn't come with a list. You came to see what's good, and then you'll decide what's for dinner.

Chock-full of 135-plus lofty, fun recipes, including rib recipes to make your mouth salivate and your fingers sticky, this must-have grilling book also features recipes that I consider the essence of grilling. It is intended to make it easy for the gastro griller, with simple-to-prepare and absolutely delightful dishes such as Cinnamon-Skewered Scallops with Brown Sugar Basting Butter (page 296) and Grilled Halibut Steaks with Green Grape & Avocado Butter Sauce (page 307). There are even a few yummy grilled dessert recipes to round out the complete meal.

Gastro Grilling has something for everyone!

GASTRO CHARCOAL GRILLING

When it comes to grilling, there is nothing like the flavor of real charcoal. It is more of a production than its friend the gas grill. Gas grills are quick and easy. Open the valve, fire it up and start grilling. But with charcoal there is a process — a process that delivers the ultimate flavor to your grilled foods. Having patience is the key to working with charcoal, and the more you practice, the easier it gets.

Different charcoals provide different burn times, different temperatures and different burn characteristics and flavors.

What to Look For When Purchasing Charcoal

First, not all charcoal is created equal. Look for charcoal that is made from 100% all-natural hardwoods. No softwoods — hard wood charcoal burns more efficiently, lasts longer and has no added chemicals. You want to purchase 100% pure hardwood charcoal.

Lump vs Briquette Charcoal

LUMP CHARCOAL   These are random-sized pieces of hardwood charcoal. It is the wood that has been turned into charcoal, nothing more. Lump charcoal will burn at a higher temperature than briquettes and is normally used for grilling foods. But for some die-hard barbeque cooks, using lump charcoal gives a better, more natural flavor than briquettes, with better end results. Look for 100% hardwood lump charcoal.

BRIQUETTE CHARCOAL   Briquette charcoal is traditionally pillow-shaped. Briquettes are usually made from leftover pieces of lump charcoal. Processors take the leftover pieces, grind to a consistent size and use potato, wheat or corn starch as a binding agent. Look for 100% all-natural briquettes. The advantage with using briquette charcoal is that it burns at a lower temperature for a longer period of time.

Hardwood Charcoal Types

There are many varieties of hardwoods and thus many varieties of hardwood charcoals. Some charcoals are made from one type of wood, for example 100% hardwood maple charcoal. Other charcoals are made from a blend of woods that will create a different style of grill smoke flavor; for example, a blend made of hickory and maple or oak and mesquite. Talk to your local barbeque retailer or supplier and ask what types of charcoal

they carry. The Internet is a great source for finding information on a variety of types.

There are many different types of charcoal available on the market today and finding the one that works right for you can be a fun challenge. I like to experiment with a variety of different charcoals to see how they burn and how long they last and to see what flavor they each produce. That way I can use the right charcoal with the right foods.

Given the range of charcoal available, what I find fun is to mix and match charcoal flavors to create new flavors for your food. Creating a blend sometimes gives you an ultimate fuel that gives an even heat and lasts a good long time. Those are the things you want your charcoal doing for you: great tastes and maximum efficiency. Do some research and experiment with a variety of charcoals, even by making your own blends! Create your own unique recipes and find out what flavors you like best. Note that some charcoal smokers work better with different charcoal. The key is to have fun, experiment and make some tasty food.

I happen to have a large collection of many different types of grills and smokers. They each work a bit differently, and some even work better using a particular type of charcoal. Experimenting with a variety of charcoals will help you determine what type and flavor of charcoal works best in your grill.

COCONUT   For thousands of years, people have been using coconut shells to fuel their fires. It burns hot and offers a sweet, nutty, robust flavor to your food. Coconut charcoal is not made from the coconut tree but from shells. Coconut charcoal is best used with poultry, pork, fish and shellfish. This is a medium-flavored charcoal.

HICKORY CHARCOAL   Hickory is the most common wood used for grilling and smoking foods. This hardwood burns hot and lasts a long time. Offering a full, rich, sweet, strong flavor to foods, it is best used with pork shoulder, ribs, bacon and hams, and also with turkey and chicken. This is a full-flavored charcoal.

MAPLE CHARCOAL   Maple trees are a great source for hardwood charcoals. They burn hot and offer a sweet, buttery, nut flavor to foods. Great used on poultry, ribs, steaks, lamb and game meats. This is a full-bodied charcoal.

MESQUITE CHARCOAL   Mesquite is a very hard wood. Because of its density, this charcoal burns very hot and lasts a very long time. It has a very sweet, aromatic, smoky flavor with a spicy finish. This is a full-flavored, long-burning charcoal that can be used to smoke virtually any meat, beef, pork, poultry, lamb, game and seafood.

OAK CHARCOAL   Oak is a very hard wood that is best used on meats. Brisket is a Texan's delight when smoked with oak. Oak burns hot and lasts a long time. Its smoke is a medium to heavy flavor but not too overpowering. It leaves a butter-smooth, nutty finish.

ONO KIAWE CHARCOAL   Ono charcoal is a Hawaiian-style charcoal made from the *Prosopis* tree, a relative of mesquite. Like its cousin, this charcoal burns very hot, lasts a long time and has a sweet, aromatic, smoky flavor with a spicy finish. Another full-flavored, long-burning charcoal, it can be used to smoke virtually any meat, beef, pork, poultry, lamb, game and seafood. To add a boost of flavor to this charcoal, I like to scatter walnut or pistachio shells and rosemary sprigs over the hot coals.

ORANGE GROVE CHARCOAL   Orange grove charcoal is made from 100% citrus orange trees. This charcoal offers a tangy citrus note to foods and has a medium to mild flavor. When grilling with orange charcoal, I like to scatter dried orange peel, cinnamon sticks and cloves over the hot coals, giving me a sweeter aroma to add to my foods.

JERK CHARCOAL   Jerk charcoal comes from Jamaica. Made from pimento (allspice) wood, the charcoal has a sweet peppery and nutty flavor. The charcoal is traditionally made by covering a burning stack of pimento wood with earth and allowing it to slowly bake in its own earth kiln. It's kind of cool to see these big piles of smoking earth. The smell is intoxicating. When using jerk charcoal, I like to scatter pimento seeds (allspice) and pimento leaves over the hot coals to add a burst of smoky pimento flavor.

FAST LIGHT CHARCOAL   Fast light charcoal is briquette charcoal that has had a fire starter fuel mixed directly into or onto the charcoal briquettes. This makes for a quick light, but the overall flavor produced from these coals is not desirable for grilling foods. It's a great convenience and when in a pinch is ideal, but I personally don't like the flavor that is produced. I find there is always a little fuel flavor in the food.

Things You Need to Know about Charcoal Grilling

- You need patience.
- You need a desire for the best flavors.
- Read the manufacturer's manual for proper grill usage. This is important, as each charcoal grill type works a little differently. They all have similarities, but the subtle differences can mean hero to zero in no time flat. So please read the manual.
- Lump charcoal: Burns hot but burns fast, ideal for grilling foods. Approximate temperature range is 800°F (425°C) or more.
- Briquette charcoal: Burns at a lower temperature, lasts longer, ideal for smoking foods. Approximate temperature range is 600–1000°F (315–540°C).
- As long as you have charcoal, you will have a constant fuel source.
- The more oxygen you allow into your grill. the hotter the fire and the more heat that will be produced.

- Learning to control the heat takes time and patience and understanding what kind of work each type of charcoal requires. With charcoal, there never is an easy way. It requires your undivided attention.
- Always purchase 100% all-natural charcoal. This is the cleanest and most flavorful way to go. You want to know what wood is flavoring and cooking your foods. You never really know what you're getting. Pay a little extra and get the best.
- When buying lump charcoal, avoid charcoal that is in little pieces. These burn up too quickly, leaving you frustrated and out of fuel. Look for charcoal where the pieces are quite large. Larger chunks of charcoal burn longer and offer the most flavor.
- Do not use charcoal for indoor heating, cooking or smoking foods unless proper ventilation is provided for exhausting all fumes outdoors. Charcoal produces deadly toxic fumes that may accumulate and cause death.
- Never add cold charcoal to hot charcoal, always hot coals to hot coals. This keeps your temperature hot instead of cooling down your fire and losing valuable heat.
- Less is more. You don't need a lot of charcoal to create enough heat to run your smoker. Start out with a little, as it is easier to build your fire than take it away.
- Always buy more charcoal than you will need. It's no fun to run out during the middle of your cooking. Be prepared.
- Charcoal gives a more authentic flavor and is efficient and easy to use.
- Use caution when working with all fuels. Be smart and make sure you have the right tools to do the right job.
- Read the instruction manual on your grill for recommended types of fuels.
- Mix different charcoals together to make your own signature charcoal blend, such as 2 parts hickory charcoal, 1 part apple wood charcoal and 2 parts maple charcoal. Experiment and create your own blend of deliciousness!
- Never grill barefoot with charcoal. Wear proper footwear. Trust me, one time I burned the bottoms of my feet when I was at the cottage. I didn't factor in the hot small pieces of coals falling from the bottom of the charcoal chimney as I poured it into the grill. You can blister the bottoms of your feet and it takes a long time to heal. So be careful.

Arranging the Coals to Change the Temperature

How your charcoal is arranged plays a large part in temperature control when grilling. The goal is to minimize the number of times that you have to replenish the charcoal.

First open the air vents on the charcoal grill. Set up your grill with the wind at your back and away from any structure. With charcoal, you need some room to move. The coal can be lighted in a number of ways, such as with a chimney starter, a fire starter cube or an electric starter.

There are lots of ways you can place your charcoal into your grill and it usually depends on what you are grilling. Here are a few different ways to load your grill:

- Left side, right side: This is where you place the desired amount of charcoal onto one side or one half of your grill. This allows you to have a direct side with hot coals and an indirect part of the grill with nothing underneath. This allows you to grill directly and indirectly. For many of the recipes in this book, I use this method.
- Down the middle: This is where you place charcoal on either side of the grill, leaving a wide strip down the middle with nothing. This allows you to do the same direct and indirect grilling and is also good for when you are rotisserie grilling.
- Circle of heat: This is when you lay a ring of charcoal around the entire perimeter of your

charcoal grill. Great for grilling and smoking large cuts of meats. I use this a lot with the lid closed and indirect. Try this with the prime rib (page 204).

- Fill it up: This is when you are going hot and fast. Fill that kettle and let it rip. Direct grilling is perfect for T-bone steaks.

How Hot Is Your Charcoal — Here's the Tester

A tried and true method for checking the coal's temperature is the "hand test." This is done by holding your hand an inch or two (2.5 to 5 cm) above the cooking grate and doing a 1-Mississippi count until you can reach 4 or 5 seconds before it becomes too painful to hold your hand in place. If the coal is so hot that you pull your hand back after 1 to 3 seconds, it's too hot to smoke food. If your hand is just comfortably warm after 6 or more seconds, it's not yet hot enough. Look for visual cues in the center of the charcoal pile. Before you put meat in the smoker, your hot coals should have a nice even coat of gray ash, with a gentle orange glow.

Adding Extra Coal

If at all possible, add hot charcoal to your grill as needed instead of cold charcoal. This will help to keep the grill's temperature relatively even. When you see the temperature start to drop in a hot charcoal grill, preheat 10 to 12 briquettes (or about 1 lb/450 g of lump charcoal) in a charcoal chimney until they develop a solid coat of gray ash, then spread evenly over your coals.

Putting Out the Fire

When you are done grilling, putting out the fire is very important. Hot coals left unattended are a fire hazard. Before you light the charcoal, have a plan to put out the fire both at the end of your grilling session and in case of emergency. Here are two easy methods for putting out your coals:

- Slowly snuff out your charcoal by denying it oxygen. Close all doors and air vents, and

within a few hours your charcoal will have extinguished itself.

- Allow the coals to burn down to ash by fully opening all vents and doors. This will provide the added benefit of burning off grease and drippings inside the smoker, making cleanup easier.

Once your coals are cold, take a look and see what you need to do. If it has burned down to ash, clean out your grill and use the ash as fertilizer for your garden or dispose of it in a composter. Charcoal is biodegradable. If there are large chunks of cold charcoal, remove them from your grill and reserve the large pieces for the next firing of your grill.

Be careful and dispose of your coals only when they are fully cooled.

Charcoal Grill Gear

Stuff you just might want to have for getting your fire started with ease:

CHARCOAL CHIMNEY   In my opinion, the charcoal chimney is the best device for lighting charcoal. It is a charcoal lover's best friend. Fill the chimney with your favorite charcoal and set on your grill. Tuck a couple of sheets of newspaper under the chimney and light with a match. This is an easy way to get the fire started. The charcoal is contained and heats from the bottom up and quickly. Usually within 10 to 15 minutes, you can have charcoal hot enough to get your barbeque or smoker started. The added bonus of a charcoal chimney is that it allows you to replenish your smoker easily with hot charcoal so you are never adding cold charcoal to a hot fire. Get a chimney; they work the best and you will find that you won't waste charcoal. All you need to get a fire going is one full chimney. Look for a well-made galvanized steel chimney starter with a durable base and solid handles. Don't forget a pair of barbeque gloves. You will need them.

FIRE STARTER WOOD STICKS   These are made from 100% natural wood. Fire starter sticks are easy to use; light the end with a match and your charcoal will start to burn shortly.

ECO GEL   Eco gel is a 100% natural liquid gel fire starter made from sugar cane. This fuel starter is a clean and a natural way to start your fire.

ELECTRIC STARTERS   Using an electric starter is an easy and efficient way to start your charcoal. Set the coil in the charcoal and plug it in. Be careful not to keep the electric starter in the charcoal too long, 10 minutes maximum or just until the charcoal starts to burn. There are a variety of electric starters on the market today, some that have an old-school coil burner and now some that have air blowers and heaters in them to help get the fire going. The only drawback is that you might need an extension cord, and in the wild there just might not be an outlet.

PAPER AND MATCHES   When it comes to doing things the old way, I like to crumple up a ball of newspaper (not too tightly crumpled) topped with a few coals. This is the easiest and most efficient way to start your fire. Stack your coals in a pyramid-shaped pile on top of crumpled paper. Strike a match and let it go. Not too many coals; start out small to get the fire going and then add more coals to build your fire. It takes a bit of talent, but once you get it down, it is easy to do and cost effective too.

FLAME THROWER   This is what I use! When it comes to lighting a lot of charcoal to fire a big smoker, I like to use a weed-burning, flame-like torch. Powered by propane, this burner is tradiitionally used to burn up the weeds in your driveway or patio. Not recommended for everyday use. Professionals use this kind of starter. It's fast and easy and saves you time so you can get grilling sooner.

LIQUID FUEL STARTERS   I do not recommend using liquid fuel charcoal starters. Most liquid charcoal starters are usually some type of "gasoline" fuel, are not 100% natural and in the end leave a chemical flavor in your charcoal and thus in your foods. Some people may argue that the fuel burns off during the initial start, but most barbeque professionals would say the flavor of the fuel still lingers long after the fire is gone and the coals are just embers.

If you choose to use a liquid charcoal fire starter to fire up your charcoal, then please note that turpentine and gasoline are not fire starters for food! Be smart and be careful!

If you want to give the purest charcoal flavor to your food, don't use liquid fuel starters.

Must-Have Accessories When Charcoal Grilling

Stuff you really need for effective grilling:

BELLOWS   Go to your local fireplace store and look for a solid pair of bellows. Bellows are a safe and easy way to add a little air to the coals. This will help keep the fire hot. A little burst or two of air makes it easy to keep things toasty.

HEAVY-DUTY GLOVES   Be sure to get yourself a thick pair of elbow-long grill gloves — ones that will keep the heat from scorching your hands and arms. Better safe than sorry!

SMALL SHOVEL   Having a little garden shovel on hand to move hot coals quickly in your grill can be a nice accessory. You never know when you might want to bury your steaks in hot coals and grill it old-school (see Steaks on a Hot Bed of Coals, page 196).

BUCKET   Grab a bucket to hold cold water in case of an emergency, or a hose in your backyard will do too.

GAS GRILLING

If you lack the patience for a charcoal grill and you enjoy immediate gratification with minimum muss or fuss, then a gas grill is for you. You just push the button and in about 15 minutes you're ready to get sticky. Gas grills need the fat that drips onto the lava rocks to produce some smoke, but you can easily create more smoke when grilling with gas by using the untreated hardwood chips that are readily available these days. After soaking, they can be put either directly on the lava rock or, preferably, in a tube-like "log" of foil with holes poked in it for the smoke to escape. You can even put them in a foil pan placed on top of the rocks.

With gas grills, once you get over the initial investment, they are actually inexpensive to grill on. The heat source of most gas grills either comes from propane or natural gas, both of which are less expensive than supplying your grill with charcoal. Look for sturdy construction of rust-proof materials, as well as temperature controls designed to stay cool. Fuel tanks should be easy to change in the ideal gas grill and the ignition button should light the grill within one or two tries. If your budget will allow, go for a gas grill with two burners that will allow you to set the two sides at different temperatures.

When lighting your grill, follow your manufacturer's instructions. Be sure to turn your face away from the grill when igniting it and be careful not to allow the gas to build up. If after a few tries, your grill doesn't start, turn off the gas and allow the gas to dissipate with the lid open. Try again in a few minutes, either with the igniter or with matches (see your manufacturer's instructions for lighting your gas grill with matches).

For the most part, the following procedure for lighting a gas grill should bring you success:

1. Always open the lid! Never start a barbeque with the lid shut unless you want to launch your grill into the atmosphere.
2. Open the gas tank valve.
3. Turn the temperature control knob to high (if using a two-burner grill, turn on the right side only to start).
4. Turn your face away from the open grill and press the ignition button immediately.
5. Turn the left-hand burner knob to high and the right side should ignite the left.

Always preheat your gas grill before grilling. You need to ensure that the lava rocks are evenly heated for efficient cooking and that the rack is hot enough for searing. Preheat grill on the highest setting for a minimum of 15 minutes. If you're searing, leave the burners on high but then reduce to your grilling temperature for the remainder of grilling time. On high, most gas grills can reach temperatures of up to 700°F (370°C). Gas grills cook most evenly and with the fewest flare-ups at medium or low heat with temperatures in the 250–450°F (120–220°C) range. Remember to suit your temperature to your recipe. Sear on high, cook fattier foods over medium and warm over low. If you should get a flare-up, close the grill lid, turn the heat down and if necessary remove food from grill until the temperature is under control.

INFRARED GRILLING

Infrared energy is a form of electromagnetic energy that has a wavelength just greater than the red end of the visible light spectrum. Most foods readily absorb infrared radiation, causing a rapid increase in temperature. Charcoal is the traditional way of infrared cooking. The glowing briquettes emit infrared energy to the food being cooked, with very little drying effect. Any juices or oils that escape from the food drip down onto the charcoal and vaporize into smoke, giving the food its delicious grilled taste.

Infrared grills cook in the same way. In each burner, ports that each have their own tiny flame cause the surface of the ceramic to glow red. This glow emits the same type of infrared heat to the food without the hassle or mess of charcoal. It also provides a more consistent heated area that is far easier to regulate than a charcoal fire. For instantaneous searing, the burners can be set to high, yet they can also be turned down for slower cooking. Infrared grills produce searing heat for juicier, tastier steaks, hamburgers and other meats.

So when you are looking for hot and fast, the infrared grill can certainly do the job. Most infrared grills can achieve extreme heat of approximately 1800°F (980°C) in about 30 seconds. Now that's hot and fast!

PLANK GRILLING

If you haven't tried grilling foods with a wooden plank, you are missing a fast and delicious way of smoking food.

Planking is an ancient method of cooking that traces its roots to the Haida people of the Pacific Northwest. In my humble opinion, it is a hot, fast way of grilling food and an easy way to infuse smoke into your foods without the use of a smoker. It can be done on a gas grill or a charcoal grill or even over an open fire with delicious moist and juicy, smoky results. Just make sure your grill has a tight-fitting lid to keep the smoke in.

Compared with conventional smoking, plank smoking uses higher heats to create a very hot smoke to infuse quickly into the foods and cook them quickly. Some may argue that planking is more grilling than smoking. I would disagree. You are using a grill as the source for a heat-smoking chamber. The fire heats the soaked wooden plank and creates smoke that flavors the food as it cooks.

You can use a variety of woods to plank on, depending on the taste sensation you're trying to create — apple, cherry, maple and oak are all woods you can use.

When you are planking, you should soak the wood in advance for a minimum of 1 hour. This will reduce the risk of the wood catching fire. Soak the wood in water or juice or even beer.

Preheat grill to desired temperature. I recommend keeping your grill around medium heat, 350–450°F (180–230°C). Place plank on grill, close barbeque lid and preheat the plank for 2 to 3 minutes, until it begins to crackle and smoke.

Carefully open the barbeque lid and place the meat onto the heated plank. Close barbeque lid and let the cooking begin. Check every 4 to 5 minutes to see that the plank is not on fire. If there is a fire, use a spray bottle of water to put out the flames and reduce the heat to medium-low.

There's no turning or flipping; just leave the food on the plank. Let it smoke, nice and easy so you don't have to fuss.

When the food is cooked, carefully remove the plank from the grill, place on a serving platter and enjoy.

Let the plank cool before throwing it out. I usually use my planks a second time — in the fireplace.

Although every recipe and grill is different, it's key that you achieve consistent heat to have good results. So keep the lid closed as much as possible to maintain heat and smoke. The lower the temperature, the less the chance of the plank igniting. It is important to have even heat and even smoke. Keep flames to a minimum.

The following table will help you follow the recipes accurately and keep the grill at the appropriate temperature when using either gas or charcoal grills. I recommend plank smoking at temperatures of medium (350–450°F/180–230°C or lower) for best results.

Be patient!

High heat: 550°F (290°C) or higher
   (use caution when planking at a very
   high temperature)
Medium-high heat: 450–550°F (230–290°C)
Medium heat: 350–450°F (180–230°C)
Medium-low heat : 250–350°F (120–180°C)
Low heat: less than 250°F (120°C)

Safety and Planking Tips

It is important to use caution when plank smoking. Even properly soaked planks can catch fire. Plank smoking is a lot of fun, but please exercise caution and common sense when preparing these recipes. Follow the rules and you shouldn't have any trouble.

Always remember, planks are made of wood and have a tendency to smoke and possibly catch fire. Smoke is good; fire is bad.

Recommended Safety Equipment

- High-heat thermometer suitable for the grill
- Squeeze or spray bottle filled with water
- Garden hose
- Fire extinguisher, just in case
- Phone: To dial 911 — better safe than sorry
- Goggles: Swimming goggles, snow goggles or sunglasses will work, but some type of eye protection is necessary when checking planks during smoking and when removing from the grill
- Sturdy pair of long, well-made grilling tongs: Tongs need to be able to hold the weight of a plank with food on it
- Large, metal container filled with water, should a fire break out
- Thick, heat-resistant barbeque gloves to keep your hands safe

Safety Tips

- All planks should be made out of natural, pure, untreated wood.
- Soak all planks in cold water for a minimum of 1 hour prior to planking.
- Never brush planks with any type of oil — this is literally adding fuel to a piece of wood that can potentially ignite.
- Keep all children and pets away from the grill while planking.
- Never leave your grill unattended once planking has commenced. Keep to your post and be prepared.
- Soak used planks in water for a minimum of 30 minutes before putting in the garbage.
- Consider wind direction when plank grilling and adjust position of grill as needed.
- Should a plank ignite, reduce temperature or turn burners off. Lift the lid and douse flames with the spray bottle that is ALWAYS standing by. Replace lid and resume plank grilling.
- Place a foil pan that is larger than the plank under the grate to catch drippings. This will reduce the number of flare-ups.
- Transfer hot planks from the grill to a heatproof platter, another raw soaked plank or baking sheet to prevent burning tabletops or counters, as the underside of the planks are very hot.
- Always transfer cooked food onto a new soaked plank or serving platter outside before bringing food inside. I like to use funky-shaped planks that we have cut specially for doing the final service.
- Be careful!

Planking Tips

- Always soak planks in cold water for a minimum of 1 hour or up to 24 hours before planking.
- Soak planks in different liquids to impart different flavors. Try wine, beer or juice. Herbs and spices will also add a new dimension to the flavor of the wood.
- Remove bark from planks, as the bark produces a bitter smoke.
- Use sandpaper to remove any splinters from the wood before rinsing and soaking the plank.
- Quick and easy recipes are best for charcoal barbeques. Having to add more charcoal to the grill means losing precious smoke and increasing the cooking time.
- Neither the plank nor the food needs to be flipped or rotated once on the grill.
- Refrain from opening the grill lid too often when planking. This will keep the beautiful smoke in and the cooking time on schedule.
- When mashed potatoes or vegetables are too fresh, they will run off the plank, leaving a nasty mess on the grill, so prepare them the day before planking.

- Try cutting planks into different shapes for an impressive presentation.
- Never waste leftovers! Get creative or make a sandwich. With the addition of a little mayonnaise, leftover planked salmon makes an out-of-this-world salmon salad sandwich.
- Planking takes time, so be patient; it will all be worth it in the end!

SOAK Soak all planks in cold water for a minimum of 1 hour. Weigh the plank down with something heavy to keep it submerged under water. For best flavor and smoke results, soak the plank for 4 hours.

SMOKE Preheat grill to the appropriate temperature (the thickness of the plank and the type of food will dictate temperature) with the grill lid closed. Place the plank on the grill; close the lid and heat for 3 to 5 minutes or until plank begins to crackle and smoke.

FLAVOR For added flavor, season the plank with coarse sea salt, cracked black pepper and/or fresh herbs.

EAT AND ENJOY Carefully remove the hot plank from the grill using heavy-duty tongs and set on a presoaked raw plank. Transfer the smoked cooked food to serving plates or platters. Place the hot plank in a bucket of cold water to cool down.

PLANK SMOKING

Dos	Don'ts
Soak plank	Leave grill unattended
Season plank	Flip food
Keep lid closed	Flip plank
Be careful	Peek constantly
Have fun	Be careless

Varieties of Wood

Suitable woods for plank grilling are much like fine wines; there are many different types and they vary from region to region. The Pacific Northwest produces a great deal of western red cedar and alder; maple and oak are abundant in Canada and the northern US; hickory and nut woods are common in the southern US; and fruit woods (including apple, peach and pear) are available in many parts of Canada and the US.

Semi-hard or hard wood (e.g., western red cedar, maple and oak) are the most suitable for planks, as they have less sap and do not burn as quickly as soft woods. Western red cedar is the most commonly used wood to make planks. It imparts a sweet smoke, is especially aromatic and is the most versatile for plank grilling. Avoid using soft woods, such as pine, as they tend to produce a bitter smoke, resulting in Pine Sol–tasting food. Bark also imparts a bitter flavor to food, so be sure to remove all bark before soaking planks. Bark also tends to ignite more easily than clean wood.

Here is a list of the different woods I recommend using for plank grilling, as well as the flavors they impart, suggested flavorings for soaking and suggested foods for each variety of plank:

HICKORY A hard wood with a very bold flavor from the southern US. It's very much a "good ol' boys" kind of wood. Hickory can be difficult to find, so when you do find it, buy a ton and hold onto it. It works really well when slowly plank grilling a large cut of meat over low heat. For soaking, use water, beer, bourbon, ginger ale, cola, apple juice, pineapple juice or cabernet sauvignon. These planks are best used with pork (ribs, chops and bacon), turkey, ham, steaks, game (venison, ostrich, buffalo, pheasant) and portobello mushrooms.

MAPLE   A hard wood with a subtle sweet smoke with a nice balance. Soak this plank in water, apple juice, chardonnay, cabernet sauvignon, honey brown lager or even a maple-flavored lager. Use maple for plank grilling poultry (chicken, turkey, duck, quail), trout, salmon, arctic char, pizza and steaks.

PECAN   A hard wood with mildly sweet and nutty flavors from the South. These planks are especially hard to find, but well worth the search. Try soaking this plank in water, strong dark beer, cabernet sauvignon or merlot, chardonnay, apple juice or ginger ale. Pecan is awesome for plank baking desserts, fruits, vegetables, mushrooms, quail, chicken, turkey, and pork.

RED OAK   A hard wood with a deeply rustic smoke flavor; it's best paired with strong flavors. Cover this plank with water, cabernet sauvignon, merlot, pale ale, grape juice, cranberry juice or orange juice. Grill beef, game, poultry, cheese and desserts on this plank.

WESTERN RED CEDAR   A semi-hard, aromatic and sweet wood from the Pacific Northwest. It is easy to find and perfect for plank grilling. Cedar produces big smoke and big flavor. Try soaking the plank in water, chardonnay, hard cider, pilsner, Dr. Pepper or cherry juice. This plank complements salmon, seafood, cheese, poultry, game meats, beef, pork, veal and lamb. Cedar is even great for fruits, vegetables and desserts. Like I said before, cedar is a very versatile plank.

ALDER   A semi-hard wood with a delicate and slightly sweet smoke flavor from the Pacific Northwest. Alder is best when soaked in water, chardonnay, sauvignon blanc, Riesling, pinot noir, apple juice, lager or ale. Alder is great for cooking vegetables, salmon, halibut, arctic char, pork, chicken and fruit.

APPLE   A semi-hard wood that produces a subtle fruity and sweet smoke. For soaking, use water, apple juice, apple ale, apple wine, apple cider, chardonnay, pinot noir or pineapple juice. Use apple planks for planking poultry, fish, shellfish, pork chops and pork tenderloin, veal, assorted vegetables and fruits.

CHERRY   A semi-hard wood that creates a tart, fruity smoke. Try soaking cherry wood in water, pinot noir, shiraz, sauvignon blanc, chardonnay, cherry whiskey, cherry cola or cherry juice. Cherry planks are perfect for venison, beef, turkey, pork chops, pork tenderloin, cheese and fruits.

MESQUITE   A hard wood that lets out a sweet smoke. It is an exotic wood, making it hard to find, but is great for long cooking times because of its thickness. It is extra delicious when soaked in water, beer, cider, pineapple juice, lemonade or ginger ale. Mesquite is a strong flavor, so it works best with beef, pork and poultry.

Where to Find and Buy Planks

I've been planking for nearly 15 years now and when I started doing this there weren't many places you could buy planks. In fact, there was only one place I could get planks — the lumberyard. I would go in and buy a great big piece of wood and ask the guys to cut it into 10-inch (25 cm) long planks. This obviously piqued their curiosity and they would ask how I was going to use them. When I explained I was cooking on the wood, it really opened the floodgate of questions. They began to think I was crazy until other customers, seemingly normal people, were also asking for their wood to be cut into planks. All these years later, the lumberyard is still the best place to get planks.

There are a few more options out there these days. Many grocery stores and gourmet shops carry planks, as well as many home improvement-type stores, although they usually only have untreated western red cedar. While cedar is a great wood to plank with, there are so many other wonderful flavors of wood. Red oak and maple are hard woods that produce a good amount of smoke for long periods of time and don't usually ignite. Alder has a slightly nutty flavor, and hickory is a great hard wood with a not too sweet flavor. These varieties of wood are harder to find but worth the search, as they each impart a different flavor to food.

Planks are available in different sizes and thickness. Use small planks for small portions, wider planks for roasts and longer planks for longer items like whole sides of salmon. The length and width of a plank is not as important as its thickness.

Thickness is the most important thing to consider when buying planks. The thinner the plank, the shorter the time it can stay on the grill. Recipes that have a quick cooking time can get by with a thin plank, but longer cooking time will need either a regular or a thick plank. Every recipe in this book will specify what thickness of plank to use.

THIN PLANK
> Approximately ¼ to ½ inch
> (0.5 to 1 cm) thick
> Maximum of 15–20 minutes of cooking time
> (mashed potatoes, risotto, vegetables, garlic)

REGULAR PLANK
> Approximately ¾ inch (2 cm) thick
> 20–60 minutes of cooking time
> (salmon or other fish fillets, steaks, pork loin, ribs, tuna, roast chicken and game)

THICK PLANK
> Approximately 1 inch (2.5 cm) or more thick
> 60 minutes plus of cooking time

(turkey, prime rib, veal roast, pork loin roast, whole fish)

Thin planks tend to warp when heated. To avoid warping, place the plank over high heat (without food) for a couple of minutes, turn the plank over and place the food on the lightly heated side. Hard woods are less likely to warp than semi-hard woods, but take this easy precaution just to be safe. Soaking the plank for a longer amount of time will also help to prevent the plank from warping. Why is warping such a big deal? Well, when a plank warps, the food will most likely roll off onto the grill, make a huge mess and screw up your dinner.

It is very important that you NEVER cook with treated wood — not even if you have a heap of scrap wood left over from a building project or find railway ties on the side of the tracks. Use only untreated, 100% pure, natural wood. To most people, I'm sure this all seems like common sense, but you would be surprised at the number of people I have seen using leftover wood from the cedar deck they just had built to plank grill their food. A while back I was at a party where the host could have been a bit more gracious. He was very boisterous about how good his plank salmon was and that I didn't know as much on the topic as everyone thought I did. It was then that I kindly put him in his place by telling him that the reason his fish smelled like a freshly painted washroom was because of the treated cedar deck scraps he cooked it on. A couple of weeks later, he attended one of my grilling and barbeque classes.

Another great place to find planks is on the Internet. Google "grilling planks" and you will find an outrageous number of planks, planking recipes, and even me, Ted Reader, at tedreader .com. Some of the major distributors of cedar and other wood variety planks are major grocery stores, specialty food shops and specialty barbeque supply stores. Home and garden stores (Home Depot, Lowes, Canadian Tire, Home Hardware, Bass Pro Shops, Ace Hardware, Gander

Mountain, Pro Hardware and Rona, to name just a few) also have a good selection of planks. Don't forget your local lumberyard, as they will have the hard-to-come-by woods and can cut them in a variety of lengths.

Soaking Planks

It is extremely important that planks are soaked in cold water before grilling, for both safety and flavor reasons. A minimum of 1 hour in a cold bath is necessary, 2 hours is preferred and 4 hours is ideal. Place the plank in a large bin, cover with a cold liquid and top with something heavy to keep the plank submerged. Soaking will keep the plank from igniting and it produces a clean and flavorful smoke.

Flavoring Planks

Try adding extra flavor to planks by soaking them in different liquids. A 1:1 ratio works best; 1 part water to 1 part flavoring liquid. Soak planks for 2 to 4 hours to really get the flavors soaked in there. Try apple cider for apple wood planks. Red and white wine are always a success; even fruit juice, like pineapple or cranberry, works well. Beer is awesome when paired with ribs, and bourbon is just the thing for burgers.

Salt is added to food for many reasons, but the most important is that salt brings out the natural flavors of food; it's not any different when added to wood. Season the planks with coarse sea salt prior to placing food on the plank.

Have fun, play around; try adding fresh herbs or grape leaves between the plank and the food. Cinnamon sticks, whole nutmeg or vanilla beans will also add another dimension of flavor to your food.

Plank Box

You may need an extra set of hands or a vise clamp when you make your first box, but after that, you will be able to make these with your eyes closed (hammering with your eyes closed not recommended).

1 untreated grilling plank, minimum 12 inches (30 cm) long × 8 inches (20 cm) wide × ¾ inch (2 cm) thick
4 uniform untreated cedar shims, minimum 12 to 14 inches (30 to 35 cm) long and 4 inches (10 cm) wide
8 to 16 nails, about 1 inch (2.5 cm) long with a flat head (do not use finishing nails)
1 hammer

Place the plank on one of its long edges on a flat work surface. Lay one shim onto the edge of the plank, ensuring that the thick end of the shim is square with the corner and the edge that will be the bottom of the roasting pan. Hammer a nail about 1 inch (2.5 cm) from the corner of the plank, as close to the center of its width as possible. Repeat at the other end of the shim with another nail. You may choose to hammer a nail into the center as well. From the thin side, snap off any excess shim hanging off the edge and discard. Repeat with the remaining three edges of the plank so that you have a 3- to 4-inch (8 to 10 cm) deep roasting plank.

Depending on what you're planking, you may need to add a few more nails to create a tighter seal around the corners of the shims. This can be a little tricky because the shims are thin and can split easily if the nail doesn't go in just right. These get really easy to make after the first one.

Holy Plank

This is the ultimate plank for slow roasting. Fill the wells with wine, beer, soda, whatever. Keep the wells full of liquid for the duration of the cooking time. Try the Planked Escargot with Garlic Chive Butter & Brie (page 66). Spectacular! Try a whole fish or a nice bone-in prime rib on this. Juicy!

A Forstner drill bit will give you a clean well in the wood with no hole in the middle like you get with a spade bit.

One ¾- to 1-inch (2 to 2.5 cm) Forstner drill bit

1 drill
1 large grilling plank (16 × 8 × 1 inches/
   40 × 20 × 2.5 cm)

Secure the plank to a work surface. Place the cutting end of the drill up to the edge of the plank (the minimum 1-inch/2.5 cm side) to gauge how far you can drill into the plank without going all the way through. Remember it.

Drill about 32 holes or so; I suggest 4 rows of 8. You don't have to worry about lining them up all perfect. This is barbeque we're talking about!

Dust the sawdust off the plank and rinse well with water before soaking in desired liquid.

ROTISSERIE GRILLING

Nothing says deliciousness like meats spinning slowly over the fire. So many cultures have rotisserie meats as a staple, and there are even restaurant chains that focus on this style of cooking to create some of their signature recipes. Foods that spin slowly over the fire and baste themselves with natural succulent juices makes for one tasty meal. I think that it is one of the best ways to cook foods, and it's pretty easy too.

Quite often, when you purchase a grill, it comes with a rotisserie kit. And quite often this rotisserie ends up in the garage or in the shed or tucked under the grill and never gets used. Considered an intimidating grilling accessory, it really is one of the easiest methods of cooking. It requires patience, which most grilling guys don't have, but with a little patience you can do so many wonderful recipes. Once it's up and rolling, it comes down to watching the food spin and waiting patiently for it to cook. Whether it be with gas or with charcoal, using the rotisserie produces absolutely delicious recipes.

Rotisserie grilling is low and slow cooking. It's great for cooking whole chickens, beef roasts, pork loins, and for me it is the best way to cook a whole suckling pig or lamb. Firing up your rotisserie can often mean a great party and most of your guests will be intrigued to see how it is done.

A rotisserie is pretty simple. It's a big rod with a fork on either end to secure the meat and hold it in place as it turns over the fire. Gently but firmly push the rod through the center of the meat, pushing all the way through to the other side. Center the meat on the rod. Next put the pronged fork on either end and push the tines into the meat until the meat is snug and secure. Tighten the bolts to secure the tines and meat and hold it in place. A counterweight will ensure that the meat is properly balanced and that it turns smoothly. Note that you may need to truss or tie your piece of meat prior to securing it to the rotisserie rod. There is nothing worse than having your meat flop about on the rod and having to start the whole process all over again to fix the problem. Take your time and do it right the first time. For whole chickens that you purchase at the grocery store, note that they often come already trussed. So all you will have to do is carefully look inside the cavity of the bird to ensure there is no little plastic or paper bag with the neck, liver and giblets. Remove it if it is there.

I have a buddy who invented this Brazilian-style rotisserie grill called an Epicoa. In the three models that I have, they each have seven individual motors, thus allowing you to create more than one dish at a time. Imagine smoked sausages, bacon-wrapped chicken thighs, lamb chops, pork loin, pineapple, steaks and ribs all cooking in unison over hot charcoal. It is wicked! They are pricy but worth every penny (epicoa.com). Oh, once you get one, you will drool and want to spin foods all the time.

With rotisserie cooking, it's a good idea to have a tray in the grill with some water to add moisture to the heat so that the meat doesn't dry out. Again, basting should be done in the last quarter of cooking time. Wood chips can be added as a flavoring agent to create some smoke for added flavor.

So pull that rotisserie kit out of your garage or storage bin or from under your grill and fire it up. Spin up some deliciousness for a crowd of hungry family and friends.

Rotisserie Tips

Brining your meat prior to securing to the rotisserie rod is suggested so that you have moist and tender meat.

Keep the main burners off and use only the rotisserie flames at the back of the grill. Turn the heat down to low and let the cooking begin. A good rule of thumb is 20–30 minutes of cooking time per pound. With the lid closed, your grill turns into a convection oven. For safety, always wear well-insulated cooking mitts.

ESSENTIAL GASTRO GRILL GEAR

There are a ton of grilling utensils in the marketplace. With such a huge variety of items to choose from, I have compiled a list of my favorite grilling accessories — items that will make your grilling experience a little easier — and what it comes down to is these seven items.

Grill Brush

In my opinion, the grill brush is the most important grilling utensil you should own, and you shouldn't own just one — you need to keep a small arsenal of grill brushes. The grill brush should be heavy-duty with thick, long, durable bristles that get between the grates to give a good cleaning. The bristles should be well mounted. There is nothing worse than starting to clean your grill and your grill brush starts to lose its bristles. To make sure they are firmly anchored, give them a tug when you are researching brushes.

The grill brush should have a long head and a comfortable-feeling shaft so that you can get both hands on it when you have a real mess of a grill to clean, something that is not too flexible and that is heat resistant so that you can use it when necessary during your grilling session. And lastly, the head of the brush should be large. You want a real brush that covers a lot of grill area and that can take a bit of abuse. Durability is important. A really good grill brush should last the entire season.

Cleaning your grill brush is also important. You can't clean a grill if the bristles are all clogged up with grease, food particles and carbon buildup. I suggest soaking your brushes in boiling hot, soapy water for 20 minutes to release as much of the grime as possible. Then use another brush to remove the final particles. Your grill brush will last a lot longer.

If your grill brush starts to lose its bristles or the bristles become completely flattened or there is no hope of removing the grease, it is time to replace it. Remember that a grill brush is the key to keeping your grill clean and healthy, and a healthy grill is a clean grill.

Tongs

When it comes to grilling, owning a great pair of tongs is essential to making the job easier. Tongs would be the second most important grilling utensil, next to the grill brush. You just can't grill right without a pair of tongs. They make the job easy.

You want a pair of tongs that feel right. I don't understand how some tongs are so big and cumbersome that it makes grilling difficult. Tongs should be comfortable in your hand. They should have a quick snap action that allows for gripping the food and either moving it on the grill or removing it from the grill. I like restaurant-style chef tongs. You can find this type of tong in many restaurant supply stores and specialty kitchen shops. My favorite are approximately 9 inches (23 cm) in length, as I like the quick action with them. They are heavy-duty but lightweight. They won't bend when I pick up a 3-pound (1.4 kg) steak.

Most restaurant-style chef tongs come in 9- or 11-inch (23 or 28 cm) lengths, which are both easy to handle. They also come in lengths up to 14 and 18 inches (35 to 45 cm). These are useful when working over a very hot grill, but are a little more difficult to handle. Remember to test the tongs and get what fits right.

Spatula

You can't grill burgers without a proper spatula. Spatulas come in all shapes and sizes. Some are simple and some have a few accessories attached. Some have teeth and some have a sharp cutting edge and some even have a bottle opener attached. All great stuff, but when it comes to grilling meat or a whole mess of burgers, you need a spatula that has a flexible blade that is approximately as wide as a burger patty or more. It should have a long handle to keep your hands out of the direct heat, but not so long that you can't control it. It should be lightweight but durable and it should fit comfortably in your hand. There is nothing worse than trying to use a spatula that has a shaft the size of a baseball bat.

Basting Brush

When it comes to grilling, there is nothing that completes grilled foods like the sauce, and to apply the sauce evenly, you need a great basting brush. I like a brush that is approximately 10 inches (25 cm) in length and has fine bristles that soak up lots of sauce.

Look around. There are a lot of basting brushes available, so find the one that is right for you.

A flavorful way to baste your food is to make yourself an herb basting brush. You will need the following items: a long-handled wooden spoon, about 18 inches (40 cm) of butcher twine and 2 to 3 big handfuls of fresh herbs on the stem. I like to use a mixture of rosemary, thyme, oregano, sage and lavender. You want to use firm-stemmed herbs. Lay the herbs on a flat work surface with the stem ends all facing in the same direction. Mix the herbs up a little so their flavors are combined. Next wrap the herbs around the base of the wooden spoon and, with the help of a friend, tie the herbs tightly to the spoon, leaving about 4 to 5 inches (10 to 12 cm) of herbs dangling over the end of the spoon. Soak herbs in cold water to keep fresh. Dip the herb brush in your favorite sauces, marinades, bastes and grilling oils and baste your foods with deliciousness. The herbs add a boost of big flavor to whatever you are grilling.

Injection Syringe

An injection syringe is great for injecting marinades, sauces and other liquids into the center of your burger and other grilled items. I especially love injecting butter into baked sweet potatoes, potatoes and even steaks. Plump up your grilled food with the deliciousness of an injection. Now who doesn't like a good injection every once in a while?

Grilling Stone

In this book I use a grilling stone for a variety of recipes. I first started grilling with stone about 15 years ago when I wrote a book called *The Sticks and Stones Cookbook: The Art of Grilling on Plank, Vine and Stone*. The grilling stones that I use are made from Canadian soapstone. Soapstone can range in age from 300 million to 400 million years. It is an extremely dense rock and has been used for millennia in cooking and carving materials. Soapstone grilling stones are food-safe, stain resistant and impenetrable by bacteria. It provides an even, uniform heat for easy, quick cooking. I use my grilling stones to make the best burgers and grilled cheese sandwiches. Cleaning stones is easy; use hot soapy water and scrub them with a soft brush. Do not microwave grilling stones, as there may be trace metals in the stone that could cause the microwave to arc and explode. For more information please, visit brazilianice.com.

Thermometer

A thermometer is a very important piece of gastro grilling gear. Not everyone is a chef and sometimes knowing when foods are properly cooked can be a difficult thing to judge. That's when you need a thermometer so you know when the chicken is properly cooked. I have a jar with a bunch of them sitting by my grills. Invest in a couple of good-quality thermometers. My personal favorite is the Thermapen brand of thermometers, which are quick and accurate so I can be sure my foods are cooked properly.

Remember to always have more than one. You never know when a thermometer may fail. Better to be safe than sorry. Don't forget the backup batteries in case your thermometers should run out of juice. Also be sure to check your thermometers regularly so that they give accurate readings; they don't last forever. You can add more to your list of grilling accessories, but these seven items are really all you need to get to the job of grilling foods efficiently and deliciously.

READY, SET, GO

I like to grill year-round. Pretty much daily, as a matter of fact. For those of you who don't pull your barbeque out of the garage until the snow melts, here are a few things to keep in mind before you start grilling.

Position your grill where you want to cook — close enough to the kitchen so you don't have to run back and forth, but far enough from the house so you don't fill your family room with smoke and set the roof on fire. Bring everything you need out to the grill and set yourself up before you start. You must never leave the barbeque unattended. Make sure you have access to the beverage of your choice, well iced, beside your grill.

If your grill has been sitting around the garage for a few months, the first thing you must do is give it a thorough cleaning. More than likely your grill has grease and leftovers from last season. This attracts rodents, spiders and all sorts of creatures that don't belong there. Spiders can get into the Venturi tubes (those are the tubes that feed the propane from the tank to the grill). To clean the Venturi tubes, you'll need a special cleaning brush. Follow the manufacturer's instructions to get access to the tubes.

You should also install new foil grease catchers underneath the grill. Nearly every barbeque has a spot underneath for attaching a grease catcher.

Using paper towels and an everyday household cleaner with a grease cutter, go over the entire unit, polishing it so it sparkles. A clean grill is a healthy grill and a clean grill is a safe grill and a clean grill gets hotter and stays hotter, giving you better foods. Grease buildup on the grill can lead to flare-ups and grease fires.

Always clean your grill before and after use with a stiff wire brush. Finally, a light coating of cooking oil rubbed onto the grids with a cloth will prevent food from sticking and make the grill easier to clean, or use nonstick cooking spray for an even coating to help season your grill. Never apply this when the grill is on. Never!

Before lighting the grill, check all your connections to and from the propane. Turn on the propane tank and light one burner at a time. Close the lid until the barbeque reaches the desired cooking temperature and then start cooking!

SEASONING YOUR GRILL

Seasoning a Brand Spanking New Grill

One of the many questions I get asked every year is, "How do you season your new out-of-the-box grill?" Well, when it comes to seasoning a new grill, here is what I do.

For gas or charcoal grills, the principal is about the same; once you have the grill assembled, remove the grill grates and set them aside. Fire up the grill and give it a good burn to get that new industrial manufactured smell out of it. Let it burn at least 15–20 minutes. For the grill grate, spray it liberally on both sides with a nonstick cooking spray. One designed for high heat is usually what I use. I give it a good thick spraying. I then place the grate onto the hot grill and allow the spray to get a bit of a sizzle onto the grate. Take a grill brush and scrub the grate. Remove the hot grill grate from the grill. Allow it to cool for about 10 minutes. Spray it again and place it back on the grill. Repeat this a couple of times. This bakes the spray right into the grate, giving

it a bit of extra slickness to help keep foods from sticking. New grills and grates always need a little love added before cooking on them. Turn the grill off and allow it to cool for at least 10 minutes with the lid open. Spray the head of your grill brush with a liberal amount of nonstick cooking spray and brush it into the cooling grates — this greasing of the brush helps season as it cleans. Close the lid and your grill is now seasoned and ready for cooking.

Seasoning Tip

Before you fire up your grill, make sure it is clean. The catch tray and drip pan should be kept clean so that you reduce the chance of a grease fire. I recommend cleaning these after every fourth or fifth grilling session, but this will depend on how greasy or saucy your grilled foods are. Just ensure that you make it a regular cleaning.

Keeping Your Grill Seasoned

It is important to remember that each time you grill you need to season your grill. It is to your advantage to season the grill before you fire it up and once you are done grilling. Here is what I do.

Take your grill brush and scrub the grill grate. This will help get the oil in the spray all over the grates and help remove excess grit. Put a little muscle into it. Wipe the grill grate with paper towels or a kitchen towel. (Gastro grillers don't go in the house and take your wife's good kitchen towels to do this. Head over to the hardware store and get your own batch of shop towels that you can dispose of after use if you desire. And whatever you do, don't put that greasy rag into the laundry tub.) Now you are ready to fire up your grill. Let your grill heat for a good 10 minutes to allow the nonstick spray to bake into the grates. Grill away.

Now when you are done grilling, don't just turn off the heat and close the lid and walk away — it's time to clean your grill. It's easier to clean while the grill is warm. I take my grill brush and spray the bristles liberally with nonstick cooking spray and then brush the hot grills. This will season the grill and bake in the nonstick cooking spray, keeping your grill seasoned and sealed from moisture and making sure your grill is ready for the next time you want to fire it up. Doing this routine regularly will help keep your foods from sticking to the grill grates.

GASTRO GRILLING TIPS

- High heat, lid open. Low heat, lid closed.
- Never leave your grill: Once you start cooking, keep to your post. Leaving a grill unattended may result in burning your food. Stay with it. An unattended grill is a disaster waiting to happen.
- A clean grill is a healthy grill: Keep it clean by scrubbing it with your grill brush after each cooking session. Make sure you occasionally clean the drip pan under the burners to save you from having a grease fire. Cover your grill. A clean grill is not only healthier but will last much longer.
- Patience is everything when it comes to grilling and barbequing. Low and slow is a great way to go. But remember, every time you want to touch or flip or poke or squish your food, have a sip of beer instead.
- Come to your grill prepared and ready to do some serious cooking. Make sure you have enough cold beverages to do the job and once you start grilling never leave your post.
- Any grill is a good grill as long as it gets nice and hot and does the job of helping you create delicious food. As for beer, any beer is a good beer as long it is frosty cold and quenches your thirst.
- It's not the size of your grill that matters but how you use it.
- Never touch another person's grill or smoker unless you have been invited to.
- Keep it simple and delicious.

WINTER GRILLING TIPS

When it comes to the cold weather, I much prefer to stay indoors or head south to some remote beach where I can baste in the sun and fire up my grills in the warmth rather than the cold. But the reality is I am a Canuck and living in the cold is a way of life in the Great White North. So outdoors we must go to fire up the grills and smokers and cook up something yummy.

I may not like the cold, but it is not going to keep me from my passion of eating and grilling. So here are a few tips to help you weather the cold.

Now the first and most important rule when it comes to winter grilling is never ever bring your grill or smoker indoors to cook. Not in your house or even your garage. To put it simply . . . you could die. Gas and charcoal grills produce carbon monoxide, and that is something you do not want to subject your family or yourself to. So don't bring them indoors, please!

As the summer and fall come to an end and the cold winter days set in, you will want to make sure you clean your grill really well. A clean grill is a hotter grill, and in the winter you need all the heat you can get.

Keep your grill out of the direct wind. Tuck it in a corner. The less wind, the more heat you will have.

Bundle yourself up in your warmest clothes. Now don't overdo it, since you still want to be able to move around. I wear long underwear and a thick pair of jeans, add a few layers of fleece and a windbreaker, a warm toque or balaclava (if it's really cold), ski goggles during those days when there is a blizzard, and mitts (the type where you can expose your fingers). Don't forget a pair of warm boots. I also fire up my patio heater to get a little warmer. Those hand- and foot-warming pads work too. But the reality is bundle up and get out there.

I am lucky; my grilling zone is off my garage and I keep a few heaters going inside to keep me warm. But don't get lazy, as staying in the garage can be a little risky, especially if you have a beer fridge inside, and you might just burn or overcook your foods. So stay alert and keep the warming sessions to a few minutes at a time.

Now that you're all bundled up, head outside. Keep a path shoveled to the grill or smoker. The last thing you need is to take a spill on your way to the grill. Brush off any snow from your grill or smoker. Remove the grill cover. Note: You better have a cover, since it will keep your grill lasting longer!

Now when it comes to fueling your grill in the wintertime, there are a few things to remember. Charcoal is pretty easy. Once it gets hot, you just have to monitor it and add more fuel as necessary. It also keeps you warm. But remember, in the winter you will use two to three times as much charcoal than you will in warmer weather, so make sure you stock up. Natural gas is the easiest to use. It gives you a constant fuel source that gives you an even flow. You will likely use more fuel in the winter versus the summer, but with natural gas you have a constant supply. Meanwhile, propane is the hardest to work with when you're winter grilling. The colder it gets, the less propane flows. As well, the more the tank empties, the less it flows. So I recommend keeping your propane tanks full. Have more than one tank on hand, and I sometimes even wrap the tank with a blanket. Do not store your tanks in the garage either — this is dangerous. Keep them outdoors!

Before you fire up your grill, be sure to get as much as possible of your mise en place (prep) done indoors. Marinate the meats, prepare the side dishes and salads. Get all the other stuff done first indoors and then fire up the grill. You will want to give yourself a little extra time to get the grill hot. I usually allow for 15–20 minutes to get the grill to high; hot enough to sear a steak at about 650°F (345°C) or more. After the grill is hot, bring out what you will be grilling.

Now get cooking. Do easy stuff in the winter; burgers, steaks, chops and chicken breasts are good choices. You want items that don't take too long to cook. But the rotisserie works great too, spinning slowly with the lid closed.

Always have a hot beverage with you when winter grilling. It'll keep you warm from the inside out. I like a hot cider with a shot or two of bourbon.

So don't put that grill away at the end of summer; fire it up all year long and become a winter gastro grilling expert.

GASTRO GRILLING ETIQUETTE

When it comes to the rights and wrongs of hosting a backyard gastro grilling party or attending someone else's, there are a few rules of proper etiquette that you should be fully aware of. Take it from me, I have learned a bit about this over the years.

When Attending a Gastro Grill Party

Don't touch the grill: That is the domain of the host or hostess of the grilling party and moving in on their turf, uninvited, is the biggest faux pas you can make. As a guest, you can watch but never touch. But asking questions is completely acceptable.

Do bring something: A good bottle of wine or a new brew or perhaps something you've made to add to the table. Just make sure there is enough to share with everyone.

Do be respectful: Your hosts have enough stress throwing a party that they don't need any added aggravation, so never tell the person working the grill how to do it or what they are doing wrong. Mind your manners and only offer suggestions when asked.

When Hosting a Gastro Grill Party

Make sure your grill is clean. A clean grill is a healthy grill, and it makes you look professional.

If using propane as your fuel source, make sure you have a full tank and a backup tank. There is nothing worse than running out of fuel in the middle of your cooking. Same goes for charcoal, make sure you have enough. Stock up ahead of time.

Invest in proper utensils. Make yourself look like a pro. Rusted, dirty gear can make you look unprofessional. A great pair of tongs, spatula, thermometer and other gadgets for the grill will help you look like a grilling rock star.

Ice is always a must for a grilling party, lots of it to keep your beverages frosty cold. Another important items is water — tap on ice or flat or sparkling bottled. Keeping hydrated on hot summer nights is important.

Prepare recipes that you are comfortable and familiar with. Test recipes on your family (they will forgive you), not your guests.

Prepare a checklist for your party so that you ensure you don't forget any detail.

Create a theme for your gastro grilling party: A theme will make it far easier to plan a menu and get yourself organized. Maybe it's a Seafood Celebration, or maybe it's Burgers for Gourmands and everyone is invited to bring an unusual condiment.

Be organized. Have all the foods you need at the grill, set up and ready to carry out. Have the table(s) set, have the side dishes plated and ready to set out. Nothing worse than a host who runs for 20 minutes grabbing things he/she forgot while the food gets cold.

If, for example, you are nervous about grilling a whole bunch of steaks and getting them all perfect, ask your guests if they want to grill their own. Provide a number of tongs and let the guests cook their own. Makes your job easier as a host and your guests get to have some fun.

Do have all foods ready at relatively the same time. For example, if you are grilling steaks, have all other food elements ready and the last thing you cook is the steaks.

Do have a vegetarian option. I know that meat is the mainstay of grilling and barbeque, but not all your guests may eat meat. So offer something else. I suggest grilled portobello mushroom caps topped with assorted grilled vegetables and cheese (optional).

Do have some appetizer nibbles ready to eat for when your guests arrive. I suggest Brown Sugar Butter–Crusted Shrimp with Red & White Cocktail Sauces (page 36). It is a decadent way to start a party and a recipe that will wow your guests.

Don't feel obligated to invite your neighbors. Not all parties require your neighbors.

Provide taxi rides for those who have a little too much fun.

KISS: Keep It Simple, Sexy.

And lastly, have fun. Enjoy your family and friends and don't worry. It's gastro grilling; what could possibly go wrong!

PARTY STARTERS

CHEESY GOODNESS!

My friend Maxine has a company called Brazilian Ice. She started her business by handcrafting soapstone into ice cubes. Cubes of stone that you put in your freezer and allow to get cold. They hold the cold and keep your fine whiskey chilled without the addition of water. It's a fantastic way to cool down.

But another part of her business is grilling stones. These soapstone stones can be placed directly on your gas or charcoal grills and allow for an even distribution of heat. When using them, you are basically griddling, but on the grill it's stone grilling. You have to get yourself one! **SERVES 6 TO 8**

WHAT YOU NEED: Grilling stone

2 tsp (10 mL) cold butter

3 cloves garlic, finely chopped

2 fresh red jalapeño peppers

2 fresh green jalapeño peppers

1 large white onion, thinly sliced

2 tbsp (30 mL) canola oil

Kosher salt and freshly ground
    pepper to taste

1 oz (30 mL) tequila, reposado or
    anjeo (must be 100% agave)

2 cups (500 mL) shredded
    Mexican melting cheese
    (quesadilla cheese)

1 cup (250 mL) shredded smoked
    mozzarella cheese

6 flour tortillas

6 corn tortillas

2 tbsp (30 mL) chopped
    fresh cilantro

TED'S TIP

You can add a variety of ingredients under the melted Cheesy Goodness. Try shredded chicken, barbequed pork, sliced brisket or even some delicious bacon! There are so many options to alter this recipe. Add shrimp and avocado for a wicked party starter.

Fire up your grill to 350–450°F (180–230°C).

Place your grilling stone directly over your fire source and allow the stone to heat. When ready, the stone should sizzle when you drop a little knob of butter onto it. Be careful not to overheat the stone because it will burn your food.

In a large bowl, combine the garlic, both jalapeños, onions and canola oil. Season to taste with kosher salt and black pepper. Mix well.

Open grill lid and pour the onion mixture over the grilling stone. Using a pair of tongs, spread the onions into an even layer. Let the onions sizzle away for a few minutes, then give them a stir with the tongs. Turn them about so that they start to brown on all sides. When the onion mixture is soft, tender and lightly browned, drizzle with a little bit of tequila; stand back, as it may flame. Spread the onion mixture into a uniform strip down the middle of the grilling stone, approximately 3 inches (8 cm) wide and keeping a 1- to 2-inch (2.5 to 5 cm) border on all sides of the mix. Sprinkle evenly with the cheeses. Close grill lid and allow the cheese to melt and bubble on the stone for about 5 minutes.

Warm flour and corn tortillas on grill until lightly charred and a little crisp. Remove from grill and tear or break into chip-sized pieces. Sprinkle in the Cheesy Goodness mixture and add some chopped fresh cilantro.

BACON-WRAPPED STUFFED SCALLOPS WITH HONEY ORANGE GLAZE

When buying scallops, look for fresh diver scallops that are plump and sweet-smelling. MAKES 8

WHAT YOU NEED: Cookie sheet, lined with parchment or plastic wrap; Food processor; 8 toothpicks

Fry the bacon over medium to medium-low heat until it is just starting to get crispy, about halfway done. Drain on paper towels. Set aside.

Rinse the scallops, drain well and pat dry with paper towels. Place the scallops on prepared cookie sheet and place in the freezer for 10 minutes to get the scallops very cold.

Remove scallops from the freezer and slice each of them in half through the middle. Place in the refrigerator.

Zest the orange and squeeze its juices into a bowl. You will need about ¼ cup (60 mL) of juice for the Honey Orange Glaze. Add the honey, mirin, thyme, black pepper and green onion. Season to taste with a little bit of sea salt. Set aside.

Cut the salmon into 1-inch (2.5 cm) chunks and coarsely chop the shrimp. Place the salmon and half of the shrimp into a food processor. Add the cream, tapioca starch, salt and a pinch of Bone Dust BBQ Spice. Pulse until smooth, about 30 seconds to a minute. Transfer salmon and shrimp purée to a bowl. Add remaining chopped shrimp and mix well. Mixture should be sticky and look chunky.

Spread approximately 1 oz (28 g) of salmon shrimp mix onto one side of a cut scallop, making it uniform in thickness. Next, take another scallop and place it on top of the salmon shrimp mix, similar to assembling a burger. Repeat with remaining scallops and salmon shrimp mix. Return to the refrigerator and allow to rest for at least 1 hour.

Using the 1 tsp (5 mL) Bone Dust BBQ Spice, sprinkle the scallops. Wrap each scallop tightly with a slice of partially cooked bacon. Secure each with a toothpick.

Fire up your grill to 450–550°F (230–290°C).

Grill scallops, over direct heat with the lid open, for 4–5 minutes. Turn scallops over and baste with Honey Orange Glaze. Continue to cook for approximately 4–5 minutes, basting a few more times until the scallops are just cooked through and the bacon is crisp. Remove from grill. Remove toothpick and serve immediately. Drizzle with extra Honey Orange Glaze.

8 slices smoked bacon
8 fresh jumbo scallops, U10 size, trimmed of muscle

HONEY ORANGE GLAZE

1 orange
¼ cup (60 mL) honey
1 tbsp (15 mL) mirin
1 tsp (5 mL) chopped fresh thyme
½ tsp (2 mL) freshly ground black pepper
1 green onion, finely chopped
Sea salt to taste

4 oz (115 g) fresh salmon, boneless and skinless
4 oz (115 g) fresh shrimp, peeled and deveined
2 tbsp (30 mL) heavy cream (35% MF)
1 tsp (5 mL) tapioca starch
Pinch of sea salt
Pinch + 1 tsp (5 mL) Bone Dust BBQ Spice (page 212)

BROWN SUGAR BUTTER-CRUSTED SHRIMP WITH RED & WHITE COCKTAIL SAUCES

When in Chicago on business, I tend to find myself at a steakhouse and quite often I will order a shrimp cocktail. On one occasion, I ordered a shrimp cocktail that consisted of a bowl of ice with shredded iceberg lettuce on top and then topped with 5 jumbo shrimp and of course the standard red cocktail sauce. Not that this was bad or anything, but I was in a mood for something tastier. I just happened to have a half a glass of Maker's Mark in front of me, and the next thing I knew I was dipping my shrimp into the bourbon and eating them up. The bourbon was far superior to the cocktail sauce. This became "my thing" and now, if I'm on the road, I order the shrimp and some Maker's Mark and call it a great meal. Have a blast with this one. It's incredibly tasty. **SERVES 6**

WHAT YOU NEED: Cookie sheet, lined with parchment or plastic wrap

RED COCKTAIL SAUCE

¼ cup (60 mL) freshly grated horseradish

1 tbsp (15 mL) extra-hot prepared horseradish (find one that has a good kick of heat to it)

½ cup (125 mL) ketchup

½ cup (125 mL) chili sauce

2 tsp (10 mL) freshly squeezed lemon juice

Splash of cane vinegar

2 tsp (10 mL) TABASCO® Chipotle Sauce

Sea salt and freshly ground black pepper to taste

WHITE COCKTAIL SAUCE

½ cup (125 mL) mayonnaise

¼ cup (60 mL) cream cheese, softened

¼ cup (60 mL) ranch dressing

¼ cup (60 mL) freshly grated horseradish

2 tbsp (30 mL) extra-hot prepared horseradish

2 tsp (10 mL) freshly squeezed lemon juice

Splash of cane vinegar

Sea salt and freshly ground black pepper to taste

18 fresh wild jumbo shrimp (approx. 2 lb/900 g), size 8/10 or 10/12 per pound

2 tbsp (30 mL) sea salt

1 cup (250 mL) Maker's Mark

½ cup (125 mL) unsalted butter

½ cup (125 mL) brown sugar

To make the Red Cocktail Sauce, stir together the horseradish, ketchup, chili sauce, lemon juice and cane vinegar in a small bowl. Season to taste with TABASCO® Chipotle Sauce (2 tsp/10 mL will give it a real kick; add less if you don't like it too hot), sea salt and black pepper. Transfer to a self-sealing container and refrigerate until needed. Let the sauce sit for at least 1 hour so that the flavors come together and the heat builds.

To make the White Cocktail Sauce, whisk together the mayonnaise, cream cheese and ranch dressing until smooth in a small bowl. Add the fresh and prepared horseradish, lemon juice and cane vinegar. Season to taste with sea salt and black pepper. Transfer to a self-sealing container and refrigerate until needed. Let the sauce sit for at least 1 hour so that the flavors come together and the heat builds.

continued...

To make the Grilled Shrimp with Brown Sugar Butter Crust, peel the shrimp, leaving the tail portion intact. Using a sharp knife, cut down the length of the top side of the shrimp from head to tail, exposing the digestive tract. Rinse under cold water to remove the dirt. Repeat with remaining shrimp. Pat dry with paper towels. Place shrimp in a bowl and sprinkle liberally with sea salt, then toss to coat evenly. Let the shrimp stand refrigerated for 15 minutes in the salt, as this will enhance the flavor of the shrimp.

Remove shrimp from refrigerator and rinse quickly under cold water to remove excess salt. Pat dry one more time with paper towels. Place shrimp into a bowl and pour the Maker's Mark over them, making sure that all of the shrimp are submerged in the whisky. Place them back in the refrigerator for another 15 minutes. While you wait, have a shot of whisky to pass the time!

Melt the ½ cup (125 mL) of unsalted butter.

Remove the shrimp from the whisky marinade. Brush each shrimp with a lot of melted butter. If the shrimp are cold enough, the butter will harden almost as soon as you brush it on. Place the butter-glazed shrimp on the prepared cookie sheet. Repeat with remaining shrimp. If you are a diehard whisky fan, then you will not waste the marinade; save it and use it for something else or drink it up!

Roll each butter-glazed shrimp in a little bit of brown sugar. Be sure to cover both sides and then place back into the refrigerator.

Fire up your grill to 450–550°F (230–290°C).

With the grill lid open, grill the shrimp directly over the heat for about 3–5 minutes per side, until the shrimp are just cooked through and opaque. Remove from grill and serve immediately with both the Red & White Cocktail Sauces.

FIRE-ROASTED ONION SOUP WITH SMOKED CHEDDAR DUMPLINGS

For this recipe, I like to fire up my charcoal grill and fire-roast the onions over hot coals until the outside is completely charred and the flesh is hot, moist and tender on the inside. I then peel away the outer layers, as inside is where the "love" is. Make this soup; your friends will drool over it. **SERVES 8**

WHAT YOU NEED: Large soup pot

Fire up your grill to 450–550°F (230–290°C).

Place the whole onions above the coals, close lid and roast for 45–60 minutes, turning occasionally, until the onions are charred on the outside and tender on the inside. It is important that you make sure you don't turn them into mush. Remove onions from grill and allow them to cool slightly. Peel and then thinly slice them. Set aside.

In a large soup pot, heat ¼ cup (60 mL) butter over medium heat. Add the roasted onions and garlic and sauté for 15–20 minutes, stirring constantly, until the onions are lightly browned and extremely tender. Deglaze the onions and garlic with the whiskey. Stand back as you add the whiskey, as it may flambé. Stir to scrape up any brown bits. Add the thyme sprigs, bay leaves, peppercorns, beef stock and salt to taste. Bring to a rolling boil, reduce heat to medium-low and simmer, stirring occasionally, for 30 minutes. Adjust seasoning with salt and pepper. Discard bay leaves.

Meanwhile, prepare the dumplings by sifting the flour, baking powder and salt into a large bowl. Stir in 1 cup (250 mL) cheese, parsley, black pepper and cayenne pepper. Make a well in the center and add the melted butter and ½ cup (125 mL) buttermilk. Stir together to make a soft dough, adding more buttermilk if necessary.

Drop 16 spoonfuls of the dumpling batter on top of the simmering smoky onion soup. Continue to simmer, uncovered, for 8 to 10 minutes or until the dumplings are puffed and cooked through.

To serve, ladle onion soup mixture into bowls. Top each bowl with at least 2 dumplings. Drizzle with a little bit of birch syrup and garnish with a little extra crumbled smoked cheddar cheese. Serve immediately with a shot of spiced whiskey on the side.

Now this is a gastro way to warm up your bones!

FIRE-ROASTED ONION SOUP

8 large sweet onions, sliced

¼ cup (60 mL) butter

12 cloves garlic, finely chopped

½ cup (125 mL) spiced whiskey

4 sprigs fresh thyme

2 bay leaves

1 tsp (5 mL) cracked black peppercorns

12 cups (3 L) beef stock

Salt and freshly ground black pepper to taste

APPLE WOOD SMOKED CHEDDAR DUMPLINGS

2½ cups (625 mL) all-purpose flour

2 tsp (10 mL) baking powder

1 tsp (5 mL) salt

1 + ½ cups (375 mL) shredded apple wood smoked cheddar cheese

1 tbsp (15 mL) chopped fresh parsley

¼ tsp (1 mL) freshly ground black pepper

Pinch of cayenne pepper

¼ cup (60 mL) melted butter

½ to 1 cup (125 to 250 mL) buttermilk

8 teaspoons (40 mL) birch syrup

FIRE-ROASTED MUSSELS WITH ORANGE WHEAT BEER & BUTTER

Fire-roasting mussels adds a sweet smokiness to the succulent flesh. This recipe is quick and easy with big flavor results. Be sure to have plenty of napkins on hand. **SERVES 4**

WHAT YOU NEED: Grill topper

Rinse mussels under cold running water.

The beard (a hair-like strand the mussel uses to attach itself to rocks or coral, or in the case of cultivated mussels to the wooden posts in the ocean) will need to be removed. Hold a mussel between your fingers with the beard facing up. Using a damp paper towel or kitchen towel, grab hold of the beard and pull to remove. Repeat with remaining mussels. Cover with damp paper towels and refrigerate until right before you are going to grill them.

Fire up your grill to 450–550°F (230–290°C).

Set grill topper directly onto the grill, close grill lid and allow it to heat.

Place the mussels into a large bowl. Add smoked and sea salt, black pepper, thyme, rosemary and garlic, then toss to coat. Crack open that bottle of beer and drizzle the mussels with about a quarter of the bottle (4 oz/125 mL). Continue to toss the mussels to evenly coat.

Open grill lid and carefully pour the seasoned mussels onto the preheated grill topper. Close the lid and grill-roast until the mussels open. This should take approximately 8 to 10 minutes. About halfway through open grill lid and squeeze 3 orange halves over the mussels and drizzle with extra beer. Close lid and continue to cook until all the shells are open, a couple more minutes.

Carefully remove mussels from the grill and place in a large bowl, add a few cubes of butter and squeeze the final orange half over top. Discard any unopened shells. Drizzle with a little more beer, toss and serve immediately. Serve with lots of toasted baguette and bottles of ice cold beer.

3 lb (1.4 kg) large fresh mussels

1 tbsp (15 mL) coarsely ground smoked salt

2 tbsp (30 mL) coarsely ground sea salt or kosher salt

1 tbsp (15 mL) freshly cracked black pepper

2 tbsp (30 mL) roughly chopped fresh thyme

3 tbsp (45 mL) roughly chopped fresh rosemary

8 cloves garlic, minced

1 bottle (12 oz/341 mL) Shock Top (or other Belgian-style wheat ale)

2 oranges, halved

¼ cup (60 mL) cold butter, cut into ½-inch (1 cm) cubes

TED'S TIP

- When you are cleaning your mussels, if you come across any shells that are open, give them a squeeze to close the shell. If the shell stays closed, they are alive; if they don't close, then the mussel is dead and should be discarded.
- You can find smoked salt in specialty food shops as well as many grocery store chains. One of my favorite branded smoked salts is called Maldon, a flaked sea salt with a light smoky flavor. Smoked salt is great for adding that smoky flavor to your dishes without having to fire up your smoker. It's a staple in my pantry.

FIRE-ROASTED OYSTERS WITH CRAWFISH BACON BBQ BUTTER

When buying your oysters, find a reputable fishmonger that has a variety of fresh oysters available. Buy them fresh, never frozen. For the gastro grill chef in me, I like to do this recipe best over burning hot charcoal. The charcoal adds a wonderful smokiness to the roasting oysters. **MAKES 12**

WHAT YOU NEED: Oyster knife; Grill topper (optional)

1 cup (250 mL) crawfish tail meat (fresh steamed is best when in season, but in a pinch use thawed and drained frozen)

6 slices bacon, cooked crispy and diced

2 cloves garlic, minced

2 green onions, minced

2 tbsp (30 mL) smoky barbeque sauce (I personally use my Beerlicious™ BBQ Sauce, but as a gastro griller you can use whatever kind you like the most)

1 stick (4 oz/115 g) unsalted butter, softened

1 or 2 dashes of TABASCO® brand Pepper Sauce

Kosher salt and freshly ground black pepper to taste

12 large fresh oysters (deep-welled oysters work best for stuffing)

½ cup (125 mL) freshly grated Parmesan cheese

½ cup (125 mL) panko breadcrumbs

In a bowl, mix together the crawfish tail meat, bacon, garlic, green onions, barbeque sauce and butter. Season to taste with a dash or two of TABASCO® brand Pepper Sauce, salt and black pepper. Set aside.

Rinse the oysters under cold running water to remove excess mud and grit. Using an oyster knife, shuck the oysters, being careful to reserve the oyster liquor in the shell. Place the shucked oysters, evenly spaced, onto a grill topper accessory. If you do not have a topper, use a cookie sheet for now.

In a separate small bowl, combine Parmesan cheese and panko. Set aside.

Place 1 heaping tbsp (15 mL) crawfish barbeque butter mixture on top of each of the oysters, gently patting the butter mix to cover the oyster completely. Sprinkle the Parmesan mixture evenly over the surface of each oyster to make a crust. Cover with plastic wrap and refrigerate for 10–15 minutes so that the butter mixture firms up.

Fire up your grill to 450–550°F (230–290°C).

Place the grill topper onto the grill. If you did not use a grill topper, remove oysters from the cookie sheet and then place them carefully onto the grill, shell side down and stuffing side up. Close the lid and fire-roast for 8–10 minutes, until the oysters are bubbling in crawfish bacon barbeque butter and the crust is golden brown and crisp.

Carefully remove from the grill and serve immediately.

TED'S TIP

If you cannot find crawfish, then substitute with crab or lobster meat. Better yet, just double up on the bacon. And if you don't eat bacon (oh, how can you not?), then switch it out for another delicious ingredient.

FIRE-ROASTED TOMATO BRUSCHETTA

This is a really simple and delicious recipe to bring out the gastro griller in you — bruschetta with charred tomatoes, fresh garlic, olive oil and basil. Topped with a goat's milk Pecorino Crotonese cheese, it's wickedly delicious! **SERVES 8**

Fire up your grill to 450–550°F (230–290°C).

Cut the plum tomatoes in half. Place the tomato halves, cut side down, onto the hot grill and quickly char the surface of each. Turn and grill the tomatoes until the skin is lightly charred, as this should take just a minute or two. You don't want to cook the tomatoes, as this will make them mushy — just a little char to add some grill flavor.

Remove tomatoes from grill. Peel and discard the charred skin. Coarsely chop the charred tomato pieces and place them into a medium-sized bowl. Season to taste with a little kosher salt and black pepper. Drizzle with extra virgin olive oil, mix and set aside.

Toast the rustic bread on both sides until golden brown and crispy; set aside and keep warm. Take a clove of garlic and rub it all over one side of the bread; repeat with remaining bread pieces.

Add freshly chopped basil to the charred tomato mixture. It is best to do this right before serving so that the basil is fresh and doesn't turn black. Spoon the bruschetta mixture onto the grilled bread; drizzle with a little extra virgin olive oil and balsamic vinegar. Garnish with shaved Pecorino Crotonese cheese and serve immediately.

4 ripe, plump plum tomatoes
Kosher salt and freshly ground black pepper to taste
Extra virgin olive oil
8 slices rustic bread, cut approx. 1 inch (2.5 cm) thick
2 to 4 cloves garlic
1 cup (250 mL) fresh basil leaves
Drizzle of aged balsamic vinegar
16 shavings of Pecorino Crotonese cheese

TED'S TIP

Use a good-quality extra virgin olive oil along with an aged balsamic. I have a nice 40-year-old balsamic that I love to drizzle on this recipe.

FULLY LOADED GASTRO SKINS

Fully loaded with bacon, marbled cheddar cheese, chives and ranch dressing, and using locally farmed fingerling potatoes, these little loaded potatoes will be mouth-popping happiness. **MAKES 24 SKINS**

WHAT YOU NEED: Grill topper

24 fingerling potatoes (approx. 2 to 3 lb/0.9 to 1.4 kg)

¼ cup (60 mL) olive oil

Kosher salt and freshly ground black pepper to taste

¼ cup (60 mL) ranch dressing (good quality), plus extra for serving

6 slices bacon

½ cup (125 mL) marbled cheddar cheese, grated

¼ cup (60 mL) chopped fresh chives

Pinch of cayenne pepper

TED'S TIP

When buying the potatoes, try to find ones that are uniform in size and shape.

Wash and scrub the fingerling potatoes to remove any excess dirt and grit. Pat dry with paper towels and place in a large bowl. Drizzle with olive oil and season with kosher salt and black pepper to taste.

Preheat oven to 375°F (190°C)

Place potatoes in an even layer on a baking sheet. Bake fingerling potatoes in preheated oven for 30–45 minutes, until they are tender and a toothpick pushes easily into the flesh. Remove from oven and allow to cool for approximately 10 minutes.

Meanwhile, in a frying pan over medium-high heat, cook the bacon until nice and crispy. Drain off grease, pat bacon dry with paper towels and then dice. Set aside.

Cut the top off each potato lengthwise about a quarter from the top. Using a small spoon, scoop out the potato flesh from the bottoms and tops, reserving the flesh for the filling and being careful not to break the outer skin; you want to make fingerling potato "canoes." Set aside.

Take the remaining scooped fingerling potato tops and finely chop. Add to the scooped mashed potatoes. Don't waste this crispy goodness — be sure to add it back in.

To the warm potato flesh, add the crispy bacon, ranch dressing, marbled cheese and chives, and season to taste with kosher salt and black pepper and a pinch of cayenne pepper. The mixture should be slightly sticky; therefore, if it is too dry add a little extra ranch dressing.

Using a small spoon, fill the fingerling potato "canoes" with the potato bacon cheese mixture. Load 'em up so that the mixture is piled above the edge of the skins. Once full, place them skin side down onto a grill topper and set aside. Repeat for all skins.

Fire up your grill to 450–550°F (230–290°C).

Place grill topper onto the grill. Close lid and grill-roast for 12–15 minutes, until the skins are crisp and the filling is hot and bubbling. Remove from grill. Drizzle with a little extra ranch dressing and serve immediately.

GRILLED CHICKEN STICKS WITH SPICY MAPLE SOY GLAZE

This recipe is a crowd pleaser. I use chicken tenderloins for my sticks, but if you cannot get chicken tenderloins, you can substitute chicken breast meat cut into approximately 6 or 8 strips. These won't take long to grill for your guests. Medium-high heat, lid open and grill 'em up! **MAKES 24 STICKS**

WHAT YOU NEED: 24 bamboo skewers (I call them sticks as it's a little more rustic), each about 8 inches (20 cm) long; Basting brush

Place 20 of the skewers into a rectangular container and pour over warm water and 1 cup (250 mL) sake. Add 1 tsp (5 mL) ginger and a pinch of salt and black pepper. Swish it all about and let stand for at least 1 hour. The sticks will infuse with flavor.

Carefully thread 1 chicken tenderloin onto one end of each skewer. Place the skewered chicken tenderloins into a glass dish large enough to hold them in a single layer.

In a bowl, whisk together the remaining ¼ cup (60 mL) of sake, rice wine vinegar, mirin, soy sauce, sesame oil, ginger, lemongrass and chili sauce. Pour over chicken sticks, turning to coat. Cover and marinate chicken, refrigerated, for 4 hours.

Fire up your grill to 450–550°F (230–290°C).

To make the Spicy Maple Soy Glaze, whisk together the maple syrup, hoisin sauce, soy sauce, lime juice, chili sauce, cilantro, green onions and sesame seeds in a bowl. Season to taste with salt and black pepper.

Remove chicken sticks from marinade, discarding leftover marinade. Grill chicken sticks with the lid open for about 3–5 minutes on one side. Turn the sticks over and baste with reserved Spicy Maple Soy Glaze until the chicken is fully cooked and the glaze is sticky. These should take no longer than 8–10 minutes to fully cook.

Serve immediately. No dip required.

TED'S TIP
- Always soak your wooden skewers (sticks) in water or a flavored water mixture to keep them from catching fire.
- Wrap each stick with a little bit of tinfoil, starting where the meat ends.
- Grill your sticks with the lid open and with the non-meat part of the stick sticking out over the edge of the grill, away from the direct flame.

1 cup (250 mL) warm water
1 + ¼ cups (300 mL) sake
1-inch (2.5 cm) knob fresh ginger, minced (1 + 1 tsp/10 mL)
Salt and freshly ground black pepper to taste
24 fresh chicken tenderloins
¼ cup (60 mL) rice wine vinegar
¼ cup (60 mL) mirin
2 tbsp (30 mL) soy sauce
1 tbsp (15 mL) Asian sesame oil
2-inch (10 cm) stalk lemongrass, squished to crack and thinly sliced
1 tsp (5 mL) Asian chili sauce

SPICY MAPLE SOY GLAZE
¼ cup (60 mL) pure maple syrup
½ cup (125 mL) hoisin sauce
2 tbsp (30 mL) soy sauce
2 tsp (10 mL) freshly squeezed lime juice
1 tsp (5 mL) Asian chili sauce
1 tbsp (15 mL) chopped fresh cilantro
2 green onions, thinly sliced
1 tsp (5 mL) sesame seeds
Salt and freshly ground black pepper to taste

LAMB STICKS WITH LEMON OUZO BASTE

These are amazing gastro meat sticks; fresh rosemary sprigs for skewers and tender lamb loins are your meat. This recipe is fast and easy to grill, making them the perfect appetizer for a great party. **MAKES 24 STICKS**

WHAT YOU NEED: Basting brush; 24 sprigs of fresh rosemary, approx. 8 to 10 inches (20 to 25 cm) long

2 boneless lamb loins (approx. 6 to 8 oz/170 to 225 g each)

2 tbsp (30 mL) olive oil

1 lemon

6 plump cloves garlic, minced

2 oz (60 mL) ouzo

3 tbsp (45 mL) honey

Kosher salt

1 tsp (5 mL) freshly ground black pepper

½ cup (125 mL) crumbled feta cheese

TED'S TIP

- The fresh rosemary should have a pretty thick stem so that it can support the weight of the lamb. If you cannot find thick-stemmed fresh rosemary, use metal or bamboo skewers.
- Always soak your wooden skewers (sticks) in water or a flavored water mixture to keep them from catching fire.
- Wrap each stick with a little bit of tinfoil, starting where the meat ends.
- Grill your sticks with the lid open and with the non-meat part of the stick sticking out over the edge of the grill, away from the direct flame.
- Do not overcook these sticks. Lamb loins are very lean and the small medallions that you cut will take no time at all to cook. Fast and easy. No dip required.

Take a sprig of rosemary and peel away about 2 to 3 inches (5 to 8 cm) of the leaves from the bottom part of the stem, exposing the stem. Reserve the rosemary leaves for the marinade. Repeat with remaining rosemary sprigs. Place rosemary sticks into a dish and cover with warm water for at least an hour so that the rosemary absorbs some moisture to prevent burning on the grill.

Slice the lamb loins into ½-inch (1 cm) thick medallions. You should get approx. 12 medallions per lamb loin. Thread one slice of lamb onto the bottom end of one rosemary stick. Repeat with remaining slices of lamb loin and rosemary sticks. Brush each slice of lamb on both sides with a little olive oil and set aside.

To prepare the basting sauce, zest the lemon and place the zest in a bowl. Cut the lemon in half and juice. Add juice to the lemon zest. Coarsely chop the reserved rosemary leaves (you will need about 1 tbsp/15 mL worth of rosemary) and add to the lemon zest and juice. Set aside.

In a small saucepot, heat remaining oil over medium heat for about a minute. Add garlic and sauté for 1–2 minutes, until tender. Remove from heat; add ouzo, honey and lemon-rosemary mixture. Season to taste with kosher salt and black pepper. Set aside.

Fire up your grill to 450–550°F (230–290°C).

Season lamb on both sides with a little salt and black pepper. Grill lamb sticks with the lid open for about 1–2 minutes on one side. Turn the sticks over and baste with reserved ouzo lemon baste. At this point, they should be done. Remove from grill. Garnish with crumbled feta cheese and serve immediately.

MARGARITA CHICKEN LOLLIPOPS

Nothing says a party like a Margarita — tequila and lime — plus adding a few ice cold beers into the mix! You don't have to go to the extent of making the lollipops if you are not comfortable; you can just use regular chicken wings instead of drummettes to keep it simple. It's up to you, but the lollipops look so much more gastro grillesque. Cheers! **SERVES 4**

Zest the lime and place the zest in a small bowl. Add the black pepper, salt, cilantro, cumin, a pinch of cayenne (to add some kick) and oil to the lime zest and mix. The mixture should be a little slushy.

Cut the lime in half and squeeze the juice into a separate small bowl. Set juice aside for use in the Margarita Wing Sauce.

Using a sharp paring knife, slice around the knuckle of each drummette to loosen the skin and meat from the bone. Scrape and push the meat down the length of the bone, forming a ball of chicken at the end of the drummette. Repeat with remaining drummettes.

Place chicken lollipops in a large bowl and toss with the lime zest mixture. Cover and refrigerate for 1 hour.

To prepare the Margarita Wing Sauce, whisk together the honey, mustard, reserved lime juice, tequila, orange liqueur, green onion, minced jalapeño and cilantro in a bowl. Set aside.

Fire up your grill to 450–550°F (230–290°C). Prepare grill for indirect grilling.

Grill chicken wing lollipops for 5–6 minutes, turning frequently to get them a little bit charred. Move wings to the indirect part of the grill, close lid and allow wings to cook for 12–15 minutes until fully cooked, golden brown and a little crispy. Indirect grilling allows you to keep the flare-ups to a minimum and makes for easier grilling, allowing you more time to gastro party!

Transfer grilled lollipops to a bowl and toss with reserved Margarita Wing Sauce and butter. Mix well. Sprinkle with crushed cashews and crumbled cheese, toss and serve immediately.

1 fresh juicy jumbo lime

1 tsp (5 mL) coarsely ground
black pepper

2 tsp (10 mL) kosher salt

2 tsp (10 mL) dried cilantro or 2 tbsp
(30 mL) fresh coriander leaves

¼ tsp (1 mL) ground cumin

Pinch of cayenne pepper

1 tbsp (15 mL) vegetable oil

3 lb (1.4 kg) jumbo chicken
drummettes (approx. 36 pieces)

MARGARITA WING SAUCE

½ cup (125 mL) honey

¼ cup (60 mL) prepared mustard

2 tbsp (30 mL) freshly squeezed
lime juice

2 oz (60 mL) tequila (100% agave;
reposado tequila is best)

1 oz (30 mL) orange liqueur

1 green onion, minced

1 jalapeño pepper, minced

2 tbsp (30 mL) chopped
fresh cilantro

2 tbsp (30 mL) butter

¼ cup (60 mL) crushed
salted cashews

½ cup (125 mL) queso fresco
(Mexican cheese)

PIG NUTS

Plank Grilled Bacon-Wrapped Smoked Sausage & Ground Pork Stuffed Meatballs with Spiced Whiskey Maple BBQ Sauce is much too long to say, so I have since dubbed this recipe "Pig Nuts." Pig Nuts is a heck of a lot easier to say. Not only will their name be a hit at your backyard party, but so will their flavor. Give 'em a go! **MAKES 12**

WHAT YOU NEED: Maple grilling plank (12 × 8 × ½ inches/30 × 20 × 1 cm), soaked in water for a minimum of 1 hour; Basting brush

3 smoked sausages (approx. 4 oz/115 g each)

1¼ lb (500 g) ground pork

2 tbsp (30 mL) chopped fresh cilantro

1 to 2 jalapeño peppers, seeded and finely diced

1 green onion, minced

2 tsp (10 mL) Bone Dust BBQ Spice (page 212)

12 slices smoked bacon

SPICED WHISKEY MAPLE BBQ SAUCE

¼ cup (60 mL) gourmet-style barbeque sauce

2 tsp (10 mL) TABASCO® Chipotle Sauce

¼ cup (60 mL) pure maple syrup

1½ oz (45 mL) spiced whiskey or rum

Cut 2 smoked sausages into 6 equal-sized chunks, approx. ½ oz (14 g) each. Set aside. Take 1 smoked sausage and finely chop; place in a large bowl. Add ground pork, cilantro, jalapeño, green onion and Bone Dust BBQ Spice. Mix well.

Divide mixture into 12 equal-sized portions, approximately 1½ oz (42 g) each. Place a portion of meat into the palm of your hand and flatten slightly. Place a chunk of smoked sausage onto the ground pork mixture. Wrap the meat mixture around the sausage so that the entire sausage is covered by the meat. Roll between your hands to make into a nice round meatball. Repeat with remaining ground pork and smoked sausage chunks.

Lay a slice of bacon on a flat work surface and run your fingers across the entire length of the bacon to stretch it by almost one-third. Wrap each meatball tightly with the stretched slice of bacon, making sure to cover the entire surface of the meatball. Refrigerate, covered, for at least 1 hour.

In a small bowl, combine barbeque sauce, TABASCO® Chipotle Sauce, maple syrup and spiced whiskey. Set aside.

Fire up your grill to 350–450°F (180–230°C). Prepare grill for indirect grilling.

Place bacon-wrapped smoked sausage–stuffed pork balls, evenly spaced, onto a presoaked grilling plank. Place plank into grill, not directly over the flame or heat source, and close lid. Plank grill for 8–10 minutes. Turn the grilling plank 180°, close lid and continue to plank grill for another 8–10 minutes, until the bacon begins to crisp. Baste with Spiced Whiskey Maple BBQ Sauce and continue to plank grill for 5 more minutes, until the bacon is crispy and the sauce sticky. Remove from grill. Serve immediately.

PLANK GRILLED LOBSTER CAKES WITH BROWN BUTTER DRIZZLE

This recipe requires a bit of preparation but is well worth the effort that goes into it. I use my grill to bake the potatoes for this recipe; it adds a bit of extra smokiness to the recipe. For ease, you can bake them in your oven or give 'em a nuke in the microwave! Whatever makes your life easier, which goes for boiling up the lobsters too. If you wish to use fresh or frozen already cooked lobster meat, go ahead. This recipe is for you to have fun. A shot of vodka might help too! **SERVES 8**

WHAT YOU NEED: Large pot (holds 2 gallons/2 L); Ice cream scoop (optional); Maple grilling plank (12 × 8 × ½ inches/30 × 20 × 1 cm), soaked in water for a minimum of 1 hour

Fire up your grill to 350–450°F (180–230°C).

Place potatoes into the grill, close lid and bake for 45–60 minutes, turning occasionally, until fully cooked and the flesh is tender.

While the potatoes are baking, take the time to prepare the lobsters. Fill a large pot with cold water and, over high heat, bring to a rolling boil. Add in the sea salt. (It may seem like a lot of salt, but if you want to get the best flavor from boiling a lobster, then heavily salt the water. Personally I add ½ cup/125 mL of sea salt because I want to taste the sea!). Plunge your lobsters head first into the boiling water. Cover and return the lobsters to a rolling boil, then reduce heat to medium just so they are cooking at a bubble, not a full-on boil. Cook lobsters for about 10 minutes. You want the meat to be firm and opaque, not rubbery and overcooked. Remove lobsters from boiling water and allow lobsters to cool. Do not rinse under cold water, as you will wash away the entire wonderful sea salty flavor that you just added to the meat.

Break apart the lobster tail, claws, and body and get all the meat out of the shell. It's a bit of work but rewarding. Place the lobster meat into a bowl and set aside.

Remove the potatoes from grill and allow them to cool for about 5 minutes. Once cool, cut each potato in half and scoop out the hot flesh of the potato into a large bowl. Gently mash with a fork. Add 2 tbsp (30 mL) butter and stir until the butter has melted and mixed evenly through the mashed potato mixture. Set aside to fully cool. You will need about 1½ cups (375 mL) of butter mashed potatoes.

¾ lb (340 g) gold-fleshed potatoes (approx. 2 to 3 large potatoes)
2 fresh/live Atlantic lobsters (approx. 1½ to 2 lb/675 to 900 g each)
¼ cup (60 mL) sea salt
2 tbsp + 3 tbsp + ½ cup (200 mL) butter
½ cup (125 mL) mayonnaise
1 large egg yolk
2 green onions, thinly sliced
¼ cup (60 mL) red onion, diced
1 tbsp (15 mL) chopped fresh dill
½ lemon, juiced (approx. 1 tbsp/15 mL)
1 tsp (5 mL) Bone Dust BBQ Spice (page 212)
Sea salt, freshly ground black pepper and TABASCO® brand Pepper Sauce to taste

continued...

After you remove the meat from the lobster shells, do not throw out the shells — save them. I like to put them in a self-sealing bag and freeze them. Once I have a large amount, I will use them for a soup stock.

Shred the lobster meat into small strips or chunks and place into a large bowl. Add in the buttered mashed potato mixture and gently mix together. Keep it light and fluffy. Add in the mayonnaise, egg yolk, green onions, red onion and dill. Squeeze in the lemon juice and sprinkle in the Bone Dust BBQ Spice. Season to taste with salt, black pepper and a few drops of TABASCO® brand Pepper Sauce. Gently mix until everything binds together. You may need to add a little more mayo, so keep the jar at hand.

Form into 8 small cakes. You can use an ice cream scoop to make this a little easier. Place each lobster cake onto the soaked grilling plank, evenly spaced.

Melt 3 tbsp (45 mL) butter and brush each lobster cake with it, cover with plastic wrap and refrigerate for at least 1 hour to allow the cakes to settle.

Place the grilling plank on the grill and close lid. Plank grill for 20–25 minutes, until heated through and the lobster potato cakes are golden brown.

Just before the lobster cakes are done cooking, heat a small pan over medium-high heat, add the ½ cup (125 mL) butter and heat until the butter starts to bubble and spurt. Give it a stir and allow the butter to brown. You want the butter to take on a nutty flavor. Remove from heat and set aside.

Remove lobster cakes from plank and serve drizzled with browned butter and sprinkled with a little extra sea salt. Serve immediately.

THIN CRUST PLANK-GRILLED PIZZA

This is a gastro sexy pizza; hot plank grilled thin crust pizza topped with juicy sweet grilled pineapple, Gorgonzola cheese and speck. Give this a go — you and your family and friends will not be disappointed. This can be served either as an appetizer or even as a dessert pizza. It's up to you. Have fun! **SERVES 4 TO 6**

WHAT YOU NEED: Hand-held blender or blender; Maple grilling plank (12 × 8 × ½ inches/30 × 20 × 1 cm), soaked in water for a minimum of 1 hour; Pizza peel

BLACKBERRY SYRUP
8 oz (225 g) fresh blackberries
3 tbsp (45 mL) packed light brown sugar
¼ cup (60 mL) pure maple syrup
2 tbsp (30 mL) water
½ oz (15 mL) spiced rum or ½ tsp (2 mL)
    rum extract (optional)

LEMON CREAM CHEESE
½ cup (125 mL) cream cheese, softened
2 tbsp (30 mL) icing sugar
½ oz (15 mL) spiced rum or ½ tsp (2 mL)
    rum extract (optional)
½ teaspoon (2 mL) grated lemon zest
½ teaspoon (2 mL) lemon juice
Freshly ground black pepper to taste

PIZZA DOUGH
2 cups (500 mL) all-purpose flour
¼ cup (60 mL) freshly grated Parmesan cheese
1 tbsp (15 mL) Bone Dust BBQ Spice (page 212)
2½ tsp (12 mL) baking powder
¼ cup (60 mL) butter, diced
½ to ⅔ cup (125 to 150 mL) milk
Salt and coarsely ground black pepper to taste
2 to 3 tbsp (30 to 45 mL) cornmeal
¼ cup (60 mL) olive oil

TOPPINGS
6 slices fresh pineapple, peeled and sliced
    (approx. ¼ inch/5 mm thick)
8 slices speck (smoked prosciutto)
½ cup (125 mL) Gorgonzola cheese, crumbled

MINT SALAD
1½ cups (375 mL) fresh crisp mint leaves
½ green onion, finely chopped
Drizzle of lemon juice
Drizzle of olive oil
Drizzle of Blackberry Syrup
Kosher salt and coarsely ground black pepper to taste

To prepare the Blackberry Syrup, place berries into a small saucepot and mash with the back of a wooden spoon. Add brown sugar, maple syrup and water. Bring to a bubbling boil.

Reduce heat to medium to medium-low and, stirring occasionally, cook until the berries are very tender, about 15 minutes. The mixture should be sticky and coat the back of the wooden spoon. Remove from heat and stir in the rum or rum extract (if using). Purée with blender. Strain through fine-mesh sieve and let stand at room temperature.

continued...

To prepare the Lemon Cream Cheese, whisk together softened cream cheese, icing sugar and spiced rum (if using) in a bowl until smooth. Add lemon zest and lemon juice and season to taste with black pepper. Set aside.

To prepare the Pizza Dough, stir together all-purpose flour, Parmesan cheese, Bone Dust BBQ Spice and baking powder in a large bowl. Add cold butter to flour mixture. Season to taste with a pinch of salt and a little coarsely ground black pepper. Using your fingertips, rub butter and flour together until mixture resembles coarse breadcrumbs. Stir in enough milk to form a dough. Turn dough out onto a lightly floured surface and knead for 6–8 minutes or until dough is smooth and elastic. Wrap dough in plastic wrap and allow to rest for about 30 minutes at room temperature.

Fire up your grill to 450–550°F (230–290°C).

While dough is resting, prepare toppings for pizza. Start with grilling pineapple slices for 3–5 minutes per side, until lightly charred. Remove from grill and allow to cool slightly. Cut each slice in half. Set aside.

Place dough ball onto a floured surface and flatten slightly. Roll into a tube about 12 inches (38 cm) long. Using rolling pin, flatten out dough into a crust 2 inches (5 cm) shorter than the length of the grilling plank and about ¼ inch (5 mm) thick.

Remove plank from water. Pat dry with paper towels and sprinkle one side of the plank with cornmeal. Lay pizza dough onto plank and brush lightly with olive oil. Place plank onto grill and bake crust for about 8–10 minutes or until top is light golden brown and the dough is just starting to get a little crisp. Open lid of grill and carefully flip pizza dough over directly on the plank.

Take the Lemon Cream Cheese and spread it evenly over the entire surface of the pizza crust, spreading it to just within the edge of the crust. Garnish pizza with slices of pineapple and speck. Layer it up and sprinkle with crumbled Gorgonzola. Continue to bake for 8–12 minutes, until the crust is crispy to your liking and the toppings are hot. Check occasionally so that the plank does not ignite and the pizza burn. Easy does it!

While the pizza is cooking, prepare the Mint Salad. Combine mint leaves and green onion. Drizzle with a little lemon juice and olive oil and finish with a little drizzling of the Blackberry Syrup. Season to taste with a little kosher salt and black pepper.

Remove pizza from grill. Drizzle with Blackberry Syrup and garnish with a sprinkling of Mint Salad along the entire length of the pizza. Slice it up and serve immediately.

TED'S TIP

- If you soak your mint leaves in icy cold water for 10 minutes, it will keep the mint nice and crisp for the salad.
- Your leftover Blackberry Syrup goes great on your pancakes or French toast.

PLANK SMOKED BURRATA CHEESE

Burrata is similar to fresh mozzarella, only the main difference is in the stretching technique. Burrata is made from cow's milk and should be eaten within 1–2 days of being purchased. When you cut into burrata, there is a creamy filling. Rich and buttery in flavor, burrata is traditionally served at room temperature, but for this recipe I quickly hot plank smoke the cheese. It is pretty wicked when spread onto grilled Italian bread, drizzled with grilled peaches and olive oil. **SERVES 4 TO 6**

WHAT YOU NEED: Maple grilling plank (12 × 8 × ½ inches/30 × 20 × 1 cm), soaked in water for a minimum of 1 hour

Fire up your grill to 450–550°F (230–290°C).

Cut the peaches in half and remove the stone. Place the peaches cut side down onto the hot grill. Close lid and char grill for about 4–5 minutes. Using a spatula or tongs, turn the peaches over. Squeeze the half an orange over top of the peaches and close lid. Continue to grill for a couple more minutes. Open grill and remove peaches. Peel away and discard skin, then slice the peaches into thin slices. Place them into a bowl, add mint, season to taste with kosher salt and black pepper and set aside.

Place the grilling plank onto the grill and close lid. Let the plank heat up. When you see a little smoke coming from the grill and you hear a little crackling, open the grill lid and flip the plank over. This should take about 5–6 minutes.

Remove the burrata from the refrigerator and place on the plank. You want to keep the cheese cool before smoking it, as this will help prevent it from melting into a big mess. Season burrata with a little kosher salt and black pepper. Close lid and plank smoke for 8–10 minutes, until the cheese has taken on a smoky almond color and is warm throughout. Remove the cheese and the plank from the grill and set aside.

Grill-toast rustic bread. Spoon the hot smoked burrata onto the bread. Add a little of the peach mixture and drizzle with extra virgin olive oil. Serve immediately.

2 ripe peaches
1 orange, halved (only using one half)
2 tsp (10 mL) chopped fresh mint (approx. 2 medium sprigs)
Kosher salt and freshly ground black pepper to taste
1 fresh burrata cheese (approx. 8-oz/225 g ball)
6 slices rustic Italian bread
Drizzle of extra virgin olive oil

TED'S TIP
For an extra twist, garnish with shaved prosciutto or even a dollop of caviar.

PLANKED ESCARGOT WITH GARLIC CHIVE BUTTER & BRIE

The first time I had snails was with my older brother at a French bistro in Stowe, Vermont, back in 1978. The flavor stuck with me forever. My version, inspired by this first experience, is done on a grilling plank. SERVES 6

WHAT YOU NEED: 2 Holy Planks (page 18), soaked in water for a minimum of 1 hour

GARLIC CHIVE BUTTER
1 lb (450 g) unsalted butter, softened
8 plump cloves garlic, minced
¼ cup (60 mL) shallot,
    finely chopped
½ cup (125 mL) finely chopped
    fresh chives
½ cup (125 mL) finely chopped
    fresh parsley
2 tsp (10 mL) coarsely ground
    black pepper
2 tbsp (30 mL) freshly grated
    Parmesan cheese
Sea salt to taste

24 large escargots (snails), tinned in
    brine (approx. 24 per can)
Drizzle of cognac
Sea salt and freshly ground black
    pepper to taste
24 tsp (120 mL) Garlic Chive Butter
1 wheel Brie cheese (approx.
    ⅔ lb/300 g)
¼ cup (60 mL) hemp seeds

To make the Garlic Chive Butter, place the softened butter into a large bowl and whisk until slightly whipped. Add the garlic, shallot, chives, parsley, black pepper and Parmesan cheese. Season to taste with sea salt. Whisk until mixed. Transfer to a self-sealing container and set aside.

Open the tin of escargots and drain. Rinse under cold water, drain and pat dry with paper towels. Place snails into a bowl and drizzle with a little cognac (approximately 2–3 tsp/10–15 mL) and season to taste with sea salt and black pepper. Mix, cover and refrigerate, allowing the snails to marinate for 1 hour.

Slice the Brie cheese into twenty-four 2-inch (5 cm) squares, cover and refrigerate until needed.

Remove Holy Planks from water, drain and pat dry with paper towels.

Smear about a tsp (5 mL) of the Garlic Chive Butter into each of the reservoirs of the Holy Planks. You want to fill each reservoir completely with the butter. Remove the snails from the refrigerator and push one snail into each of the butter-filled reservoirs. Push it in so the butter pushes up the sides around each snail. Refrigerate, allowing the butter to harden for approximately 15 minutes.

Fire up your grill to 350–450°F (180–230°C).

Place the Holy Planks onto the grill, snail side up. Close lid and plank grill for 5–8 minutes, until the snails are bubbling in the hot butter. Be careful when you open the grill lid, as it might be a bit hot and smoky. Drizzle the smokin' bubblin' buttery snails with cognac. Watch for the flambé. Top each snail with one slice of Brie cheese and sprinkle with hemp seeds. Close grill lid and continue to plank grill for a few more minutes, until the hemp is smoky and toasty and the Brie melting. Remove plank from grill and serve immediately with fresh baguette and a glass of champagne.

STUFFED PORTOBELLO MUSHROOMS

When it comes to grilling mushrooms, I would have to say that portobellos are king; nice and meaty like a steak. The key to this recipe is mushroom tenderness. You don't have to rush it. Tender is better than undercooked. **SERVES 6**

Brush any dirt off the mushrooms. Cut off and discard the stems. Put the mushroom caps into a large bowl and cover with the hot water; let stand for 10 to 15 minutes to allow the mushrooms to soften. Drain and pat dry with paper towels.

In a bowl, mix together the olive oil, balsamic vinegar, garlic, oregano and red pepper flakes. Season to taste with kosher salt and black pepper. Add mushroom caps, turning to coat well, and let marinate for approximately 30 minutes while you prepare the stuffing.

In a separate bowl, stir together the Parmesan, Gorgonzola, breadcrumbs and mozzarella cheese. Set aside.

Fire up your grill to 450–550°F (230–290°C).

Grill the mushrooms, gill side down, for 6–8 minutes or until slightly charred and just tender. Keep the lid open to watch for flare-ups. Turn mushrooms over and sprinkle the cheese breadcrumb mixture evenly over the gill side of the mushroom. Close the lid and cook for 7–8 more minutes or until the cheese is hot and bubbling. Remove from grill, drizzle with a little more aged balsamic vinegar and serve immediately.

6 medium portobello mushroom caps, approx. 3 to 4 inches (8 to 10 cm) in diameter

3 cups (750 mL) hot water

3 tbsp (45 mL) extra virgin olive oil

⅓ cup (75 mL) aged balsamic vinegar, plus extra for drizzling

6 cloves garlic, minced

1 tbsp (15 mL) chopped fresh oregano

Pinch of red pepper flakes

Kosher salt and freshly ground black pepper to taste

¼ cup (60 mL) freshly grated Parmesan cheese

½ cup (125 mL) Gorgonzola cheese, crumbled

½ cup (125 mL) panko breadcrumbs

1 cup (250 mL) mozzarella cheese, shredded

SIDE KICKS

AVOCADO CUCUMBER QUINOA SALAD WITH GRILLED HALOUMI CHEESE

Quinoa is one of those ancient grains that is full of things that are good for you. It should be one of those superfoods that you include in your diet regularly. Yes, I said this! I hope that this salad becomes part of your summertime diet; it's fresh and easy to do. **SERVES 8**

Prepare quinoa as per package instructions. Allow to cool. Stir in cucumber, avocado, onion, green onion, cilantro, oil, lemon juice and zest, mirin and balsamic vinegar. Season to taste with kosher salt and black pepper. Chill for 20–30 minutes.

Fire up your grill to 450–550°F (230–290°C).

Grill haloumi cheese for 1–2 minutes per side with the grill lid open, until it is lightly charred and starting to get soft and creamy. Season to taste with a little salt and black pepper. Remove from grill. Dice cheese and fold warm into quinoa salad. Serve immediately.

2 cups (500 mL) cooked white, black or green quinoa

½ cup (125 mL) seedless cucumber, diced

1 large ripe avocado, peeled, pitted and diced

½ cup (125 mL) sweet onion, diced

2 green onions, chopped

1 tbsp (15 mL) chopped fresh cilantro or dill

2 tbsp (30 mL) canola oil

1 tbsp (15 mL) lemon juice

1 tsp (5 mL) lemon zest

1 tbsp (15 mL) mirin

1 tbsp (15 mL) white balsamic vinegar

Kosher salt and freshly ground black pepper to taste

8 oz (225 g) haloumi cheese, cut into 4 slices approx. ½ inch (1 cm) thick

BAKED SWEET POTATOES WITH HOT BUTTERED LOVE INJECTION

Sweet potatoes are delicious, especially when baked over hot charcoal. The skin gets crisp and the flesh is tender with a hint of smokiness. Take it one step further and inject those tender grilled baked potatoes with hot buttered honey. It's crazy delicious! **SERVES 4**

WHAT YOU NEED: Injection syringe

4 sweet potatoes
½ cup (125 mL) butter
2 tbsp (30 mL) buckwheat honey
1 oz (30 mL) spiced rum
1 tbsp (15 mL) orange juice
Kosher salt to taste

Fire up your grill to 450–550°F (230–290°C).

Place the sweet potatoes onto your grill and close lid. Grill-bake potatoes for 40–60 minutes or until they are tender when pierced with a knife.

While the potatoes are baking, prepare the butter mixture by placing the butter, buckwheat honey, spiced rum and orange juice into a small saucepot and heat until the butter is melted. Season to taste with a little kosher salt. Stir and set aside, keeping warm.

When the potatoes are baked and tender, suck up the warm butter honey rum mixture with your injection syringe. Plunge the needle into the center of the hot potato and press the plunger on the syringe, injecting the warm butter mixture into the center. Repeat with remaining potatoes.

Cut open each potato and watch the hot buttery steam rise from the hot flesh. Serve immediately.

GRILL-ROASTED POTATOES, HEIRLOOM CARROTS & PARSNIPS WITH MOLTEN BRIE

I came up with this recipe while cooking for a client in Florida. It was one of those impromptu events where I opened the fridge and cooked something from whatever I found. I found organic root vegetables, Brie cheese and striped whole bass. Yes, a fridge full of fancy stuff! I thought wood-roasted root vegetables could only get better with cheese. So it happened: hot oozing Brie drizzled over tender roasted vegetables.

SERVES 8

WHAT YOU NEED: 2 aluminum foil pans (approx. 8 × 10 × 3 inches/20 × 25 × 8 cm); Maple grilling plank (8 × 8 × ½ inches/20 × 20 × 1 cm), soaked in water for a minimum of 1 hour

Fire up your grill to 450–550°F (230–290°C).

In a large bowl, combine the potatoes, red and white onion, garlic cloves, carrots, parsnips, red pepper and mushrooms. Drizzle with olive oil and season to taste with kosher salt and black pepper. Place one aluminum foil pan inside the other and pour in seasoned vegetable mixture.

Place directly over grill flame and close lid. Grill-roast, stirring the vegetables occasionally so that they cook and brown evenly, for 45–60 minutes. Set aside in the grill, keeping warm.

Place the wheel of Brie cheese onto the center of the grilling plank. Place plank onto the grill and close lid. Plank grill cheese for 12–15 minutes, until the cheese is soft and heated through. The cheese should be slightly bulging and soft to the touch.

Transfer grill-roasted vegetables to a large bowl, drizzle with a little maple syrup and season with fresh thyme. Pierce the rind of the hot Brie cheese and drizzle the molten Brie over the vegetables. Gently toss to evenly coat. Serve immediately.

1 lb (450 g) mini red or white potatoes, washed and scrubbed

1 small red onion, cut into 1-inch (2.5 cm) chunks

1 small white onion, cut into 1-inch (2.5 cm) chunks

12 plump whole cloves of fresh garlic

½ lb (225 g) fresh heirloom carrots (orange, red, yellow, purple), peeled and cut into 2- to 3-inch (5 to 8 cm) long sticks

½ lb (225 g) fresh parsnips, peeled and cut into 2- to 3-inch (5 to 8 cm) long sticks

1 large red bell pepper, seeded and cut into 2-inch (5 cm) chunks

4 oz (115 g) cremini (brown) mushrooms, halved

3 tbsp (45 mL) olive oil

Kosher salt and freshly ground black pepper to taste

1 small wheel Brie cheese (approx. ⅔ lb/300 g)

Drizzle of pure maple syrup

1 tsp (5 mL) chopped fresh thyme

GRILLED ASPARAGUS WITH SERRANO HAM & MANCHEGO CHEESE

Make this recipe in the spring when asparagus is local and crispy fresh. **SERVES 6**

24 spears fresh asparagus (approx.
    1½ lb/675 g)
Drizzle of extra virgin olive oil
    (approx. 2 to 3 tsp/10 to 15 mL)
Drizzle of sherry vinegar (approx.
    2 to 3 tsp/10 to 15 mL)
2 cloves garlic, minced
Freshly ground black pepper to taste
24 slices Serrano-style ham or
    prosciutto, shaved
1 cup (250 mL) shaved Manchego
    cheese
1 tbsp (15 mL) chopped fresh sage

Trim the ends off the asparagus spears and place in a large bowl or pan; cover with cold water and let stand for 1 hour. This will allow the asparagus to absorb a little moisture and stay crisp and moist when grilling.

Drain asparagus. Drizzle with a little olive oil and sherry vinegar — not too much, just a little. Add minced garlic and season to taste with black pepper. Gently mix to evenly coat the asparagus.

Lay a slice of Serrano ham vertically (short end at the bottom) on a flat work surface. Place one seasoned asparagus spear across the middle of the ham at the bottom end and roll up the asparagus tightly in the ham. Repeat with remaining asparagus.

Fire up your grill to 450–550°F (230–290°C).

Cook asparagus until tender and Serrano ham crisps, for approximately 3–5 minutes per side. Remove from grill; garnish with shaved Manchego cheese and chopped sage. Drizzle with a little extra virgin olive oil and sherry vinegar. Serve immediately.

TED'S TIP
Use asparagus spears that are not too small yet not too large. Look for ones that have a stalk that is about ½ inch (1 cm) thick.

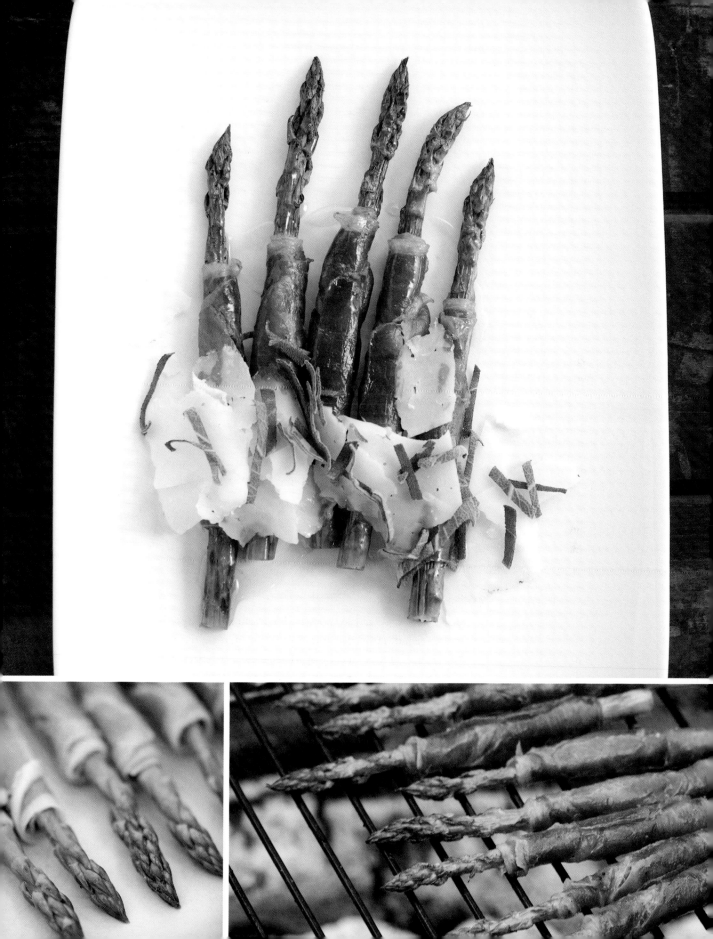

GRILLED BREAD SALAD WITH GORGONZOLA-STUFFED TOMATOES

This is one of my favorite backyard salads: grilled rustic bread, crisp cucumbers, sweet onions and small tomatoes packed with Gorgonzola cheese and fire-grilled. It's a summertime must here at Casa BBQ.

SERVES 8

WHAT YOU NEED: Espresso spoon

Cut the tops off the grape tomatoes about a quarter of the way down from the top. Using a small spoon (espresso spoon), scoop out the center of each tomato. Stuff each hollowed-out grape tomato with about ½ to 1 tsp (2 to 5 mL) Gorgonzola cheese. You may need to use your fingers to push the cheese into the tomato. Refrigerate until needed.

In a small bowl, mix together the 2 tbsp (30 mL) vinegar and 3 tbsp (45 mL) oil. Season to taste with salt and pepper. Brush liberally onto the cut sides of the bread.

Fire up your grill to 450–550°F (230–290°C).

Grill the red onion, red pepper and banana peppers for 10–15 minutes, turning occasionally, until lightly charred and tender. Coarsely chop the red onions and red pepper. Peel the skin from the banana peppers and remove seeds. Chop and add to onion mixture. Gently stir in cucumber and sun-dried olives.

Grill the bread, turning once, until lightly browned all over and crisp. Cut the bread into 1-inch (2.5 cm) cubes and add to the salad mixture.

At the same time as you are grilling the bread, grill the Gorgonzola-stuffed tomatoes with the grill lid open and on high heat. Get the tomatoes to blister quickly and the cheese to soften ever so slightly. Add into the salad. Drizzle with extra virgin olive oil and aged balsamic vinegar. Season with kosher salt and black pepper and toss thoroughly. Add lots of coarsely chopped parsley. Serve immediately.

16 ripe red grape tomatoes

16 tsp (80 mL) Gorgonzola cheese, crumbled

2 tbsp (30 mL) + a drizzle of aged balsamic vinegar

3 tbsp + ¼ cup (105 mL) extra virgin olive oil

Kosher salt and freshly ground black pepper to taste

6 slices rustic Italian bread, cut approx. 1 inch (2.5 cm) thick

2 medium red onions, cut into wedges

3 red bell peppers, halved

2 yellow hot banana peppers

1½ cups (375 mL) cucumber, peeled, halved, seeded and cut into thin strips

¼ cup (60 mL) pitted sun-dried black olives, coarsely chopped

2 tbsp (30 mL) chopped fresh Italian (flat-leaf) parsley

GRILLED FRUIT

Everybody knows you can grill a pineapple. But that barely rubs the surface. You're out there and you've done the meal and you're feeling very satisfied, but there's just one more thing. How about dessert? Why not throw some fruit kebabs brushed in butter and sprinkled with cinnamon sugar on the barbeque? A little whipped cream and chocolate sauce as dips and you hardly had to move.

Many fruits are delicious off the grill in both simple and complex recipes. The basic steps are very much the same as vegetables. The composition of most fruits is water and sugar. Grilling them concentrates the flavors and caramelizes the sugars for a much richer flavor. The result can enhance a main dish, create a unique appetizer or, of course, create a scrumptious dessert.

The easiest fruits to use are the hard fruits, apples, pears and pineapple being the best known. Softer fruits like peaches, plums or mangos need a certain amount of attention if they are grilled. They will become mushy, and since they tend to have a higher sugar content, they will burn easily. Just allow for a certain amount of caution.

BASIC GRILLED FRUIT

Prepared fruit, cut in half or in large pieces, peeled or unpeeled (your preference)
Cold water to cover
1 tsp (5 mL) lemon juice per cup (250 mL) of water
Vegetable oil for brushing grill rack or grill basket
Butter or flavored oil (walnut, sesame, etc.) or a marinade to brush fruit
Seasoning: salt or freshly ground black pepper, cinnamon, nutmeg, etc.

Place the fruit in a container filled with the cold water and lemon juice for about 20 to 30 minutes. This will preserve the flavors and juices on the grill.

Fire up your grill to 350°F (180°C), unless instructed otherwise by a specific recipe.

While grill is preheating, remove the fruit from the water bath and brush or toss in flavored oil or a marinade to coat well.

When the grill is ready, brush the rack or basket with a light coating of vegetable oil to help prevent sticking.

Place the fruit directly on the grill. Cook, basting with selected flavoring and turning frequently until lightly charred and warmed. Harder fruits will benefit from closing the lid for 3–5 minutes to allow the heat to penetrate and roast the fruit. Fruit is done when lightly charred and when the hard fruits are tender when pierced with a skewer. Take care not to allow the fruit to burn or overcook and become soft and mushy. The best flavors come from fruits that are just tender and before the natural sugars have begun to burn. Serve with your favorite ice cream or whipped cream.

GRILLED KING OYSTER MUSHROOMS

The key to grilling king oyster mushrooms is to soak them in warm water for 10–15 minutes. Doing this will allow the mushrooms to absorb more moisture so that when you are grilling the mushrooms, they will steam themselves. **SERVES 6**

Cut each mushroom in half lengthwise and place in a large bowl. Soak mushrooms in warm water for 10–15 minutes.

In a large bowl, zest and juice the lemon. Add olive oil, soy sauce, garlic, chili sauce, green onions and cilantro. Season to taste with salt and black pepper. Mix well.

Drain mushrooms and toss with marinade. Cover and refrigerate for 1 hour.

Fire up your grill to 450–550°F (230–290°C).

Remove mushrooms from marinade, reserving marinade for basting, and place onto grill. Grill mushrooms for 5–8 minutes per side, basting frequently with marinade, until tender and lightly charred. Remove mushrooms from grill and slice across the stem of each mushroom. Sprinkle with sesame seeds and chopped fresh cilantro. Serve immediately. Serve this with your favorite grilled steak.

1½ lb (675 g) king oyster mushrooms (approx. 8)
1 lemon
¼ cup (60 mL) olive oil
2 tbsp (30 mL) soy sauce
2 cloves garlic, minced
1 tsp (5 mL) Asian chili sauce
2 green onions, minced
1 + 1 tbsp (30 mL) chopped fresh cilantro
Salt and freshly ground pepper to taste
1 tsp (5 mL) toasted sesame seeds

GRILLED RAPINI SALAD WITH LEMON HONEY GINGER DRESSING

As much as I love meat, I do love my vegetables, especially when they are grilled. I picked up this method from my Italian neighbor years ago and it has become a favorite of mine. SERVES 8

1 bunch fresh rapini (approx.
    1 lb/450 g), trimmed and
    washed thoroughly

**LEMON HONEY GINGER
DRESSING**
1 clove garlic, minced
1 knob fresh ginger, peeled and
    minced (approx. 2 tsp/10 mL)
3 tbsp (45 mL) honey
1 tbsp (15 mL) white balsamic vinegar
1 tbsp (15 mL) extra virgin olive oil
1 lemon, zested and juiced (approx.
    ½ teaspoon/2 mL zest and
    3 tbsp/45 mL juice)
Kosher salt and freshly ground black
    pepper to taste
2 flatbreads (naan, pita, Greek-style
    pita, roti; your choice)
½ cup (125 mL) feta cheese,
    crumbled

Place rapini in a large bowl and cover with cold water. Allow to stand for a couple of hours so that it soaks up a little moisture. This added moisture will help the rapini steam while it grills. It will also cook faster and come out more tender.

To make the Lemon Honey Ginger Dressing, combine minced garlic and ginger in a bowl. Add honey, vinegar, olive oil, lemon zest and juice. Season to taste with kosher salt and black pepper. Set aside.

Fire up your grill to 450–550°F (230–290°C).

Drain rapini, season with salt and pepper and place in an even layer directly over the flame on the hot grill. Cook for 4–5 minutes per side, until lightly charred, bright green and tender. Drizzle rapini with a few tablespoons of the Lemon Honey Ginger Dressing. Remove from grill, cut into 2-inch (10 cm) lengths and place in a large bowl.

Brush the flatbreads with a little bit of water. Grill for about 2 minutes per side, until lightly charred and crisp. Remove and cut into 1-inch (2.5 cm) squares and add to the rapini. Add dressing to taste and toss gently. Adjust seasoning and transfer to a serving platter. Garnish with crumbled feta cheese and serve immediately.

GRILLED VEGETABLE KEBABS WITH LEMON BLACK OLIVE VINAIGRETTE

Skewer a variety of your favorite vegetables, or better yet, adjust this recipe to use fresh veggies that are in season! **MAKES 6 SKEWERS**

WHAT YOU NEED: Food processor; Rubber spatula; Six 10-inch (25 cm) wooden skewers, soaked in cold water for a minimum of 1 hour

To begin making the Lemon Black Olive Vinaigrette, combine black olives, garlic, lemon zest and juice, anchovies (if using), Parmesan cheese, sugar and vinegar in a food processor. Pulse until smooth. Slowly add the olive oil in a constant stream while the food processor is on. Stop to scrape down the sides of the bowl with a rubber spatula. Transfer to a small bowl and season to taste with black pepper. Set aside.

To make the Grilled Vegetable Skewers, cut the vegetables into uniform chunks and thread onto the presoaked wooden skewers. Brush vegetable skewers with olive oil. Set aside.

Fire up your grill to 450–550°F (230–290°C).

Grill vegetable kebabs for 10–12 minutes per side, until the vegetables are lightly charred and tender. Remove from grill and spoon 1 to 2 tbsp (15 to 30 mL) Lemon Black Olive Vinaigrette over each skewer. Serve immediately.

TED'S TIP
Vinaigrette will keep, refrigerated, for up to 2 weeks.

LEMON BLACK OLIVE VINAIGRETTE

½ cup (125 mL) sun-dried black olives, pitted (approx. 18)

4 cloves garlic

1 lemon, zested and juiced (approx. 2 tsp/10 mL zest and ¼ cup/60 mL juice)

3 anchovies (optional)

2 tbsp (30 mL) freshly grated Parmesan cheese

1 tsp (5 mL) white sugar

1 tbsp (15 mL) aged balsamic vinegar

¼ cup (60 mL) extra virgin olive oil

Freshly ground black pepper to taste

GRILLED VEGETABLE SKEWERS

1 large white onion

2 zucchini

12 brown (cremini) mushrooms

1 large red bell pepper

1 large yellow bell pepper

1 large orange bell pepper

3 tbsp (45 mL) extra virgin olive oil

GRILLED ZUCCHINI RIBBON SALAD WITH CHARRED TOMATO VINAIGRETTE

I recall first making this salad at my cottage. I had been to the local farmers' market and was inspired by the "just picked" tomatoes and firm zucchini. I decided to add the chicken for some extra flavor. You have to give it a try! SERVES 8

CHARRED TOMATO VINAIGRETTE

6 plum tomatoes

2 tbsp (30 mL) white balsamic vinegar

3 cloves garlic, minced

1 tbsp (15 mL) chopped fresh basil

3 tbsp (45 mL) extra virgin olive oil

Kosher salt and freshly ground black pepper to taste

GRILLED ZUCCHINI

4 medium zucchini

1 large sweet onion, sliced

2 tbsp (30 mL) white balsamic vinegar

2 tbsp (30 mL) roasted garlic olive oil

¼ cup (60 mL) chopped fresh basil

2 tbsp (30 mL) Parmesan cheese

Fire up your grill to 450–550°F (230–290°C).

Place the tomatoes on the grill and roast them, turning occasionally, for 5–10 minutes or until the skin is blistered and charred and tender. Let cool.

Remove and discard skin from the tomatoes. Place the tomatoes in a food processor. Add the vinegar, garlic and basil. Pulse until smooth. Turn on food processor and add olive oil in a steady stream. Season to taste with kosher salt and black pepper. Set aside.

Using a sharp knife or mandoline slicer, slice the zucchini into thin strips (ribbons).

In a large bowl, toss the zucchini and onion together. Add the vinegar, oil and kosher salt and black pepper to taste. Mix thoroughly.

Place zucchini mixture on the grill and grill for 8–10 minutes or until the zucchini and onions are tender and slightly charred. Transfer vegetables to a large bowl. Add Charred Tomato Vinaigrette and chopped fresh basil, toss well and season to taste with kosher salt and black pepper.

Take a vegetable peeler and shave the Parmesan cheese. Top grilled zucchini salad with Parmesan shavings and garnish with fresh basil leaves. Serve immediately.

GRILLED VEGETABLES

We usually think only of meat when we're at the barbeque. But there is really very little you can't use the grill for. Once the grill is lit, why not throw on some veggies? Some vegetables require more preparation than others, but the preparation can be done long before the grill is lit. Putting the asparagus next to the steaks cuts down on the run time back and forth to the kitchen.

Grilling is an effective way to concentrate the natural flavors of a vegetable while losing very little of its nutrition. Natural sugars caramelize and enhance the fresh flavors. Add a little seasoning and impress your family and friends. The basic principles apply to most vegetables. Don't be afraid to experiment, using some of the simple skills we offer here.

Vegetables are mainly water and most contain no fat. Some require brushing with a little oil, the use of a flavoring marinade with an oil base, or pouching in foil or leaves. Oils are available in many hues and flavors and you can easily create your own. Consider the health benefits of packing vegetables and flavoring into leaf (banana, lettuce, cabbage, etc.) or foil pouches and allowing them to steam alongside that pork loin. Last but certainly not least, there are the baskets, skewers and grill wok accessories that are becoming more and more popular.

With a little planning, you can set up in front of the grill and never leave until it's time to call the crowd to the table.

Success depends on the preparation. Do as much as you can ahead of time and finishing will be painless and fun.

BASIC GRILLED VEGETABLES

1 to 2 cups (250 to 500 mL) prepared vegetables *per person*
Vegetable oil for brushing grill rack or grill basket
Flavored oil or marinade, to brush vegetables
Salt and freshly ground black pepper to taste

Prepare the vegetables. Cut into pieces of approximately even size and thickness.

Fire up your grill to 350–450°F (180–230°C), unless instructed otherwise by a specific recipe.

While grill is preheating, brush or toss the vegetables in flavor-infused oils or marinades to coat well and season lightly with salt and black pepper.

When the grill is ready, brush the rack or basket with a light coating of vegetable oil to help prevent sticking.

Place the vegetables directly on the rack or pack in an even layer in the basket. Cook, basting with selected flavoring and turning frequently until browned and tender. Denser root vegetables will benefit from closing the lid for 3–5 minutes at a time to allow the heat to penetrate and roast the vegetables.

Vegetables are done when browned and tender when pierced with a skewer. Take care not to allow them to burn or overcook and become soft and mushy. The best flavors come from vegetables that are just tender and before the natural sugars have begun to burn.

Serve immediately. Grilled vegetables are delicious hot off the grill or at room temperature.

GRILLING SPECIFIC VEGETABLES

Some vegetables are better grilled after some precooking, while some are best from raw. Following is a list with preparation instructions and approximate cook times. Keep in mind that these are guidelines and personal preference will vary from person to person.

ARTICHOKES   Fresh artichokes require cleaning and cooking just until tender before placing on the grill. Tinned artichokes are also delicious after flavoring and grilling. Cut fresh into halves or quarters, leave tinned whole. Grill time 5–10 minutes.

ASPARAGUS   Remove woody ends and peel lower stems. Asparagus can be grilled from either raw or blanched. Blanched or steamed until barely tender, grill time about 3–4 minutes. Soak raw asparagus in water or a marinade for at least 30 minutes (to overnight). Grill time 7–10 minutes. Take care not to let ends burn.

BEETS   Steam or boil until barely tender. Cool and peel. Slice into equal-sized pieces ½ to 1 inches (1 to 2.5 cm) thick. Small ones can be left whole or halved. Grill time 7–10 minutes. Beets contain a lot of sugar, so take care, as those sugars will burn very easily.

BELGIAN ENDIVE, RADICCHIO OR SMALL ROMAINE   Cut into halves or quarters lengthwise, leaving enough of the stem end intact to hold leaves together. Grill quickly, taking care not to burn the delicate leaves. Grill time about 3–6 minutes.

BROCCOLI   Trim down to equal-sized spears (approx. 1½ to 2 inches/4 to 5 cm) and roughly peel any tough stems. Blanch or steam slightly to crisp-tender. Grill time about 5–7 minutes.

CARROTS OR PARSNIPS   Cook until just barely tender. Leave small ones whole, large ones sliced on the diagonal or in chunks approx. 1 inch (2.5 cm) thick. Grill time 9–12 minutes.

CAULIFLOWER   Follow the same method as broccoli above. Grill time 5–7 minutes.

CORN   Peel the husk partway down the cob of corn and remove as much silk as possible. Fold up the husk to cover the exposed cob. Soak corn in warm water for 1–2 hours to allow the corn to soak up some moisture. This moisture will create some steam to help with the cooking of the corn. Grill corn in the husk for 20–30 minutes, turning frequently, until the husk is charred and the cob of corn is hot and the kernels are tender. Peel charred husk

down to the bottom of the cob, give the ear a twist and serve immediately with butter and a bit of salt.

EGGPLANT   Leave very small ones whole. Long thin ones, such as Japanese, should be cut lengthwise in half. Larger ones should be sliced on the diagonal into ½- to 1-inch (1 to 2.5 cm) thick slices. They can also be cut lengthwise almost to the stem and fanned. Grill time 13–15 minutes. Eggplant will tolerate slightly higher and more direct heat, but take care not to burn.

FENNEL   Cut cleaned bulbs into thick slices (½ to 1 inch/1 to 2.5 cm) or wedges. Grill time 13–15 minutes.

GREEN ONIONS   Slice off roots and trim down dark green ends. Grill time 7–10 minutes.

LEEKS   Trim the root end but leave intact to hold the leek together. Trim the tough dark green tops. Split lengthwise into halves or quarters. Rinse off any soil clinging between the layers. Grill time 5–10 minutes.

MUSHROOMS   See Grilled King Oyster Mushrooms recipe on page 85.

ONIONS — RED, WHITE, SWEET SHALLOTS   Leave shallots whole. Onions can be grilled peeled or unpeeled. If onions are cut into wedges, leave root end trimmed but intact to hold wedge together. If cutting into thick slices, be sure to trim root ends off. Grill time for small whole and halved or quartered onions is 15–20 minutes. Grill time for thick slices is 5–7 minutes.

PEPPERS AND CHILES   Place peppers on the grill whole and uncut. Grill until evenly charred on all sides. Remove and immediately enclose in a paper bag or place in a bowl and cover tightly with plastic wrap. Let sit for 15–20 minutes to steam. Remove from bag or bowl and rub off skins. Slice lengthwise and remove stem, seeds and membranes. Slice into strips or chunks as preferred. Grill time 10–12 minutes.

POTATOES AND SWEET POTATOES   See Fully Loaded Gastro Skins recipe on page 48, Grill-Roasted Potatoes on page 77 and Baked Sweet Potatoes with Hot Buttered Love Injection on page 74.

ZUCCHINI AND SUMMER SQUASH   Leave small squashes whole. Cut large ones lengthwise into halves or quarters. Cut zucchini or marrow in half lengthwise into ½-inch (1 cm) thick slices on the diagonal. Grill time 7–10 minutes.

TOMATOES   Grill cherry tomatoes whole. Larger tomatoes should be cut in halves or thick slices. The best tomatoes for grilling are firm and slightly underripe or green. Grill time 8–15 minutes.

GRILL-ROASTED GARLIC

4 heads fresh garlic
¼ cup (60 mL) extra virgin olive oil

Fire up your grill to 350°F (180°C).

Take a sharp knife and slice the top off each garlic head about a quarter to a third of the way down.

Place the garlic heads in the center of a double-layered 12 × 12 inch (30 × 30 cm) square of heavy-duty aluminum foil. Drizzle the heads with olive oil, then bring corners of the foil up to create a pouch. Crimp the corners to seal.

Place the pouch of garlic on the grill and roast for approximately 1 hour or until very tender.

Remove pouch from the grill and carefully unwrap, taking care to let steam escape. Remove garlic cloves from the heads by squeezing gently to pop them out. Use a small fork to dig out any stubborn ones.

Garlic can be wrapped and stored in refrigerator for 2 weeks or frozen for up to 3 months.

HEIRLOOM TOMATO SALAD WITH GRILLED ONION & BLUE CHEESE WITH BARBEQUE DRESSING

Nothing says summer like juicy sweet local heirloom tomatoes. I love it when the tomatoes are fresh. For this recipe, I fire up my grill to grill off the onions. Once they are nicely charred, I top the onions with crumbled blue cheese — my version of this steak house classic. **SERVES 8**

To make the Barbeque Dressing, place all the tomatoes, anchovies, barbeque sauce, horseradish, vinegar, basil, garlic and Bone Dust BBQ Spice into a food processor. Pulse until smooth. Turn on the processor and slowly add the olive oil until the dressing is emulsified. Add salt and black pepper to taste. Transfer to a self-sealing container and refrigerate until needed.

Cut the tomatoes into wedges or thick slices or rounds, whichever you prefer. Arrange the tomatoes on a serving platter. Set aside.

Fire up your grill to 450–550°F (230–290°C).

Slice the red and white onions into ½-inch (1 cm) thick rounds. Brush both sides of the sliced onions with a little olive oil. Season both sides to taste with a little kosher salt and black pepper. Grill onions for 6–8 minutes on one side. Turn the onions over and continue to grill for another 6–8 minutes per side, until the onions are lightly charred and tender. Just before the onions are done, top each slice with crumbled blue cheese. Close grill lid and allow the cheese to melt for a minute or two.

Carefully remove blue cheese–crusted onions from the grill and cut into quarters. Place the grilled blue cheese onions on top of and around the heirloom tomatoes. Spoon over the dressing. Garnish with green onions and fresh basil. Serve immediately.

TED'S TIP
Cut each variety of tomato a little differently so that they each stand out in the salad. This salad is sure to impress!

BARBEQUE DRESSING

1 can (28 oz/796 mL) plum tomatoes, seeded and drained
2 anchovies
1 cup (250 mL) gourmet-style barbeque sauce
3 tbsp (45 mL) prepared horseradish
2 tbsp (30 mL) cider vinegar
1 tbsp (15 mL) chopped fresh basil
1 tbsp (15 mL) chopped garlic
2 tsp (10 mL) Bone Dust BBQ Spice (page 212)
½ cup (125 mL) olive oil
Salt and freshly ground black pepper to taste

8 heirloom tomatoes (assorted varieties)
1 medium red onion
1 medium white onion
2 tsp (10 mL) olive oil
Kosher salt and freshly ground black pepper
¼ cup (60 mL) blue cheese, crumbled
2 green onions, thinly sliced
½ cup (125 mL) fresh basil leaves, coarsely chopped

JUMBO STUFFED MUSHROOMS

You can use this stuffing recipe to stuff a variety of mushrooms: portobello, cremini or even shiitake.

SERVES 8

WHAT YOU NEED: Food processor

½ cup (125 mL) 2-day-old rustic
    bread
½ cup (125 mL) pancetta,
    finely diced
Pinch of red pepper flakes
½ cup (125 mL) diced white onion
4 cloves garlic, minced
½ cup (125 mL) smoked provolone,
    shredded
¼ cup (60 mL) freshly grated
    Parmesan cheese
1 tbsp (15 mL) chopped
    fresh oregano
Big drizzle of extra virgin olive oil
Kosher salt and freshly ground black
    pepper to taste
8 very large field (white) mushrooms

Break up the slices of bread and place into a food processor. Pulse until it forms small crumbles, not too fine yet not too chunky. Set aside.

In a small pan, fry off the pancetta until lightly crispy and the fat has been partially rendered. Add the red pepper flakes, onion and garlic and continue to sauté for a minute more. Pour the whole mixture over the breadcrumbs and mix. Add smoked provolone, Parmesan cheese and oregano. Drizzle with olive oil and season to taste with kosher salt and black pepper.

Fire up your grill to 350–450°F (180–230°C).

Remove stems from the mushrooms and clean the caps. Pat dry with paper towels. Fill the mushroom caps with the breadcrumb mixture, gently pressing the mixture into the caps. Place the mushroom caps on the grill. Close the lid and bake for 15–20 minutes or until the mushrooms are tender, the stuffing is golden brown and the cheese is melted. Remove from grill and serve immediately.

LOVE TATERS!

For those who love mashed potatoes, this is a super way to impress your friends. In my plank box potato extravaganza, creamy cheesy mashed potatoes sit atop a bed of mini new potatoes, caramelized onions and garlic. Plank box grill-bake this dish and people will be screaming how much they love taters! **SERVES 8**

WHAT YOU NEED: Potato masher; Plank box (page 18)

Place the potatoes in a large pot and cover with cold water. Bring to a boil and season with a little kosher salt. Reduce heat to medium and cook potatoes for 15–20 minutes or until just fork tender. Drain. Divide the potatoes in half. Allow one half to cool. Don't rinse them under water, just let them air cool; this keeps from adding moisture, which we don't want. Using a potato masher, mash the other half of the cooked potatoes. Add 3 tbsp (45 mL) butter and season to taste with kosher salt and black pepper. Set aside to cool.

When the whole potatoes have cooled, press firmly on the top of each potato to squish it slightly. The sides of the potato should split and expose the tender flesh. Arrange the squished potatoes into the bottom of the plank grilling box, making sure to cover the entire surface. If you have extra potatoes, squish them into the box.

In a frying pan over medium-low heat, melt 3 tbsp (45 mL) butter. Sauté the garlic and onion for 15–20 minutes, stirring frequently, until caramelized and tender. Add the herbs and salt and pepper. Spread the onion mixture evenly over the potatoes. Set aside.

In a large bowl, combine the mashed potatoes, Emmental and mozzarella cheese, eggs and sour cream. Season to taste with salt and pepper. Mix well. The mixture should be a little wet and sticky. Spread the cheesy mashed potato mixture over top of the onions and potatoes in the plank box.

Fire up your grill to 350–450°F (180–230°C).

Place plank boxed potatoes onto the grill and close lid. Plank bake for 40–45 minutes or until the potatoes are hot and the top is crispy. Remove from grill and allow to rest for 5 minutes. Serve.

3 lb (1.4 kg) mini red, white or gold-fleshed potatoes

Kosher salt and freshly ground black pepper to taste

3 + 3 + 3 tbsp (135 mL) butter

6 cloves garlic, minced

2 large onions, sliced

¼ cup (60 mL) chopped fresh herbs (such as sage, rosemary and thyme)

1 cup (250 mL) Emmental cheese, shredded

1 cup (250 mL) mozzarella cheese, shredded

3 eggs

½ cup (125 mL) sour cream

SLAW × THREE

I am a big fan of coleslaw, whether creamy or vinaigrette style, white or purple cabbage, it doesn't matter. Here are three of my favorites. Serve them with smoked ribs, brisket or beer can chicken. Nothing says a barbeque or grill-out better than a good ol' fashioned chopped fresh slaw. **EACH SERVES 8**

TRADITIONAL CREAMY SLAW

When it comes to making coleslaw, buy fresh whole heads of green cabbage. You want the cabbage to be heavy and dense and the leaves green. The whiter the leaves and the lighter the weight of a cabbage, the older it is. You want a cabbage that is full of moisture.

1 fresh cabbage, finely chopped into ¼- to ½-inch (0. 5 to 1 cm) thick squares (about 4–6 cups/ 1 to 1.5 L)

3 green onions, chopped

1 tbsp (15 mL) chopped fresh parsley

2 tbsp (30 mL) white sugar

1 tbsp (15 mL) white vinegar

½ tsp (2 mL) salt

½ to 1 cup (125 to 250 mL) mayonnaise

2 tsp (10 mL) mustard powder

1 tsp (5 mL) freshly ground black pepper

¼ tsp (1 mL) cayenne pepper

In a large bowl, combine the cabbage, green onions and parsley.

In a small bowl, whisk together the sugar, vinegar, salt, mayonnaise, mustard powder, black pepper and cayenne.

Pour the dressing over the cabbage, mix and refrigerate, covered, for at least 1 hour to allow the flavors to build and the cabbage to become a little tender.

continued . . .

MOJITO FENNEL SLAW

2 fennel bulbs, trimmed of tops
    and thinly sliced (approx.
    2 cups/500 mL)

1 cup (250 mL) green cabbage,
    thinly sliced

1 stalk celery, thinly sliced (approx.
    ¾ cup/175 mL)

½ cup (125 mL) red onion, thinly
    sliced

1 green onion, thinly sliced

1 green apple, thinly sliced and
    cut into thin strips

3 juicy limes

2 tbsp (30 mL) white balsamic
    vinegar

Splash of white rum

2 tsp (10 mL) white sugar

½ teaspoon (2 mL) freshly ground
    black pepper

Kosher salt to taste

2 tbsp (30 mL) chopped fresh mint

In a large bowl, combine the fennel, cabbage, celery, red onion, green onion and green apple. Set aside.

Zest and juice the limes. You want about ½ cup (125 mL) lime juice and about ½ tsp (10 mL) zest. Add to fennel mixture.

Place the vinegar, rum, sugar and black pepper into a small pot and bring to a quick boil; stir until sugar is dissolved. Pour dressing over fennel mixture and mix well. Season to taste with kosher salt. Let stand, refrigerated, for 1 hour, mixing at least one more time to allow the full flavors of the salad to combine.

Remove from refrigerator, add freshly chopped mint, mix and serve.

TED'S TIP

Use a sharp knife to slice the fennel, cabbage, apple and onions as thinly as you can. This will make for a more tender salad with bigger flavors. If you wish to use a food processor or mandoline to make the job easier and quicker, go for it!

RED CABBAGE SLAW

In a large bowl, mix together the cabbage, vinegar, apple juice, mustard seeds, brown sugar, mustard powder and salt and black pepper to taste. Mix thoroughly. Cover and let marinate for 2 hours or until the cabbage is tender.

Remove salad from the refrigerator and add the red onion, apple, raisins, parsley, chives and lemon juice. Mix well and adjust seasoning with salt and black pepper. Serve immediately.

TED'S TIP

Don't make this salad too far in advance or else it will lose its brilliant red color.

1 small purple cabbage, thinly sliced
(as thin as you can slice it)
¼ cup (60 mL) cider vinegar
¼ cup (60 mL) apple juice
1 tbsp (15 mL) mustard seeds
1 tbsp (15 mL) brown sugar
1 tsp (5 mL) mustard powder
Salt and freshly ground black
pepper to taste
1 red onion, thinly sliced
1 Granny Smith apple, thinly sliced
and then julienned
¼ cup (60 mL) sultana raisins
2 tbsp (30 mL) chopped
fresh parsley
2 tbsp (30 mL) chopped fresh chives
1 tsp (5 mL) freshly squeezed
lemon juice

SMOKED RISOTTO WITH FIRE-ROASTED SQUASH

When it comes to smoking rice, I had to do a lot of experimenting with different types of rice, and the one that I found to absorb the most amount of smoke is Arborio rice. This grain is high in starch and the grains of rice are nice and plump. Not as dry as long-grain or basmati rice, the Arborio is porous enough to allow for the smoke to penetrate the grain and add a nutty smoky flavor. **SERVES 8**

WHAT YOU NEED: 2 half-size steam table aluminum foil pans (a lasagna pan); Hickory or maple wood chips for smoking

4 cups (1 L) Arborio rice

1 butternut squash

Kosher salt to taste

1 medium onion, cut into ½-inch (1 cm) thick rings

6 to 8 cups (1.5 to 2 L) chicken stock (fresh made is always best)

3 tbsp (45 mL) butter

2 cloves garlic, minced

2 cups (500 mL) smoked Arborio rice

½ cup (125 mL) Creekside Estates Riesling

½ cup (125 mL) freshly grated Romano cheese

1½ cups (375 mL) Fontina cheese, cut into ½-inch (1 cm) cubes

6 fresh sage leaves, coarsely chopped

Salt and freshly ground black pepper to taste

Drizzle of balsamic vinegar syrup or glaze

To smoke the rice, prepare your smoker according to manufacturer's instructions and set temperature to 180–200°F (85–100°C).

Place one aluminum pan inside the other. Using a metal skewer or something fine, poke lots of little holes through the foil to allow for smoke to penetrate the rice but not too big because the rice will fall through the holes. Pour the grains of rice into the foil pan and spread evenly over the surface. Place into smoker and smoke for 4–6 hours, until the rice starts to color (a little golden or bronzy), stirring the rice gently every hour. This allows for a more even smoke on the rice. Remove rice from cooker and allow to fully cool.

Fire up your grill to 450–550°F (230–290°C).

Take a sharp paring knife and slash the outside skin of the butternut squash, all over the place. I like to slash it in a bit of a diamond pattern because it looks pretty, but the purpose of scoring the outside of the squash is to allow for more heat and smoke penetration into the flesh of the squash. You get full char flavor this way. Cut the butternut squash in half and remove seeds. Season the squash all over with a little bit of kosher salt. Rub the salt into the flesh a little so the coarseness tears the flesh a little. Rough it up, as this roughness is where all the flavor bits will hang out, giving a burst of grill char flavor. Close grill lid and roast for 60–90 minutes, turning it occasionally, until the flesh is tender. The tip of a knife slides easily through the hot steamy flesh.

While the squash is roasting, grill the onion for 5–6 minutes per side, until lightly charred and tender. Remove from grill, slice the rings in half and set aside.

continued...

Remove the squash from the grill and allow to cool for about 10 minutes. Scoop the flesh of the squash from the rind. Coarsely chop and set aside. You will require 1½ to 2 cups (375 to 500 mL) of fire-roasted butternut squash for the risotto.

To prepare the risotto, bring the stock to a boil. Turn heat to low, cover and hold until needed.

Melt butter over medium heat in a large heavy pot. Sauté the grilled onion and the garlic for 1–2 minutes, until the garlic is tender and the onions hot. Add the smoked rice and stir to coat the rice and lightly toast. Add the wine and simmer about 1 minute, until the wine has almost all evaporated. Stir in the chicken stock, 1 cup (250 mL) at a time, stirring constantly, for approximately 15–18 minutes. Stir gently and slowly, not quickly — you don't want to mash the grains of rice roughly, just let them absorb the stock slowly so that you allow the full smoke flavor to come out of the rice and so the risotto will have texture and be tender and creamy. Risotto should be creamy and a bit soupy, not gluey. Add more broth by ¼ cupfuls (60 mL) if risotto does not seem creamy enough. Take care not to overcook. The rice should be tender but not mushy. Stir in 1½ to 2 cups (375 to 500 mL) roasted squash and Romano and Fontina cheeses. Add chopped fresh sage and season to taste with salt and freshly ground black pepper.

Serve immediately by placing risotto in bowls and drizzling with a bit of balsamic syrup.

TED'S TIP

- You need to ensure that these pans are firm so they add some stability. There is nothing worse than having a pan buckle because it's too thin to support the weight of the food. Always double up!
- Keep your humidity level at a minimum, as you want to dry smoke so that the rice does not absorb the moisture. When stirring the rice during this smoking period, use your fingers to do the work. It will be easier to tell if the rice is getting moist or not.
- Other than color, you will not notice much of a change in the rice. If you let the rice sit for a couple of days before preparing this dish, it will allow the smoke flavor to intensify. Vacuum pack the smoked rice and store for up to 6 months.
- You can find balsamic glazes in specialty food shops as well as major grocery stores. Look for them in the vinegar section.
- Use any leftover squash for salads or as a spread on grilled flatbreads.

SPICY GRILLED VEGETABLE SALAD

I find that using a grill basket for this recipe makes the job of grilling the vegetables a lot easier. One of my favorite grilling accessories, it's worth the investment. **SERVES 8**

WHAT YOU NEED: Grill basket; Food processor

1 large red onion, sliced into ½-inch (1 cm) thick rounds

2 zucchini, sliced into ½-inch thick (1 cm) slices (cat's eye slices)

2 portobello mushroom caps, rinsed of excess dirt and grit and sliced into ½-inch (1 cm) thick slices

1 red bell pepper, seeded and cut into 1-inch (2.5 cm) thick strips

1 yellow bell pepper, seeded and cut into 1-inch (2.5 cm) thick strips

1 orange bell pepper, seeded and cut into 1-inch (2.5 cm) thick strips

1 poblano pepper, seeded and cut into 1-inch (2.5 cm) thick strips

1 bunch asparagus, cut into 3-inch (8 cm) pieces

2 tablespoons + ¾ cup (200 mL) extra virgin olive oil

2 tsp (10 mL) Bone Dust BBQ Spice (page 212)

2 chipotle peppers, puréed

½ to 1 cup (125 to 250 mL) cane vinegar

¼ cup (60 mL) honey

2 tbsp (30 mL) chopped fresh cilantro, plus extra for garnishing

Pinch of ground cumin

Pinch of cayenne pepper

1 tsp (5 mL) salt

1 lime, juiced

Kosher salt and freshly ground black pepper to taste

In a large bowl, toss the onions, zucchini, mushrooms, bell peppers, poblano peppers and asparagus together. Season with the 2 tbsp (30 mL) oil and Bone Dust BBQ Spice. Toss and then place in a grill basket.

Fire up your grill to 450–550°F (230–290°C).

To make the dressing, combine the chipotle peppers, vinegar, honey, cilantro, cumin, cayenne, salt and lime juice in a food processor. Blend until smooth. With the motor running, add the ¾ cup (175 mL) olive oil in a steady stream to emulsify the dressing. Transfer to a self-sealing container and refrigerate until needed.

Grill vegetables in the basket for 8–10 minutes per side, until lightly charred and tender. Transfer vegetables a large bowl. Toss with the dressing and extra cilantro to taste. Season to taste with salt and black pepper. Serve immediately.

SANDWICHES

APPLE CHEDDAR PORK SAUSAGE BURGER

For these sausage burgers, you will need to find a butcher that can supply you with caul fat. It looks like a spider web but made of fat with thick membrane webs with super-thin membrane-like windows between. This caul fat holds the burger together and keeps it moist with its own self-basting skin. If you can't find caul fat, you can still make this recipe by omitting the step of wrapping the burger. It works just fine. **SERVES 6**

Remove casings from sausages and place sausage meat into a bowl. Add chopped pork, apple, cheddar, onion and sage. Season to taste with salt and black pepper. Give it a splash of bourbon if you like.

Form into six 6-oz (170 g) burger patties, approx. 1 inch (2.5 cm) thick and 4 inches (10 cm) in diameter. Place burgers on a plate, cover and refrigerate for at least 1 hour.

Fry bacon in a small frying pan over medium to medium-low heat. Bacon is ready once crispy.

Lay the caul fat onto a flat work surface and spread it apart to be a uniform sheet, about 12 inches (30 cm) × 12 inches (30 cm). Place one burger in the center of the caul fat and wrap it up. Repeat with the remaining burgers and caul fat.

Fire up your grill to 350–450°F (180–230°C).

Grill burgers for 8–10 minutes per side, until fully cooked but still moist and juicy (internal temperature minimum 160°F/70°C). At the same time, grill the apple slices.

Brush hamburger buns with mayonnaise. Toast buns, mayo side down, on the grill until lightly brown and a bit crisp. Once buns are toasted, spread a little apple butter onto one side of the bun, top with a burger and garnish with some slices of grilled apple and bacon. Top with lid of bun. Serve immediately.

1½ lb (675 g) fresh sweet Italian or farmer's pork sausage

½ lb (225 g) pork tenderloin, coarsely chopped into ¼-inch (5 mm) dice

2 tart apples, 1 sliced into rings and the other seeded and diced into ½-inch (1 cm) cubes

1 cup (250 mL) white cheddar cheese, cut into ½-inch (1 cm) cubes

¼ cup (60 mL) white onion, finely diced

2 tbsp (30 mL) chopped fresh sage

Salt and freshly ground black pepper to taste

Splash of Jim Beam (optional)

12 slices bacon

8 oz (225 g) caul fat, rinsed in cold water and patted dry of excess moisture

6 hamburger buns

6 tsp (30 mL) mayonnaise

6 tsp (30 mL) apple butter

SPICY CHILI CHEESE DOG

Sounds easy and delicious, but in reality there is a bit of work to making this recipe happen.
You have to make the chilli, then inject the hot dog with hot sauce (more about that in the recipe method) and then grill the dog, assemble it and devour your creation. It is definitely worth it. For ease, you can use canned chili. I personally like my chili without beans, but if you want beans, go ahead — add 'em in. **SERVES 8**

WHAT YOU NEED: Injection syringe; Cast iron frying pan

2 lb (900 g) ground beef (regular or ground by
    your butcher)
2 tsp (10 mL) ground cumin
2 tsp (10 mL) chili powder
1 tsp (5 mL) freshly ground black pepper
1 tbsp (15 mL) Bone Dust BBQ Spice (page 212)
2 to 3 tbsp (30 to 45 mL) lard (approx.)
3 green jalapeño peppers, thinly sliced into rings
4 cloves garlic, minced
1 large onion, diced
2 tsp (10 mL) dried Mexican oregano leaves
1 bottle (12 oz/341 mL) beer
    (lime-flavored is best)

1 can (14 oz/398 mL) diced tomatoes, drained
2 tsp (10 mL) + 2 oz (60 mL) TABASCO® Chipotle Sauce
½ cup (125 mL) gourmet-style barbeque sauce (I like to
    use my Beerlicious™ BBQ Sauce or you can use your
    favorite barbeque sauce)
Salt and freshly ground black pepper to taste
2 tbsp (30 mL) butter
8 jumbo hot dogs (approx. 4 to 5 oz/115 to 140 g each)
8 soft sesame egg hot dog rolls
3 cups (750 mL) shredded jack cheese
2 cups (200 mL) corn chips
2 tbsp (30 mL) chopped fresh cilantro

Go to your local butcher and ask them to grind you a couple pounds of beef chuck. Also ask them to add a little extra beef fat into the grind. You want to have about 15–20% fat in the ground beef mixture. The fat is where the flavor comes from. Ask them to grind it twice. It's so much more fun than buying it already ground at the grocery store. Plus it tastes better.

Season the beef with the cumin, chili powder, black pepper and Bone Dust BBQ Spice.

Heat up cast iron frying pan over medium-high heat. When it starts to just smoke, add in the lard. Lard works best; however, if you wish to use oil here, that is okay. Add in the beef, a little at a time. Do this in batches. This will keep the pan hot and keep as much of the moisture in the meat as possible. Fry it quick. Add more lard if necessary. Once all the meat has been sizzled, remove it from the pan and set it aside while you sauté the jalapeños, garlic and onion.

In the same pan, bring a little more lard to a sizzle. Add the jalapeño peppers, garlic and onions and sauté for 2–3 minutes, stirring occasionally, until tender. Rub the Mexican oregano leaves in between the palms of your hands to crush and flake. This will release a bit of extra oregano flavor. Stir it into the onion mixture. Add a drizzle of lime-infused beer to deglaze the pan; stir. Add the sizzled ground beef to the mixture. Add in the diced tomatoes, 2 tsp (10 mL) TABASCO® Chipotle Sauce and barbeque sauce and simmer uncovered over

continued . . .

medium-low heat, stirring occasionally, for 45–60 minutes, until the meat is tender. If it gets too thick, add a little more lime-infused beer. Taste the chili and adjust the seasoning with a little extra TABASCO® Chipotle Sauce, salt, and black pepper. Set aside, keeping warm.

Fire up your grill to 350–450°F (180–230°C).

In a microwave-safe dish, melt the butter. Add the 2 oz (60 mL) TABASCO® Chipotle Sauce and stir. Fill your injection syringe with the warm buttered hot sauce. Set aside, keeping warm.

Grill the hot dogs, turning every few minutes, until they are plump, juicy and lightly charred. Just a minute or two before the hot dogs are done grilling, insert the tip of the syringe into one end of the hot dog in the center. Now gently push the plunger on the syringe and while removing it inject a little TABASCO® chipotle-infused hot sauce into your hot dog. Turn the hot dog around and do it again. Repeat with remaining hot dogs, replenishing syringe with extra hot sauce as necessary.

Warm buns. Sprinkle a little shredded cheese into the bun cavity all the way along the length. Add a chipotle buttered hot sauce–injected hot dog into the bun on top of the cheese. Spoon the warm chili on top of the hot dog. Sprinkle with more cheese. Crush up a few corn chips and sprinkle over top and garnish with cilantro. Repeat and serve immediately.

TED'S TIP

I use a long slender shot glass that holds about 2 to 3 oz (30 to 45 mL) of liquid. Fill it with buttered hot sauce and you can then stick the needle deep into the sauce and suck it up easily into the syringe. You'll figure it out. I have faith in you! Set aside, keeping warm. I keep it in a metal coffee cup beside my grill to keep warm.

GRILLED BACON BANH MI

This is my version of that tasty Vietnamese sandwich, the banh mi: fresh baguette topped with mashed fire-roasted sweet potatoes, grilled double-smoked bacon and a crispy crunchy salad. This sandwich will put a smile on your face. **SERVES 2 TO 4**

WHAT YOU NEED: Bread knife

2 medium sweet potatoes
1 lb (450 g) European-style double-smoked bacon
½ cup (125 mL) daikon radish, julienned
½ cup (125 mL) carrot, julienned
½ cup (125 mL) seedless cucumber, thinly sliced
2 green onions, thinly sliced into strips approx. 3 inches (8 cm) in length
2 hot red peppers (red bird chiles) (optional)
3 tbsp (45 mL) sweet rice vinegar
Salt and freshly ground black pepper to taste
3 tsp (15 mL) butter
Pinch of freshly grated nutmeg
1 French baguette, cut in half lengthwise
2 cups (500 ml) fresh cilantro sprigs
Drizzle of hoisin sauce
Drizzle of Sriracha hot sauce

Fire up your grill to 450–550°F (230–290°C).

Place the sweet potatoes onto your grill and close lid. Grill-bake the potatoes for 45–60 minutes or until they are tender when pierced with a knife. While the sweet potatoes are baking, cut the bacon into ¼- to ½-inch (0.5 to 1 cm) thick slices. You can ask your butcher or deli to do this for you. Set aside.

In a bowl, combine radish, carrots, cucumber and green onions. Finely chop the red chile peppers, if using, and add to radish mixture. Add vinegar and season with a pinch of salt, gently toss and set aside, keeping cool.

Remove potatoes from grill. Cut open and scoop the hot flesh from the skins, discard skins and place hot flesh into a bowl. Add butter and season to taste with nutmeg, salt and black pepper. Set aside, keeping warm.

Grill the cut sides of the baguette for 1–2 minutes to lightly toast. Set aside, keeping warm.

Grill the slices of bacon for 1–3 minutes per side, until lightly charred and slightly crispy.

Spread the hot sweet potato mixture over the bottom half of the grill-toasted baguette. Top with slices of grilled bacon. Mix the radish and cucumber salad with the cilantro and gently toss. Scatter across the top of the bacon. Drizzle with hoisin and Sriracha. Top with top half of bun. Cut into four equal parts and serve.

GRILLED DUCK LETTUCE WRAPS

"How do you keep duck breasts from flaring up on the grill?" This is a question that I am asked on a regular basis. The answer is you more than likely will have a flare-up; however, the key is to keep the flare-ups to a minimum. Little bursts of flame are okay, but the full-on inferno of duck fat burning on hot coals or sear plates is what you want to avoid.

After trying a number of different methods on the grill, I found that adding a double layer of aluminum foil between the fire and the duck breast helps to reduce the flare-ups significantly. What I find when searing duck on the skin side, the excess fat renders from the duck and you end up with scorched fat and grease on the duck. Not what you want. Trust me, use the foil and you will have perfect grilled duck breasts every time.

SERVES 4

2 duck breasts (approx. 8 oz/225 g each)
Freshly ground black pepper to taste
¼ cup (60 mL) seasoned rice wine vinegar
2 tbsp (30 mL) mirin
¼ cup (60 mL) honey
1½ tsp (5 mL) Asian chili sauce
4 tsp (20 mL) hot mustard powder
1 tsp (5 mL) fresh ginger, minced
1 lemon

Kosher salt to taste
2 cups (500 mL) shrimp crackers, crushed
½ cup (125 mL) crushed peanuts or cashews
Hoisin sauce
Sriracha hot sauce
Soy sauce

ASIAN PEAR SALAD

1 head green leaf lettuce, washed and patted dry
   of excess moisture
½ cup (125 mL) carrot, julienned
½ cup (125 mL) daikon radish, julienned
¼ cup (60 mL) white onion, thinly sliced
2 green onions, thinly sliced
1 Asian pear, thinly sliced and julienned
1 big handful of bean sprouts
¼ bunch fresh cilantro, chopped

Using a sharp knife, score the skin side of the duck breasts in a diamond pattern, slicing about ¼ inch (5 mm) deep into the skin and fat, being careful not to pierce the flesh. Season duck breasts on the meat side with black pepper. Place the scored and seasoned duck breasts into a self-sealing refrigerator bag.

In a bowl, whisk together the vinegar, mirin, honey, chili sauce, mustard powder and ginger. Zest the rind of the lemon and add to vinegar mixture. Add the juice of half the lemon and season to taste with a little black pepper. Divide this mixture into two equal parts. Set one part aside to baste the duck with during grilling and pour the other part over the scored and seasoned duck breasts. Seal bag, removing as much air as possible. Refrigerate for 2 hours to allow the duck breasts to infuse with the marinade. While the ducks marinate, prepare your lettuce wrap garnishes.

Wash the lettuce leaves. Drain and pat dry with paper towels. Roll up into a kitchen towel and refrigerate until needed.

continued . . .

- Let the lettuce soak for 10–15 minutes in icy cold water. This will help crisp the leaves.
- If flare-ups occur while grilling the duck, reduce heat and move duck so it is not directly over the flames.

To prepare the Asian Pear Salad, in a bowl, combine the carrot, radish, onion, green onion, Asian pear, bean sprouts and cilantro. Drizzle with a little of the reserved duck glaze; you won't need a lot, just a couple of tablespoons (30 mL). Set aside, refrigerated.

Fire up your grill to 350–450°F (180–230°C). You will need to have your grill set for direct and then indirect grilling.

Take a sheet of aluminum foil and fold it in half. Fold over the edges to secure the folded sheet together. Place foil square onto your grill directly over the fire. Using a wooden skewer or toothpick, poke a few holes in it, here and there so there are not too many; 8 or 9 will do.

Remove duck from marinade, discarding leftover marinade. Pat the duck breast with paper towels. Season with a little kosher salt. Place the duck skin side down onto the sheet of foil. With the lid open, sear the duck breast for 2–4 minutes, until the skin gets a little crispy and the knife slits open up and begin to blister. You will hear the sizzle on the foil and see the dancing duck fat as it sputters its flavor. Turn the duck breasts over, close lid and allow the ducks to roast for about 5 minutes. Be sure not to overcook. Remove duck from the grill and allow it to rest, lightly tented with aluminum foil, for 5 minutes.

Using a sharp knife, slice the duck across the breast in thin slices. The duck should be a nice medium-rare.

To assemble your wraps, take a leaf of lettuce and sprinkle with a small handful of Asian Pear Salad. Top with slices of grilled duck, drizzle with reserved basting sauce and finish off with sprinkling of crushed shrimp crackers and cashews. Repeat and serve with hoisin sauce, Sriracha sauce and soy sauce. Serve immediately.

GRILLED FISH & CHIPS SANDWICH WITH CUCUMBER SLAW

These little sandwiches are easy to prepare for the gastro griller on the go. Warm dinner rolls filled with grilled salmon, cucumber slaw and salt & vinegar potato chips for some added crunch! **MAKES 8**

WHAT YOU NEED: Nonstick cooking spray

Peel the cucumber. Cut the cucumber in half and, using the tip of a small spoon, scoop the seeds from the center. Discard seeds. Using a box grater, shred the cucumber. Squeeze the excess moisture from the cucumber. You should end up with about 1½ cups (375 mL) worth of shredded cucumber. Place the squeezed shredded cucumber into a large bowl. Add red onion, prepared horseradish, chives, dill and chopped capers. Gently mix. Add the Greek yogurt and a squeeze of fresh lemon juice. Season to taste with a pinch of cayenne pepper, sea salt and black pepper. Gently mix. Set aside, keeping cool.

Spray your cold grill grate with a little nonstick cooking spray. Caution: Do not spray the nonstick cooking spray onto grill grate while the grate is over the hot fire.

Fire up your grill to 450–550°F (230–290°C).

Rub the Bone Dust BBQ Spice into the flesh of the salmon on all sides. Rub it in so that the spices stick to the flesh. Brush seasoned salmon on all sides with a little grapeseed oil. Sear the salmon fillets directly over the hot fire on one side for 3–5 minutes. It's ready to turn when it comes cleanly from the grill grate. Turn down the temperature of your grill, just a little bit, to lower the flame. If you decided to use a charcoal grill, you will need to use indirect heat at this moment. Close lid and continue cooking for about 8–10 minutes, until the salmon is just cooked through. It should not be well done, just opaque and easily flake. Squeeze a little fresh lemon juice over the cooked salmon fillets. Transfer salmon fillets to a platter. Let rest for a few minutes.

Using the tip of a knife or a fork, gently break each fillet into coarse chunks and flakes. Season with a little sea salt.

Warm dinner rolls. Take a roll and gently tear it open. Drop in a little soft butter and spoon a few chunks of the grilled salmon into the center of the buttery dinner roll. Add a spoonful of Cucumber Slaw and top with a few crispy salt & vinegar potato chips. Squish it together. Repeat with remaining rolls and enjoy.

CUCUMBER SLAW

1 cucumber
¼ cup (60 mL) red onion, finely diced
1 tsp (5 mL) extra-hot prepared horseradish, drained of excess moisture
2 tbsp (30 mL) fresh chives or green onions, chopped
½ cup (125 mL) fresh dill, chopped
1 tsp (5 mL) capers, chopped
2 to 3 heaping tbsp (30 to 45 mL) natural Greek-style yogurt
Squeeze of lemon juice
Pinch of cayenne pepper
Sea salt and freshly ground black pepper to taste

4 tsp (20 mL) Bone Dust BBQ Spice (page 212)
4 fresh salmon fillets (approx. 4 oz/115 g each), boneless and skinless
2 tsp (10 mL) grapeseed oil
Freshly squeezed lemon juice to taste
Sea salt to taste
8 warm dinner rolls
4 tsp (20 mL) butter

2 cups (500 mL) kettle-cooked potato chips, salt & vinegar flavor

GRILLED LEMON WINE-MARINATED CHICKEN SANDWICH

Simply summer, this sandwich is. It's gastro grilltastic! **SERVES 4**

2 juicy lemons
1 cup (250 mL) Creekside Estates Riesling
4 cloves minced garlic
¼ cup (60 mL) chopped fresh herbs (parsley, chives, mint, oregano, tarragon)
2 tsp (10 mL) Dijon mustard
2 tbsp (30 mL) olive oil
Salt and freshly ground black pepper to taste
3 boneless skin-on chicken breasts (4 to 6 oz/115 to 170 g each)
1 large red bell pepper
1 large yellow bell pepper
1 large green bell pepper
Drizzle of olive oil
1 loaf olive baguette
1 log (7 oz/200 g) soft creamy goat's cheese
1 head butter lettuce, washed and drained
1 tsp (5 mL) chopped fresh thyme

Zest one lemon and place the zest into a bowl. Cut the lemon in half and juice it and add juice to the zest. Add in the white wine, garlic, herbs, mustard and olive oil. Season to taste with a little salt and black pepper and whisk.

Place chicken in a self-sealing bag and pour over marinade. Zip it shut, refrigerate and marinate for 4 hours, turning a few times to marinate evenly.

Fire up your grill to 450–550°F (230–290°C).

Fire-roast red, yellow and green peppers until charred and blistered. Place peppers into a bowl and cover with plastic wrap. Set aside for 10–15 minutes.

Uncover bowl of peppers and peel the skin from them. Remove seeds and slice the peppers into strips. Season roasted pepper strips with a little salt and black pepper, drizzle with olive oil, mix and set aside.

Slice the baguette in half and drizzle each side evenly with a little olive oil. Set aside.

Remove chicken from marinade, discarding leftover marinade. Season the outside of each chicken breast with a little salt and pepper.

Grill the chicken breasts for 6–8 minutes per side or until fully cooked and golden brown. Squeeze a little fresh lemon over top of each breast as it grills to give that boost of lemon flavor. Remove from grill and allow the chicken breasts to rest for 5 minutes.

Lightly grill the cut baguette for 2–3 minutes, until toasty and warm.

Spread both sides of the baguette with goat's cheese. Top the bottom side of the baguette with leaves of butter lettuce. Using two forks or your fingers, shred the grilled chicken breasts into strips and chunks. Season the chicken shreds with a little salt and pepper as well as some thyme. Scatter the chicken breast meat evenly over the butter lettuce. Top with roasted pepper strips and top with baguette top. Slice into four delicious pieces and serve immediately.

GRILLED SHRIMP TACO WITH MANGO SALSA & QUESO FRESCO

This recipe reminds me of a shack on a hot sandy beach in Mexico. Having fun, drinking a few cervezas and kicking back and relaxing. Mmmm, shrimp taco! **MAKES 8**

WHAT YOU NEED: Potato masher; Tequila + shot glasses; Three 8-inch (20 cm) bamboo skewers, soaked in cold water for a minimum of 1 hour

MANGO SALSA
1 ripe mango
1 fresh green serrano or jalapeño pepper, finely chopped
¼ cup (60 mL) red onion, finely diced
1 green onion, minced
1 lime
Sea salt and freshly ground black pepper to taste
Drizzle of avocado oil
2 tbsp (30 mL) chopped fresh cilantro

1½ lb (675 g) big shrimp (approx. 10–12 pieces per pound)
1 tbsp (15 mL) sea salt
Drizzle of tequila (100% agave)
Drizzle of olive oil

1 juicy lime
Freshly ground black pepper to taste
Pinch of cayenne pepper

½ cup (125 mL) seedless small cucumber, thinly sliced
¼ cup (60 mL) red onion, thinly sliced
1 cup (250 mL) cilantro leaves, picked from the stem
2 cups (500 mL) iceberg lettuce, shredded
12 flour or corn tortillas, 5 to 6 inches (12 to 15 cm) in diameter
Dash or two of TABASCO® brand Pepper Sauce (optional)
½ cup (125 mL) crumbled queso fresco
8 wedges lime

To prepare the Mango Salsa, peel the mango. Cut the mango flesh from the pit and coarsely chop. Take a potato masher and mash the mango. This is to extract all the sweet flavor for the salsa. Add the serrano chile, red onion and green onion. Squeeze over a little fresh lime juice and season to taste with salt and black pepper. Drizzle with a little avocado oil. Mix and set aside.

To prepare the shrimp, peel the shrimp by taking the entire shell off them and discard the shells or save them for stock. Rinse the shrimp under cold water and drain. Add sea salt and mix about to coat all of the shrimp. Let stand, refrigerated, for about 5 minutes. This will help increase the flavor of the shrimp, especially when using frozen shrimp.

Rinse shrimp to remove excess salt and pat dry with paper towels. With a sharp knife, cut each shrimp in half lengthwise through the middle. Pick the black vein bits out from the flesh. Rinse under cold water, drain and pat dry with paper towels again. It is a lot easier to work with partially dry rather than sloppy wet shrimp — also safer when working with knives. Skewer the shrimp halves onto a couple of bamboo skewers, about 10 to 12 pieces per skewer. Don't put the shrimp onto the skewer facing the same way. Change it up and put them any way you like. It looks pretty funky once the shrimp are grilled!

continued . . .

Just before you are about to serve your tacos, add the chopped fresh cilantro to the Mango Salsa. You don't want to add it too early because it will turn black and alter the taste. It's the truth. Last minute is best here.

Place shrimp skewers in a dish large enough to hold them in an even layer. Drizzle them heavily with tequila and a little olive oil. Zest a lime and add to the dish, then juice the lime over the skewers. Season with a little black pepper and a pinch of cayenne pepper. Mix it around and let it marinate, refrigerated, for about 20 minutes.

In a bowl combine cucumber, red onion, cilantro and iceberg lettuce. Refrigerate until needed. Don't make this too far ahead, as you want it to be crisp and green.

Fire up your grill to 450–550°F (230–290°C).

Remove the shrimp from the tequila lime marinade, reserving marinade for basting. Grill shrimp skewers for about 6–8 minutes, turning frequently and basting with marinade. Watch for flare-ups when basting as there is tequila in that marinade. Grill until the shrimp are just cooked through and opaque. On a hot grill, this will not take too long.

Warm the tortillas on the hot grill. Remove shrimp from grill and remove the skewers. Put hot shrimp into a large bowl. Add a dash or two of TABASCO® brand Pepper Sauce (if using) and then sprinkle the queso fresco over the hot shrimp. Toss.

Cut a warm tortilla in your hand. Sprinkle in the lettuce and cucumber salad. Add a few grilled shrimp and a spoonful of Mango Salsa. Squeeze in some lime juice. Wrap and enjoy with a shot of tequila.

GRILLED TUNA MUFFULETTA

This recipe is inspired by my many trips to New Orleans and the muffuletta sandwiches that I have consumed at Central Grocery in the French Quarter. **MAKES 1 LOAF**

To make the Olive Salad, combine the olives, jalapeño, red onion, celery, roasted red pepper, green onions, garlic, Parmesan cheese, olive oil, vinegar and parsley in a bowl. Season to taste with a little salt and black pepper. Mix well, cover and refrigerate.

Slice the top off the loaf of bread. Scoop out the middle to make a bread bowl, leaving a wall about ½ inch (1 cm) thick. Set it aside.

Fire up your grill to 450–550°F (230–290°C).

Brush zucchini slices with a little olive oil and season to taste with salt, black pepper and hot pepper flakes. Grill zucchini for 1–2 minutes per side, until lightly charred and a little tender. Don't over-grill, as it will become mushy. Set aside.

Season the tuna steaks with sea salt and black pepper to taste. Leaving the lid open, grill tuna for 1–2 minutes per side for rare. Take care to not overcook. At the same time, grill the pancetta until crisp.

Spoon half of the olive salad on the bottom of the loaf of bread. Top with arugula and sliced tomatoes. Slice the tuna steaks into ¼-inch (5 mm) thick slices. Add the slices of tuna, followed by the grilled zucchini and pancetta. Add remaining olive salad and cover with bread lid. Cut loaf into six pieces and serve immediately.

OLIVE SALAD

1 cup (250 mL) sliced pimento-stuffed green olives, drained
1 to 2 jalapeño peppers, seeded and finely chopped
1 small red onion, diced
1 stalk celery, finely diced
1 roasted red bell pepper, diced
1 green onion, minced
2 cloves garlic, minced
¼ cup (60 mL) freshly grated Parmesan cheese
2 tbsp (30 mL) olive oil
2 tbsp (30 mL) red wine vinegar
1 tbsp (15 mL) chopped Italian (flat-leaf) parsley
Salt and freshly ground black pepper to taste

GRILLED TUNA MUFFULETTA

1 loaf round Italian bread with sesame seeds
1 medium green zucchini, sliced into strips about ½ inch (1 cm) thick
Sea salt and freshly ground black pepper to taste
Small pinch of red pepper flakes
3 fresh tuna steaks (approx. 4 to 5 oz/115 to 140 g each), about 1½-inches (4 cm) thick
8 slices pancetta
1 cup (250 mL) baby arugula leaves
2 tomatoes, thinly sliced

HOT ENGLISH CHEESE STEAK WITH PALE ALE & STILTON

It's pretty simple math: grilled steak + Stilton cheese + sautéed mushrooms + rustic bread + cold beer = deliciousness! **MAKES 4 TO 8**

WHAT YOU NEED: Large cast iron frying pan

4 center-cut beef tenderloin steaks (approx. 6 to 8 oz/170 to 225 g each), at least 3 inches (8 cm) thick

¼ cup (60 mL) hot English-style mustard

¼ cup + ½ cup (185 mL) Alexander Keith's IPA

2 tbsp (30 mL) Steak Spice (page 169)

3 tbsp (45 mL) canola oil

2 tsp (10 mL) butter

4 cups (1 L) quartered white or brown small "button" mushrooms

4 cloves garlic, minced

1 tsp (5 mL) chopped fresh thyme

½ cup (125 mL) Stilton cheese, crumbled

Kosher salt and freshly ground black pepper to taste

4 slices rustic bread, cut into 1-inch (2.5 cm) thick slices

Butter

Baby arugula

TED'S TIP

When buying your steaks, go to a good butcher, as you want quality meat and the perfect cut. They will know what you want. You may, however, pay a premium for this cut, but it is well worth it.

Cut each steak into two equally thick parts about 1 inch (2.5 cm) thick. You will now have eight 1-inch (2.5 cm) thick steaks.

Spoon the mustard into a small bowl and drizzle with the ¼ cup (60 mL) beer. Stir until combined. Brush each steak evenly over the entire surface with the mustard mixture. Season the steaks with Steak Spice, pressing the spices into the meat. Rub it in! Set aside.

Heat a large cast iron frying pan over high heat for 5 minutes. Add the oil and heat until it just starts to smoke. You want a good hot pan so that the mushrooms cook fast and the moisture in the mushrooms evaporates quickly so that you have crispy browned tender mushrooms, not a soupy mess. Add the butter and mushrooms; sauté for 3 to 5 minutes, stirring, until golden brown and a little crispy. Add the garlic; sauté for another minute. Add the ½ cup (125 mL) pale ale and let the liquid reduce to almost nothing. Remove from heat and stir in the thyme and Stilton cheese. Season to taste with salt and lots of black pepper. The cheese will melt all over the mushrooms. Set aside, keeping warm.

Fire up your grill to 450–550°F (230–290°C).

Grill the steaks over high heat, grill lid open, for about 1–2 minutes per side. It's beef tenderloin, so you don't want to overcook it. Best served rare or medium-rare or medium at a maximum. Move steaks to indirect area of grill.

Toast bread on grill. Butter toast, spread on a little hot English mustard and season with a little black pepper. Top with a heaping spoonful of Stilton mushrooms and spread it about. Slice each steak in half across the middle. Layer the steak slices onto the buttered toast (two to four slices per sandwich). Garnish with crisp baby arugula. Serve immediately.

INSIDE-OUT GRILLED CHEESE STEAK

I originally thought about putting the grilled steak inside the grilled cheese sandwich, but as I was making this recipe I had second thoughts and felt the need to switch it up. This version is easier to eat with a knife and fork but fun to prepare since I use a grilling stone. **SERVES 6**

WHAT YOU NEED: Grilling stone

In a bowl, combine Emmental and Edam cheeses. Set aside.

Slice the baguette into 12 rounds about 1 inch (2.5 cm) thick. Butter one side of each slice of bread. Place 6 slices of bread butter side down. Sprinkle each with 2 to 3 tbsp (30 to 45 mL) of the mixed cheese. Top with a slice of bread, butter side up. Repeat for remaining sandwiches and set aside.

Fire up your grill to 350–450°F (180–230°C).

Place your grilling stone directly over your fire source. The stone should sizzle when you drop a little knob of butter onto it. Be careful not to overheat the stone because, as even a heat as it is, it can still burn your food.

Open grill lid and drop a teaspoon (5 mL) of butter onto the hot stone. As it melts and sizzles, add the red onion and shallots and sauté on the stone. Using a pair of tongs, spread the onions into an even layer. Let the onions sizzle for a few minutes, then give them a stir with the tongs. Turn them about so they start to brown on all sides. Set onions aside in a small bowl or a corner of the stone. Keep warm.

Season all sides of the filet mignons with kosher salt and black pepper. Set aside.

Stone grill the sandwiches for 2–3 minutes per side, turning frequently to prevent burning, until the bread is golden brown and crisp and the cheese is melted.

At the same time as you are grilling the cheese sandwiches, drop another teaspoon (5 mL) of butter onto the hot stone and place seasoned steaks onto the bubbling butter. Stone fry the steaks for 2–3 minutes per side for medium-rare doneness. Remove steaks from grill stone and set aside to rest for 5 minutes. Remove grilled cheese from grill. Thinly slice each steak into four, on the bias. Place two slices of steak atop the grilled cheese. Garnish with caramelized red onions and fresh thyme. Serve immediately.

1 cup (250 mL) Emmental or Swiss cheese, shredded

1 cup (250 mL) Edam cheese, shredded

1 bakery fresh demi baguette, about 10 to 12 inches (25 to 30 cm) in length

4 tbsp (60 mL) unsalted butter, softened

1 large red onion, thinly sliced

2 shallots, thinly sliced

2 filet mignon (approx. 6 oz/170 g each), cut about 1½ inches (4 cm) thick

Kosher salt and freshly ground black pepper to taste

PLANKED BISON SLIDERS

For these burgers, I recommend grinding your own meat. Find a good butcher who sells game meats. They will often have already ground fresh or frozen game meats. But I find that those meats are usually too high in moisture and the burgers just don't cook up as well as when you grind the meat yourself. Once you start grinding your own meats, you will want to create a variety of mixes to make burgers, chilies and even sausages. Read your grinder's manual and have fun. It truly makes a better burger.

MAKES 10–12 SMALL BURGERS

WHAT YOU NEED: Cooling rack; Cookie sheet; Meat grinder with grinding blade and 1/8-inch (3 mm) grinding plate; Oak or maple grilling plank (12 × 8 × ½ inches/30 × 23 × 1 cm), soaked in water for a minimum of 1 hour; 3-oz (85 g) ice cream scoop

1¾ lb (790 g) bison sirloin
¼ lb (115 g) beef fat

BLACKBERRY WHISKEY COMPOTE
1 cup (250 mL) fresh or frozen
    blackberries
1 ripe pear
¼ cup (60 mL) honey
1 oz (30 mL) Jim Beam
1 sprig fresh sage
Salt and freshly ground black
    pepper to taste

2 cups (500 mL) caraway Gouda,
    grated
12 small rustic rolls

To prepare the meat, unwrap the bison sirloin or roast and pat it dry with paper towels. Place bison on a cooling rack over a cookie sheet. Refrigerate for at least 4–6 hours (or even overnight) to allow the meat to air dry. This reduces the moisture in your ground meat and allows for a burger that is not too wet and sloppy; they tend to fall apart.

Set up your meat grinder according to the manufacturer's instructions. Cut the bison sirloin into 1- to 2-inch (2.5 to 10 cm) chunks. Chop up the beef fat. Grind the bison meat and the beef fat together. When all the meat has been ground once, give it a quick stir or mix and then grind it again. Place ground meat back into the refrigerator and allow it to rest.

To make the Blackberry Whiskey Compote, combine blackberries, pear, honey and whiskey in a small saucepot. Add in the sprig of fresh sage and a grind or two from your pepper mill. Heat over medium to medium-low heat, stirring occasionally, until the mixture reaches a low boil. Simmer for 10–15 minutes, stirring occasionally, until the mixture is slightly thick. Remove from heat, remove and discard sprig of sage and season to taste with a little salt. Set aside.

Fire up your grill to 350–450°F (180–230°C).

Remove grilling plank from water and pat dry with paper towels.

Remove bison from refrigerator. Season the meat liberally with a little salt and black pepper. Scoop the bison meat (approx. 3 oz/85 g) and firmly but gently pack the ground meat into the scoop. Unmold the little ball of meat and place on grilling plank, flat side down. Repeat with all meat. You should be able to get about 12 small balls onto each

continued …

If you wish to make bigger burgers, go ahead. Just double up a couple of smaller balls, roll into a baseball-sized ball and plank grill. It will take about 25–30 minutes for them to cook.

plank. Squish 'em a little if you must or grab a second plank. Never buy just one, always have a backup!

Place plank onto hot grill. Close lid and let bison balls plank grill for about 15–18 minutes, until the burgers are cooked to an internal temperature of 145°F (63°C), medium doneness. You don't want to overcook these burgers as they will get dry and tough. They are much better moist and juicy. Just before the burgers are done, sprinkle the caraway Gouda cheese evenly over top of them. Close lid for a minute or so until the cheese is melted.

Warm the rolls, then take one and tear it open. Spoon in a little Blackberry Whiskey Compote and add a burger. Repeat and serve immediately.

ROTISSERIE OF BERKSHIRE PORK LOIN SANDWICHES

You know that rotisserie kit that came with the gas grill you bought? The one that is probably still in the box and packed away in the back of your shed? Well, it's time to open it up and get the party started.

This is the key to making the best shaved pork. Hit your local butcher and get a boneless Berkshire pork loin. Berkshire pork is well marbled with delicious succulent fat. This marbling will help keep the meat moist and juicy as it smokes. For me, I find that cooking the pork loin over an open fire of hardwood or hot coals while spinning it slowly on a rotisserie spit is about the only way to truly do this. Spinning it slowly over a nice even heat will provide you with the juiciest of results. **SERVES 8**

WHAT YOU NEED: Roasting pan or self-sealing heavy-duty food-grade storage bag; 1 rotisserie rod with 2 tines, 1 counterweight and 1 rotisserie motor (for proper use, refer to your manufacturer's instruction manual); Thermometer; Sharp carving knife

To prepare the Honey Mustard, whisk together the honey and prepared mustard. Set aside.

To begin preparing the pork, place pork loin into the roasting pan or storage bag.

In a large bowl, mix 1 tbsp (15 mL) Bone Dust BBQ Spice, 3 bottles of beer, water, sugar and salt. Stir to dissolve sugar and salt.

Pour the brine over the pork loin, making sure to cover as much of the loin as possible. Refrigerate for 24 hours, rolling the loin over every 4–6 hours.

Fire up your grill to 350–450°F (180–230°C) and set up rotisserie unit as per manufacturer's instructions. I personally do not put a drip pan under the pork loin for this recipe. I want the natural juices and fats to drop from the meat and land on the hot grill or coals and sizzle into flavor vapor.

Remove pork from brine, discarding leftover marinade. Pat dry with paper towels. Using the tip of a very sharp knife, score the pork loin on all sides in a diamond pattern — not too deep, just a little so that these nooks and crannies can pick up and hold the flavor of the spices. It also looks great for a rustic appeal and crispy bits.

Rub the outside of the pork loin with the ½ cup (125 mL) Bone Dust BBQ Spice, making sure to massage and rub the seasonings into the

HONEY MUSTARD

2 tbsp (30 mL) honey

4 tbsp (60 mL) prepared mustard

1 boneless pork loin (approx. 3 lb/1.4 kg), 10 to 12 inches (25 to 30 cm) long

1 tablespoon + ½ cup (140 mL) Bone Dust BBQ Spice (page 212)

3 + 1 bottles (12 oz/341 ml each) Leffe Blonde (Belgian pale ale)

4 cups (1 L) water at room temperature

¼ cup (60 mL) white sugar

½ cup (125 mL) kosher salt

Bakery fresh soft Kaiser rolls (approx. 4 inches/10 cm in diameter), at least 1 bun per person with a few extra for those who are very hungry

Sprinkle of red pepper flakes

continued . . .

meat. Skewer the pork loin with the rotisserie rod through the center of the length of the loin. Secure with the rotisserie spikes, making sure to push the loin from both ends to plump it up before skewering. Plumping will help keep it juicy. Check for balance on the rod. Once you start the rotisserie, you might find the pork loin to be flopping about on the spit. Remove, adjust tines to make it a little more secure and add a counterweight to help with balancing the loin. With a pork loin, it's a pretty uniform cut of meat, so it works pretty easily. Place pork on the grill, over hot coals, and start the motor. Let the pork spin slowly for 60–75 minutes, until an internal temperature of 150°F (65°C) is reached.

Remove pork from the rotisserie and with the rod still in place cover loosely with a sheet of aluminum foil and then with a couple of kitchen towels. This will allow the meat to rest and retain most of its precious juices before being sliced. Carefully remove rotisserie rod.

While the meat is resting, slice your fresh rolls, toasted if you wish, but I like them bakery fresh for this sandwich.

Take a very sharp knife and shave the pork loin as thin as you can. The thinner the better! Stack four to six pieces of the shaved rotisserie pork on a Kaiser roll. Sprinkle with a few crushed red pepper flakes and drizzle with Honey Mustard. Garnish as you please with whatever your heart desires and enjoy with an ice cold beer.

TED'S TIP

- For added flavor, sprinkle the outside of the spinning cooking pork loin with a little extra Bone Dust BBQ Spice. Do this a few times during the rotisserie process, as it boosts the flavors.
- For gas grill users, use a smoking tube or box to add a natural smoke flavor to the pork loin as it rotisseries.

STONE-GRILLED BUTTER BURGERS

I love burgers! I love 'em so much I wrote a whole book on the subject. I even went as far as securing a Guinness Book of World Records entry for the World's Largest Commercially Available Hamburger. At that time, my record stood at 590 pounds (268 kg). For me, the quest for the ultimate burger has been lifelong. Until now! But first my story.

Years ago, I wrote a recipe for Better Butter Burgers. They were pretty darn tasty and fans have told me for years that they love that burger. Well I like it too, but I wanted it to be even better. But in order to do that, I needed to (1) grind my own meat and (2) not grill it but "stone grill" it. Even heat, buttery sizzle, no big greasy flare-ups, just nice and easy cooking on a stone. Trust me, this recipe rocks. **MAKES 12**

WHAT YOU NEED: Cooling rack; Cookie sheet; Meat grinder with grinding blade and 1/8-inch (3 mm) grinding plate; Grilling stone

3 lb (1.4 kg) beef chuck
2 sticks (8 oz/225 g) cold butter

HONEY MUSTARD ONIONS

2 large sweet onions
4 cloves garlic, minced
Salt and freshly ground black
     pepper to taste
Drizzle of canola oil
2 tbsp (30 mL) prepared
     yellow mustard
1 tbsp (15 mL) honey
1 oz (30 mL) Canadian Club
     Small Batch

WOOZY MOP

10 cloves garlic, minced
1 tsp (5 mL) freshly ground
     black pepper
1 tsp (5 mL) kosher salt
1 tbsp (15 mL) mirin
3 tbsp (45 mL) Worcestershire sauce
2 tbsp (30 mL) canola oil

12 buns
12 slices Swiss cheese (optional)

Go to your local butcher and get a few pounds of beef chuck. Unwrap the beef chuck and pat it dry with paper towels. Place beef on a cooling rack over a cookie sheet and place into the refrigerator for at least 4–6 hours (overnight is best) to allow the meat to air dry a little. This reduces the moisture in your ground meat and allows for a burger that is not too wet and sloppy.

Set up your meat grinder according to the manufacturer's instructions.

Cut the beef chuck into 1- to 2-inch (2.5 to 5 cm) chunks. Cut both sticks of cold butter into ½-inch (1 cm) cubes. Keep the butter cold, as it will grind more easily. Grind the beef chuck and the cubed cold butter together, alternating between a few chunks of meat and a little butter. This way the butter grinds right into the meat. When all the meat has been ground once, give it a quick stir or mix and then grind it again. Place ground meat back into the refrigerator and allow it to rest.

While the ground beef and butter mixture is resting, prepare the Honey Mustard Onions. Slice the onions and place them into a bowl. Add the garlic, salt and black pepper to taste. Drizzle with a little canola oil. Set aside.

In a bowl, whisk together the mustard, honey and whiskey. Set aside.

Prepare the Woozy Mop. In a bowl, combine garlic, pepper, salt, mirin, Worcestershire sauce and canola oil. Stir; this should be a little slushy. Set aside.

continued . . .

- Do not squish or press the burgers while they are cooking. Leave them be. Every time you want to push, press, squish and/or cut the burger, go have a sip of your beer or cocktail instead. This will make for a juicier burger.
- This recipe calls for grinding your own beef. If you do not have a meat grinder readily available, you can still prepare this recipe. When using butcher- or grocery store–bought ground beef, you will need to soften the butter slightly before mixing it into the cold ground beef. This will allow for an even coating of butter on the meat. Proceed with the same cooking procedure.

Fire up your grill to 350–450°F (180–230°C).

Place your grilling stone directly over your fire source. The stone should sizzle when you drop a little knob of butter onto it. Be careful not to overheat the stone because it can still burn your food.

Open grill lid and drop a teaspoon (5 mL) of butter onto the hot stone. As it melts and sizzles, add the onion mixture on the stone. Using a pair of tongs, spread the onions into an even layer. Let the onions sizzle for a few minutes, then give them a stir with the tongs. Turn them so they start to brown on all sides.

Drizzle sautéed onions with the mustard mixture. Stir and season to taste with a little salt and black pepper. Set onions aside in a small bowl or a corner of the stone. Keep warm.

While the onions are sautéing, scoop the ground meat mixture into 3- to 4-oz (85 to 115 g) balls. Don't overpack them, gently press the meat together. Drop another few cubes of butter onto the hot stone and top with 4 to 6 burgers. Using a flat, sturdy spatula, press the balls of meat to flatten. Don't squish them too much, just a little so that they are flat on the top and thick in the middle. Stone grill butter burgers for 3–5 minutes, until the burgers are browned evenly on the bottom side. Flip the burgers over, adding a cube or two of extra butter if needed.

Baste a little Woozy Mop mixture over the top of each burger. Continue to stone grill the burgers for 3–5 more minutes, until just cooked through and still juicy. When the burgers are almost done, toast your buns on the grill or grill stone for 1–2 minutes, until lightly browned and crisp.

Place burger on bun, top with sautéed Honey Mustard Onions and add your favorite burger garnishes. Some of my favorites are melted Swiss cheese, mayonnaise, thinly sliced raw jalapeño peppers and thinly sliced raw red onions.

TURKEY BACON CLUB WITH STUFFING & CRANBERRY SAUCE

I don't know about you, but to me the best part about Thanksgiving or Christmas dinners is the leftovers of roasted turkey made into a sandwich. You know the one you might make, with layers of tender turkey, a little bit of cranberry sauce and stuffing. Why wait for leftovers when you can have it hot and fresh any time!

SERVES 6

WHAT YOU NEED: Large roasting pan; Oak or maple grilling plank (12 × 8 × ½ inches/30 × 20 × 1 cm), soaked in water for a minimum of 1 hour

1 boneless skinless turkey breast (approx.
  2 to 3 lb/0.9 to 1.4 kg)
¼ cup (60 mL) kosher salt
4 cups (1 L) apple juice
2 cups (500 mL) water
½ cup (125 mL) Jim Beam
2 tbsp (30 mL) Bone Dust BBQ Spice (page 212)

STUFFING

3 cups (750 mL) white rustic sourdough bread
  cubes (day old and stale), diced
8 + 12 slices smoked bacon
⅓ cup (75 mL) butter
1 medium onion, diced
1 stalk celery, diced
3 tbsp (45 mL) milk
Salt and freshly ground black pepper to taste
1 tbsp (15 mL) chopped fresh sage

CRANBERRY SAUCE

1½ cups (375 mL) frozen cranberries, thawed
  and picked through for stems and leaves
⅓ cup (75 mL) white sugar
¼ cup (60 mL) water
¼ cup (60 mL) orange juice
1 oz (30 mL) Jim Beam

GARNISH

1 loaf rustic sourdough bread, cut into
  12 uniformly thick slices
3 tsp (15 mL) butter, softened
3 tsp (15 mL) mayonnaise
½ cup (125 mL) red onion, thinly sliced
2 vine-ripened tomatoes, thinly sliced
6 slices Swiss cheese
1 avocado, peeled, pitted and cut into thin slices
1 cup (250 mL) baby arugula

Rinse turkey breast with cold water and pat dry with paper towels. Using a sharp thin-bladed knife, make a pocket in the turkey breast for the stuffing mixture. The easiest way to do this is to start at the thick end of the turkey breast, insert the tip of the knife into the middle of the end of the breast and push into the breast, going almost the entire length but stopping short about 2 inches (5 cm). Place turkey breast into a large roasting pan.

In a bowl, combine kosher salt, apple juice, water and bourbon. Pour over turkey breast. Cover and refrigerate, allowing the turkey breast to brine for 24 hours. During this brining process, turn the turkey breast a few times so the brining is even.

Meanwhile, prepare the stuffing mixture by placing the bread cubes into a large bowl and set aside.

continued . . .

Fry off 8 slices of bacon over medium to medium-low heat until it is just a little bit crispy. Remove bacon from pan and pat dry with paper towels. Coarsely chop bacon and add to bread cubes.

Drain bacon fat from pan and reserve for further use. Add butter and 2 tbsp (30 mL) bacon fat back into the pan. Sauté onions and celery for 3–5 minutes, stirring, until tender. Add milk and pour over top of the bacon and bread cubes. Season to taste with salt and black pepper. Add chopped fresh sage and mix well so that the stuffing is a little moist and sticks together. Cover and refrigerate.

To make the Cranberry Sauce, wash and drain cranberries. Put berries, sugar, water, orange juice and bourbon in a large saucepan. Slowly bring to a boil, stirring occasionally. Cover and cook for 10 minutes or until the cranberries burst and are tender. Skim and cool.

Remove turkey breast from brine, discarding brine. Pat turkey breast dry with paper towels and make sure you get inside the incision too. Stuff the cavity of the turkey with the bread stuffing, pushing the mixture in firmly so it is well packed. Rub the outside of the turkey with Bone Dust BBQ Spice, making sure to press the seasonings into the meat. Place turkey breast, centered, onto the grilling plank, tenderloin side (flat side) down.

Next you will need to wrap the turkey breast with slices of bacon. Run your fingers along the surface of a slice of bacon to stretch it longer by almost one-third. Cut each slice of bacon in half. Starting at one end, wrap the bacon over the top of the turkey breast, tucking the bacon underneath the breast so it holds in place. Repeat until the turkey is completely covered and place back on plank.

Fire up your grill to 350–450°F (180–230°C).

Place planked bacon-wrapped stuffed turkey breast onto the grill directly over the heat source. Close grill lid and plank smoke for 10–15 minutes. This will get a good burst of smoke flavor into the turkey. Be sure to keep the lid closed as much as possible to keep the smoke inside. Reduce heat directly under plank and grill-roast for 60–75 more minutes, until a meat thermometer measures an internal temperature of 160°F (70°C). Remember that as the bacon renders and gets crisp, the fat will drip into your grill. Watch for flare-ups.

Remove planked turkey breast from grill, cover loosely with aluminum foil and a couple of kitchen towels and let rest for 10–15 minutes.

Peel the cooked bacon from the outside of the turkey and set aside.

Carve the stuffed turkey breast into thin slices across the breast.

Toast your sourdough bread. Butter one side of each slice of toast and lay, butter side up, on a clean work surface. Spread on a little mayo, add sliced red onion, one or two slices of tomato, three to four thin slices of stuffed turkey breast and a slice of Swiss cheese. Continue with a couple of slices of avocado, top with a piece or two of the crispy bacon wrap, add a handful of arugula and season to taste with a little salt and black pepper. Top sandwich with the other slice of sourdough. Repeat and serve immediately.

MEAT

BEEF

TERIYAKI FLANK STEAK   199

SMOKED & GRILLED BEEF RIBS WITH BEER SCHMEER   200

BEER BUTTER-BASTED ROTISSERIE OF PRIME RIB   204

MAUI SHORT RIBS   207

PLANKED MEATLOAF & MASHED POTATOES WITH BEER BBQ GRAVY   208

PORK

FIVE RIB RUBS   212

FOUR BBQ SAUCE RECIPES FOR GRILLING, GLAZING, DIPPING & LICKING!   218

PLANK-ROASTED RACK OF PORK STUFFED
WITH GRILLED APRICOT & SHALLOT STUFFING   229

GRILLED PORK CHOP WITH CANDIED CHILI GLAZE   233

BOURBON STREET GRILLED PORK TENDERLOIN WITH PRALINE BBQ SAUCE   234

LAMB

CINNAMON CHIPOTLE-RUBBED LEG OF LAMB WITH RAITA   237

GRILLED LAMB CUTLETS WITH FIRE-ROASTED SHALLOT,
MINT & GOAT'S CHEESE PESTO   238

GRILLED LAMB KIDNEYS WITH PRUNES & PORT WINE REDUCTION   241

GRILLED LAMB T-BONES WITH PINK PEPPERED POMEGRANATE GLAZE   242

SMOKED LAMB RIBS WITH SPICY PEANUT SAUCE   245

VEAL

GASTRO GRILL ABCS: GRILLED APPLE, BACON & CALF'S LIVER
WITH ICE SYRUP   246

GRILLED VEAL RACK CHOPS WITH BLACK OLIVE TAPENADE   249

GRILLED VEAL SWEETBREADS WITH HORSERADISH GREMOLATA   250

GRILLED VEAL T-BONES WITH CHANTERELLE FRICASSEE
& BUFFALO MOZZARELLA   253

GAME

GRILLED BUFFALO STEAKS WITH HONEY DATE BUTTER   254

GRILLED VENISON RACK CHOPS WITH PISTACHIO NUT CRUST
& PARTRIDGE BERRY GLAZE   257

GRILLED FIGS & FOIE GRAS   258

GRILLED STEAKS

I have been in love with steak for as long as I can recall. I'm pretty sure it all started with my dad and his wheelbarrow grill and those big juicy sirloin steaks marinated in red wine (page 174). The heat and smell of the hot charcoal, the fat sizzling and dripping onto the hot coals, the tenderness of beef and the overall juicy steakalicious goodness. I love steak!

I would have to say that my favorite food is steak. I am a big fan of a big juicy steak. And yes, I could eat a steak every day. I love it, period.

My favorite steak is the rib steak. Bone-in or boneless, it has the most flavor. My next favorite cut would be the strip loin steak. I usually order them about 1½ to 2 inches (4 to 5 cm) thick, 12 to 16 oz (340 to 450 g) each and brought to room temperature before I even begin. Seasoned with salt, pepper and garlic and cooked blue-rare, about 90 seconds per side — delicious!

I like my steaks cooked differently based upon the cut. Tenderloin raw or blue-rare to rare. NY strip loin blue-rare to rare. Rib steak medium-rare to medium, to allow the internal fat to render a little, which adds lots of flavor.

BUYING STEAKS

When purchasing steaks as part of a meal, here are a few rules that I live by:

RULE #1   Buy the best-quality steak that you can afford. Not all good top cuts (rib eye or strip loin) are always tender. There are many grades of meat, A, AA, AAA, with A being the worst quality and AAA being the best. At least here in Canada, that's how it works. Keep in mind that usually the more expensive the cut of meat is, the better-quality it is likely to be. Here are a few grades of meat to look out for that will give you great quality: CAB (certified Angus beef) is expensive but delicious. USDA choice is reasonably priced and you can often get a very tasty piece of meat. Then of course there is PRIME, which is the best quality of meat you can get in the US. It's expensive, but providing you can afford it, it's worth it. There is also Japanese Kobe beef, which is loaded with internal marbling and fat and very expensive. But again, if you have the means, I highly recommend it.

RULE #2   For a steak to be tender, it needs some age. By age I mean the older it is, the more tender it will be. There are two methods to age meat.

The first, which is a relatively new method of aging meat, is called wet aging. This is done primarily by the meat packing industry. It essentially means that the meat has been vacuum sealed in a plastic bag, which allows the meat to retain its moisture and age a little quicker than the old-school method of dry aging. Now there is nothing wrong with buying wet-aged meat; it is usually a little less expensive than dry-aged and it is ready to eat. For me, if I am buying wet-aged beef, I am looking for beef that has at least 21 days' worth of age on it from the date of packing. Your local butcher can assist you with finding the right wet-aged beef for you.

But if you want the best when it comes to steak, for me it is dry aging. This is the old-school method of aging beef. The meat is hung in a temperature-controlled refrigerator for a period of time, thus allowing the moisture to escape or evaporate from the meat. This produces a more tender and flavorful steak than wet-aged. I find with wet-aged steaks the meat tastes a little "bloody," which in turn overpowers the true deliciousness of the beef. For dry-aged beef, the big question becomes, how long does one age the beef for? Personally I like beef to be dry aged for anywhere between 35 and 42 days. Many butchers will dry age for approximately 21 to 28 days. The longer the meat ages, the more moisture loss and the more expensive the cut.

For dry aging, it is always best to find a great butcher who does their own dry aging, but if you wish to dry age your own meat, then here is my method of doing so:

You want to dry age in a refrigerator that will not be opening all the time. It is best to use a secondary refrigerator where you can ensure that the door is kept closed, maintaining a constant consistent temperature. A beer fridge is a good place to start, whether in your garage or basement, but for me I bought a fridge that I dedicate to aging my beef. Buy a refrigerator thermometer or two and place in the refrigerator. I like to have one beside the meat and one on the top shelf of the fridge (traditionally the warmest spot) so that I can keep my temperatures true.

Maintain a constant temperature of between 36°F and 40°F (2.2°C to 4.4°C). You don't want the fridge to be too cold and yet not too warm. Too cold will not allow for even drying. As well, you don't want your refrigerator to be too moist, so maintain a humidity level of about 35–40%. To monitor the humidity, you can purchase a sling psychrometer from butcher or restaurant supply stores. They are not that expensive, about $60 to $75. It's worth the investment, since butchers charge a premium for dry-aged beef and you don't want to have any issues. A whole strip loin might cost you $100 — that's a lot of money and meat to throw out because you didn't want to invest in a little piece of equipment

Purchase a whole primal cut of beef (short loin or prime rib, bone in, are best). Remove any packaging from the beef and pat dry with paper towels to remove the excess external moisture. Wrap the beef in two to three sheets of cheesecloth. Sprinkle a layer of kosher salt or coarse sea salt onto the bottom of a stainless steel pan (pan should be approximately 16 to 18 inches/40 to 45 cm long, 10 to 12 inches/25 to 30 cm wide and 3 inches/8 cm deep). A nice even layer, about 2 cups (500 mL), of salt will add flavor and help draw the moisture from the beef as it ages. Place a fitted wire rack over top of the salt in the stainless pan. Place cheesecloth-wrapped beef onto rack and let stand for 48 hours; this is to absorb any blood dripping in the first couple of days. Remove and discard cheesecloth and return beef to fridge unwrapped. Place in refrigerator and continue to age for 1, 2, or 3+ weeks, checking the meat weekly to see how it is coming along. You will notice that the meat will get dark red and begin to dry and shrink. Watch for mold spores that will begin to grow on the outside of the beef. It's okay to see mold as long as the meat is dry and not wet and slimy. You will know by the smell as well when you open the fridge. It should be sweet smelling rather than sour.

After aging, remove beef from refrigerator and trim away any dark discoloration and bits of mold you may see. Trim the hard dry fat and excess sinew and cut into steaks.

Fire up your grill!

RULE #3   To put it simply, fat equals flavor. The more internal fat, the more flavorful and tender your steak will be. Internal fat or marbling is what gives a steak its succulence and juiciness. You want a steak to be well marbled: the more marbling, the more flavor. External fat — the fat that is on the outside of the steak — is also important. This adds great flavor while your steak grills, but this outer fat should really not be eaten. It's not good for your heart, and believe me, I love that crispy fatty outer layer of goodness, but it does not do me any good. So nibble with care!

RULE #4   Find yourself a good butcher. A thicker steak will cook more evenly and give you a little wiggle room in case you get distracted. You can't go back once it's overcooked, but you can always throw it back on the grill if it's underdone. It will have far less chance of drying out on the grill. Keeping the juices in your steak will yield better flavor and satiation value.

Talk to your butcher about dry-aged versus wet-aged beef.

HOW TO GRILL THE PERFECT STEAK

When it comes to grilling a great steak, the debate begins with gas versus charcoal. Simple answer is that charcoal gives you the best flavor and gas gives you convenience. Use whatever you have to cook on, just make it taste great.

Once you have spent some serious dough on some great steaks, you do not need to marinate them to tenderize. Only marinate if you want to add flavor. Personally I like to take a huge rib steak or porterhouse and marinate it for a couple of hours in a bottle of dark beer. Season your steaks at the last minute with lots of coarsely ground sea salt, freshly ground black pepper and loads of garlic.

For cooking a great steak, I prefer to use charcoal since it gives the best flavor, but use whatever grill you have. But make sure you get it hot, 600°F (315°C) or hotter if you can. Once you start cooking the steaks, remember high heat, lid open. Be patient, never leave your grill, don't poke, cut or stick your steaks, and have a beer. Place steaks on a hot grill on a 45° angle at 11 o'clock. Grill for 2 to 5 minutes to sear, depending on thickness and doneness you want. Turn steaks 45° to 2 o'clock and cook for another 2 to 5 minutes. Flip steaks over and baste grilled surface with your favorite baste or sauce, like my Ted's World Famous BBQ™ Beerlicious™ BBQ Sauce or whatever brand you prefer. Continue to grill for 2 to 5 minutes on a 45° angle. Turn steaks 45° and cook for another 2 to 5 minutes. Flip steaks and baste again. Now you have that fancy chef/steakhouse diamond pattern. Remove steaks from grill and let rest for 3 to 5 minutes before serving.

STEAK CUTS

TENDERLOIN   Of all of the steak cuts, the tenderloin is the most tender. The tenderloin comes from the short loin of beef; it lies between the rib and the sirloin and never really does anything but lie there and be tender. The tenderloin may be cooked whole or cut into wonderfully tender steaks. Be careful not to overcook this cut. It does not have a lot of fat, so it tends to dry out and become tough the more it cooks. Quite often steak joints will wrap it with a strip or two of bacon to keep it moist and succulent.

STRIP LOIN   The strip loin steak is one of the most popular cuts of beef. It comes from the top loin muscle in the short loin of beef. It is best grilled to medium-rare and is often served with a peppercorn sauce. This steak is known by many names, the most popular being the New York strip steak. A bone-in strip loin steak is known as a Kansas City steak or shell steak. I think a bone-in strip offers the ultimate flavor, as the bone and extra fattiness bring out added flavor. My favorite way to eat a NY strip loin steak is rare. Brought to room temperature and grilled over charcoal hot and fast.

RIB-EYE STEAK   This steak is cut from between the rib and chuck section. The bone-in rib steak is also known as the cowboy steak. The rib steak is an extremely tender cut of beef. This steak is heavily marbled with fat, giving it maximum flavor. It is best to grill this steak to medium-rare, which allows the internal fat to melt and bring out the natural juices and flavor.

T-BONE STEAK   This steak is named after the shape of its bone, a large T that separates the strip loin from the small tenderloin. Cut from the center of the short loin, this is a large steak, often best shared, but if you're truly hungry it is a real meal for one. I like to serve this steak with lots of sautéed onions and mushrooms and topped with crumbled blue cheese.

PORTERHOUSE STEAK   A porterhouse steak is cut from the large end of the short loin and also has the same T-shaped bone as the T-bone. It has a larger tenderloin portion and is truly a meal for two — it's sometimes called the king of steaks. It is often cut into 2-inch (5 cm) thick portions weighing approximately 36 oz (1 kg). Rub this steak with garlic, black pepper and fresh rosemary and grill it over medium-high heat.

SIRLOIN STEAK   Cut from the area between the short loin and round, the sirloin has three main muscles. Cut into steaks, they are quite flavorful but require marinating to make them a little more tender. A teriyaki marinade is the most popular marinade used on sirloin steaks. This cut gives you the best of both worlds; the strip and the tenderloin. Delicious! A steak for one or more, if you feel like sharing.

FLANK STEAK   The flank steak comes from the lower hind region of beef. It is a tougher cut of steak that requires marinating to make it tender. As it does not have a lot of internal fat, be careful not to overcook it. Marinated in an Asian marinade, this steak will have great flavor. It is best sliced thinly when served and is a great steak for a salad or steak sandwich.

SKIRT STEAK   This piece of meat is the diaphragm muscle that is cut from the flank steak. It's a tough piece of meat that needs to be well trimmed of its fat and sinew and marinated for a long period of time to garner flavor and tenderize the meat. I go usually 24 to 48 hours. I also like to tenderize this cut with either a meat mallet or a needler. A needler is a meat instrument that has 48 little stainless steel blades that, when pushed into the meat,

cut through the flesh and membrane to make everything tender. You can find this utensil in most restaurant supply stores.

HANGER STEAK   The hanger steak hangs between the rib cage and loin cage. Hanger steaks have a slightly stronger flavor than regular steaks and need to be very fresh. Ask your butcher for this tender cut of beef, which isn't usually found in grocery stores. Marinate it with stronger-flavored herbs and spices and lots of garlic. It is best cooked rare to medium and sliced thinly.

COOKING STEAK: HOW DO YOU LIKE YOUR STEAK COOKED?

Blue-rare: A blue-rare steak is quickly charred on the outside and barely cooked on the inside. For best results, bring the steak to room temperature before cooking.

Rare: A rare steak has a cool red center.

Medium-rare: A medium-rare steak has a warm red center.

Medium: A medium steak has a pink center and the juices are clear.

Medium-well: A medium-well steak has a hot pink center and the juices are clear.

Well-done: A well-done steak is gray throughout without any trace of pink and the juices are clear.

Super-well-done: This steak is weighted with a brick until heavily charred on the outside and without any trace of pink and no juices inside.

HOW TO TEST FOR DONENESS FOR YOUR PERFECT STEAK

The best way to test for doneness on a steak is to use a meat thermometer.

Blue-rare	130°F (55°C)
Rare	130 to 140°F (55 to 60°C)
Medium-rare	140 to 145°F (60 to 63°C)
Medium	145 to 150°F (63 to 65°C)
Medium-well	150 to 160°F (65 to 70°C)
Well-done	160 to 170°F (70 to 76°C)
Super-well-done	170°F (76°C) or more

The next best method to test for doneness is the *hand touch method*. Shake one hand loose so that it is completely relaxed: With your other hand, touch the soft fleshy part of your relaxed hand at the base of your thumb. This soft texture is similar to the texture of a blue-rare to rare steak. Now touch your thumb and forefinger together and again touch the base of your thumb. This texture is similar to a medium-rare steak. Next, touch your thumb to your middle finger. This firmer texture is similar to the texture of a medium steak. Next, touch your thumb to your fourth finger. The semi-firm texture at the base of your thumb is similar to a medium-well steak. Last, touch your thumb to your pinky finger. The very firm texture at the base of your thumb is similar to a well-done steak.

This method of testing for a steak is relatively easy and you will never find yourself looking for a thermometer while grilling.

One last note, and maybe the most important of all: Never cut the meat to test for doneness. Cutting the steak lets all the natural juices escape, leaving you with a dry and tasteless piece of meat.

STEAK SPICE

This is a recipe for your pepper grinder. A steak spice that you grind yourself, allowing you to get the full flavor of the spices. MAKES ABOUT 2 CUPS (500 ML)

Combine the salt, black peppercorns, white peppercorns, Szechuan peppercorns, onion flakes, garlic, mustard seeds, coriander seeds, ancho pepper and dill seeds.

Fill a pepper grinder with as much of the Steak Spice as it can hold. Store remaining Steak Spice in an airtight container in a cool, dry place away from heat and light.

⅓ cup (75 mL) coarse sea salt
¼ cup (60 mL) whole black
　　peppercorns
¼ cup (60 mL) whole white
　　peppercorns
¼ cup (60 mL) Szechuan
　　peppercorns
¼ cup (60 mL) dried onion flakes
3 tbsp (45 mL) coarse
　　granulated garlic
2 tbsp (30 mL) mustard seeds
2 tbsp (30 mL) coriander seeds
1 tbsp (15 mL) crushed or flaked
　　ancho pepper
1 tbsp (15 mL) dill seeds

SMOKED SALT STEAK SPICE

When you want to add a bit of smokiness to your meats, try this smoked salt steak rub. If you are a diehard barbeque griller or smoker and you want to smoke your own salt, go for it, but for ease you can find a variety of smoked salts in specialty food shops and grocery stores. It makes life a little easier. MAKES ABOUT 1 CUP (250 ML)

To prepare the rub, mix together smoked salt, both peppers, garlic, red pepper flakes, sugar, thyme and coriander seeds. Set aside.

In a frying pan over medium heat, toast cumin and mustard seeds for about 1 minute, until the seeds start to pop and are fragrant. Allow to cool. Add toasted cumin and mustard seeds to smoked salt mixture. Mix well to combine.

Store in an airtight container in a cool, dry place away from heat and light.

½ cup (125 mL) smoked salt
2 tbsp (30 mL) cracked black pepper
1 tbsp (15 mL) cracked white pepper
2 tbsp (30 mL) granulated garlic
1 tbsp (15 mL) red pepper flakes
2 tsp (10 mL) white sugar
1 tbsp (15 mL) dried thyme
1 tbsp (15 mL) cracked
　　coriander seeds
1 tsp (5 mL) cumin seeds
1 tsp (5 mL) mustard seeds

SMOKY GARLIC & HERB GRILLING OIL

I use this for baste on pretty much everything I grill. Store it in a canning jar and use for grilling on all your favorite steaks, chops, ribs, chicken, seafood and vegetables. It adds a boost of flavor and will help keep your foods moist, tender and succulent. MAKES ABOUT 2 CUPS (500 ML)

WHAT YOU NEED: Hickory wood chips, soaked; High-heat thermometer; 2-cup (500 mL) canning jar

3 heads garlic
½ cup (125 mL) olive oil
Salt to taste
1 juicy lemon
1 cup (250 mL) canola oil
1 drop all-natural liquid smoke,
    hickory flavor
2 tbsp (30 mL) chopped
    fresh rosemary
2 tbsp (30 mL) chopped
    fresh oregano
2 tbsp (30 mL) chopped fresh thyme
2 tbsp (30 mL) chopped fresh sage
¼ cup (60 mL) chopped
    fresh parsley
1 tsp (5 mL) coarsely ground
    black pepper

Fire up your grill to 350–450°F (180–230°C). Set grill for both direct and indirect grilling.

Cut the stem off the top of the head of garlic, exposing the inner cloves. Drizzle with olive oil and season with a little salt. Place the heads of garlic, cut side down, onto the grill and char for a few minutes, until the top is nice and dark. If you would like to throw a few wood chips onto the fire as the garlic sears for a little extra smokiness, go for it. Turn the heads over and char for a few minutes more, until the outer skin of the garlic is nicely darkened. Remove from grill and set each head of garlic on an 8-inch (20 cm) square sheet of aluminum foil. Drizzle heads with a little more olive oil and a pinch more of salt. Wrap it up into a little pouch, not too tightly but sealed, leaving some room in the foil for steam, return to indirect part of the grill and close lid. Grill-roast the garlic for approximately 45 minutes, until the garlic is soft. Remove from grill and unwrap the garlic. Let it cool.

Remove all of the roasted cloves from the skins. Get all of that precious smokiness out of the skins — it's all great sweet flavor. You should have about ½ cup (125 mL) garlic. Set aside.

Zest the lemon and set aside.

Place the grill-roasted garlic cloves and lemon zest into a saucepot and cover with canola oil. Add a drop of liquid smoke, and I mean just a drop. You don't need much. Heat over medium-low heat to a temperature of 200°F (100°C) and hold temperature, simmering the garlic in the oil for 10 minutes. Remove from heat and stir in the fresh herbs and black pepper. Set aside to cool.

Once cool, pour into a canning jar, seal lid and refrigerate.

Smoky Garlic & Herb Grilling Oil will keep refrigerated for up to 3 weeks. When you want to use it, remove from the refrigerator and let it come up to room temperature. Shake up the jar really well to mix up the roasted garlic herb mixture. Fire up your grill and as your foods grill, give them a light brushing.

CLASSIC FILET WITH SAUCE BÉARNAISE

When I was a young pup working in kitchens, I had a job in a local steakhouse that wrapped the beef tenderloin steaks in bacon and served them with sauce béarnaise (hollandaise sauce with tarragon) and a huge baked potato fully loaded. I love this type of steakhouse! **SERVES 6**

WHAT YOU NEED: Toothpicks

Fry the bacon for 2–3 minutes per side or until slightly done. You do not want to fry the bacon crisp or you will not be able to wrap it around the filets. Remove from pan and pat dry with paper towels to remove excess fat. Set aside.

Take a sprig of tarragon and skewer it through the middle of the side of the steak. Run it all the way through so that there are a few inches of tarragon sticking out two sides of the steak. You may need to make a small incision with the tip of a knife to get it started.

Rub the filets all over with the Steak Spice, pressing the seasoning into the meat. Fold the end of the tarragon sticking out around the steak and then wrap each steak with a slice of partially fried bacon. Use a half slice extra if the bacon does not quite make it all the way around. Secure with a toothpick and set aside at room temperature.

Meanwhile, make the Sauce Béarnaise. In a small saucepot, bring the vinegar, tarragon sprigs, shallot, water and peppercorns to a boil. Reduce heat and simmer for 3–4 minutes or until the liquid has reduced by half. Remove from heat and strain. Discard solids and let the liquid cool.

In a medium bowl, whisk the egg yolks, white wine, sherry and cooled vinegar mixture. Place over a pot of simmering water and whisk constantly until the mixture is thick enough to form a ribbon when drizzled from the whisk. Be careful not to turn this into scrambled eggs. Remove from heat. Whisking constantly, slowly add the clarified butter a little at a time until all the butter has been absorbed. Season with chopped tarragon, mustard, lemon juice, TABASCO® brand Pepper Sauce, Worcestershire sauce, salt and pepper. Remove from heat and keep warm over the hot water.

Fire up your grill to 450–550°F (230–290°C).

Grill beef for 5–6 minutes per side for medium-rare doneness and the bacon is crispy. Remove toothpicks and serve filets drizzled with Sauce Béarnaise.

6 to 8 thick slices bacon

6 petite filet mignon — center-cut beef tenderloin steaks (approx. 6 oz/170 g each), cut about 1½ to 2 inches (4 to 5 cm) thick

6 sprigs fresh tarragon (approx. 6 to 8 inches/15 to 20 cm in length)

2 tbsp (30 mL) Steak Spice (page 169)

SAUCE BÉARNAISE

¼ cup (60 mL) cider vinegar

2 sprigs fresh tarragon

1 small shallot, diced

2 tbsp (30 mL) water

4 black peppercorns

4 egg yolks

2 tbsp (30 mL) dry white wine

1 tbsp (15 mL) dry sherry

1 cup + 2 tbsp (280 mL) clarified butter

1 tbsp (15 mL) chopped fresh tarragon

1 tbsp (15 mL) Dijon mustard

1 tsp (5 mL) lemon juice

Dash of TABASCO® brand Pepper Sauce

Dash of Worcestershire sauce

Kosher salt and freshly ground black pepper to taste

TED'S TIP
Look for tarragon sprigs with a good firm stalk as these are best for skewering the meat.

DAD'S GRILLED STEAK

This is where it all started for me. My dad's grill. As a child, we had a crappy three-legged charcoal grill. I say crappy because the bottom had rusted out of it and my dad was using quadruple folded sheets of aluminum foil as a new bottom. Finally the whole thing collapsed as my dad was firing it up. I learned a few choice words that day, I tell you.

So off my dad went to the shed and pulled out his rusty ol' red wheelbarrow. Filled it with charcoal, fired it up with a container or two of lighter fluid and we were back in action. I stood there in awe. He was nuts. He then went in the house and took a shelf out of my mom's fridge and set that over the coals. "There," he said "perfect."

So true it was. Best steak ever came off that grill, by the hands of my pop and his frugalness.

Love ya, Dad. **SERVES 4 TO 6 WITH PLENTY OF LEFTOVERS FOR STEAK SANDWICHES**

1 sirloin steak (approx. 4 lb/1.8 kg and 3 inches/8 cm thick)

¼ cup (60 mL) freshly ground black pepper

12 cloves garlic, minced

1 cup (250 mL) Creekside Estates Cabernet Shiraz

¼ cup (60 mL) vegetable oil

¼ cup (60 mL) ketchup

2 tbsp (30 mL) chopped fresh herbs (such as parsley, sage, rosemary)

1 tbsp (15 mL) Worcestershire sauce

Salt to taste

Rub the steak with the black pepper, pressing the seasoning into the meat.

In a glass dish large enough to hold the steak, whisk together the garlic, wine, vegetable oil, ketchup, herbs, Worcestershire sauce and salt. Add steak, turning once to coat. Marinate, covered and refrigerated, for 6 hours or overnight.

Fire up your grill to 450–550°F (230–290°C).

Remove steak from marinade, discarding marinade. Pat dry with paper towels. Season steak with salt.

Grill steak for 12–15 minutes per side for medium-rare to medium doneness, drizzling with a little red wine occasionally to add some sizzling moisture. Remove from the grill and let rest for 5–10 minutes. Thinly slice the steak across the grain and serve.

ESPRESSO-CRUSTED T-BONES WITH GORGONZOLA CHEESE

I am a big fan of T-bone steaks; it's like having two steaks in one, the filet and the strip all in one beautiful steak.

When shopping for your T-bones, make sure the steaks you buy have a good-sized eye of tenderloin. Some T-bones are often bone and strip steak and you get cheated out of the tenderloin. Be fussy; find yourself a great butcher who can help you make the best choices for your steaks. **SERVES 4**

WHAT YOU NEED: Cast iron frying pan

Using the bottom of cast iron frying pan, crush the espresso beans. In a bowl, mix together the crushed espresso beans, garlic, chopped rosemary, black pepper, olive oil, coffee liqueur, molasses and Worcestershire sauce. The mixture should be a bit slushy. Set aside.

To prepare the Espresso Gorgonzola Butter, fold together the softened butter, Gorgonzola cheese and coffee liqueur in a small bowl. Season to taste with salt and black pepper. Transfer to a small serving dish and set aside.

Rub each steak with the Espresso Paste, pressing the seasoning into the meat. Allow steaks to sit at room temperature for 1 hour. This will allow for flavor penetration into the steak.

Fire up your grill to 550-650°F (290–345°C).

Grill the steaks for 6–8 minutes per side directly over the fire; top each steak with a dollop of the Espresso Gorgonzola Butter. As the butter begins to melt and sizzle, brush it all over the steaks using the bunch of fresh rosemary. The oils from the rosemary with add flavor to your steaks. Remove steaks from grill and allow to rest for 3–5 minutes. Top each steak with an extra dollop of Espresso Gorgonzola Butter and serve immediately.

TED'S TIP
Make the Espresso Paste a day in advance so that the espresso beans soften slightly and the flavors become quite bold and pronounced.

ESPRESSO PASTE
½ cup (125 mL) espresso beans

8 cloves garlic, minced

2 tbsp (30 mL) fresh rosemary leaves, coarsely chopped

2 tbsp (30 mL) cracked black peppercorns

Splash of olive oil

2 oz (60 mL) coffee liqueur

2 tbsp (30 mL) molasses

2 tbsp (30 mL) Worcestershire sauce

ESPRESSO GORGONZOLA BUTTER
1 stick (4 oz/115 g) butter, softened

¾ cup (175 mL) crumbled Gorgonzola cheese

2 oz (60 mL) coffee liqueur

Salt and freshly ground black pepper to taste

4 T-bone steaks, each about 1 to 1½ inches (2.5 to 4 cm) thick

1 bunch fresh rosemary

GAUCHO RIB STEAKS WITH CHIMICHURRI

Chimichurri is an Argentinean sauce made with fresh herbs (parsley, oregano and cilantro is what I use), chiles, garlic and vinegar. It is full of flavor and is an excellent sauce for this big steak. Try it on grilled lamb too! MAKES 4 BIG STEAKS

CHIMICHURRI SAUCE

1 cup (250 mL) Italian (flat-leaf) parsley

½ cup (125 mL) fresh oregano

¼ cup (60 mL) fresh cilantro

4 green onions, cut into 2-inch (5 cm) lengths

8 cloves garlic

1 jalapeño pepper, halved lengthwise and seeds removed

¼ cup (60 mL) malt vinegar

Drizzle of Alexander Keith's Red

¼ cup (60 mL) olive oil

1 tbsp (15 mL) cracked black pepper

1 tsp (5 mL) red pepper flakes

1 tsp (5 mL) ground cumin

Kosher salt to taste

4 bone-in rib steaks (approx. 1½ lb/675 g each), cut 1½ inches (4 cm) thick

¼ cup (60 mL) Bone Dust BBQ Spice (page 212)

To prepare the Chimichurri Sauce, combine parsley, oregano, cilantro, green onion, garlic, jalapeño and vinegar in a blender. Blend until smooth. With the motor running on the blender, drizzle in a little splash of dark ale and the olive oil in a steady stream to incorporate. Add black pepper, red pepper flakes and cumin. Season to taste with a little kosher salt. Set aside.

Rub the steaks with the Bone Dust BBQ Spice, pressing the seasoning into the meat.

Fire up your grill to 450–550°F (230–290°C). Set grill for both direct and indirect grilling.

Sear the steaks for 1–2 minutes per side. After the initial sear, move the steaks to an indirect part of your grill and baste with Chimichurri Sauce. Close lid, maintaining a grill temperature of about 350–450°F (180–230°C), and let the steaks indirectly roast for 12–15 minutes for medium-rare to medium doneness. Remove steaks from grill and let rest for 5 minutes. Serve with extra Chimichurri Sauce.

GRILLED BEEF TENDERLOIN WITH FIRE-ROASTED RED PEPPER & GOAT'S CHEESE

Let's just say this is a heavenly dish, plus it is pretty simple when all is said and done. This recipe is sure to put a smile on your face. **SERVES 6**

Season the filets with the Steak Spice, pressing the seasoning into the meat. Set aside.

Roast peppers on the grill, turning periodically, until the peppers are charred and blistering. Place peppers in a bowl and cover with plastic wrap. The heat from the peppers will produce steam that makes the skin easier to peel. After 10 minutes, peel and seed the peppers and cut into ½-inch (1 cm) wide strips, place in a bowl and allow to cool.

At the same time as you are grilling the peppers, grill the onions. Remove them from the grill, cut the onion rings in half and add to the red peppers. Season with a drizzle of olive oil, balsamic glaze and fresh oregano. Season to taste with salt and black pepper and a squeeze of fresh lemon juice. Mix well and set aside.

Crumble the soft goat's cheese and refrigerate until needed.

Fire up your grill to 550-650°F (290–345°C).

Add the crumbled goat's cheese to the roasted red pepper mixture. Season to taste with a little more salt and pepper. Gently mix.

Grill the filets for 3–4 minutes on one side. Turn steaks and top each with a handful of roasted red pepper and goat's cheese mixture. Close the lid and cook for 3–4 more minutes for medium-rare doneness. Remove from grill and serve immediately.

6 beef tenderloin filets (approx. 6 to 8 oz/170 to 225 g each), cut 1½ inches (4 cm) thick
2 tbsp (30 mL) Steak Spice (page 169)
2 red bell peppers
1 medium red onion, sliced into rings
2 tbsp (30 mL) olive oil
2 tbsp (30 mL) balsamic glaze
1 tbsp (15 mL) chopped fresh oregano
½ juicy lemon
½ cup (125 mL) goat's cheese
Salt and freshly ground black pepper to taste

GRILL-ROASTED WHOLE BEEF TENDERLOIN WITH SPICED WHISKEY BUTTER INJECTION

If you have a crowd coming over for dinner and you want to impress them, this is the recipe! This tenderloin is wickedly delicious. **SERVES 6 TO 8**

WHAT YOU NEED: Injection syringe; Butcher twine

½ cup (125 mL) unsalted butter, melted and cooled
1 + 1 tbsp (30 mL) Dijon mustard
¼ cup (60 mL) spiced whiskey
1 beef tenderloin (approx. 3 lb/1.4 kg), trimmed of tough silver skin
2 tbsp (30 mL) Steak Spice (page 169)
8 cloves garlic, minced
2 tbsp (30 mL) olive oil
1 tbsp (15 mL) Worcestershire sauce

In a bowl, whisk the melted butter, 1 tbsp (15 mL) Dijon mustard and spiced whiskey together.

Place tenderloin on a flat surface and pat dry with paper towels. Fill the injection syringe with the spiced whiskey butter mixture. Stab and inject the tenderloin in multiple places. Cover in plastic wrap and refrigerate for 2 hours.

In a small bowl, mix the Steak Spice, garlic, olive oil, Worcestershire sauce and remaining 1 tbsp (15 mL) Dijon mustard together. Remove tenderloin from the refrigerator and rub with a small amount of olive oil and then massage well with the spice mixture. Set aside for 30 minutes to come to room temperature.

Fire up your grill to 550-650°F (290–345°C). Set grill for both direct and indirect grilling.

Place the beef tenderloin on the grill and sear quickly, about 2–3 minutes a side. Move tenderloin over to the indirect part of your grill and close grill lid, maintaining a grill temperature of about 350–450°F (180–230°C). Roast for 15–18 minutes for medium-rare doneness, internal temperature 135–140°F (58–60°C). Remove from grill and allow to rest for 5 minutes. Slice and serve.

MY KANSAS CITY STRIP STEAK

My favorite steak is a bone-in "Kansas City" strip steak. You'll need to order this cut of beef through your butcher. If you can't get a bone-in strip steak, use a boneless NY strip steak. **SERVES 2 TO 3**

WHAT YOU NEED: Cooling rack; Cookie sheet

Unwrap the steaks and pat dry with paper towels to dry them off. Place steaks on a cooling rack over a cookie sheet and let air dry, refrigerated, for 24 hours.

Prepare the Woozy Mop by combining the garlic, black pepper, kosher salt, mirin, Worcestershire sauce and canola oil in a bowl. Stir; this should be a little slushy. Set aside.

Remove steaks from refrigerator and, using the tip of a sharp knife, score the fat on the meat part of the steak. Score it in a ¼-inch (5 mm) diamond pattern; when the steak grills, this will allow the fat to render more quickly. Let stand at room temperature for 1 hour. This will allow the meat to go on the grill at a little warmer temperature so that the cooking will be faster and reduce toughness.

Season the steaks all over with kosher salt, rubbing it into the flesh so it adheres.

Fire up your grill to 550–650°F (290–345°C). Set grill for both direct and indirect grilling.

Place the steaks over the hot fire and sear for about 1–3 minutes, turning the steak once a quarter turn. Flip the steak over and continue to sear for another 1–3 minutes, turning the steak once a quarter turn. Move the steak to an indirect side of the grill. Spoon a heaping spoonful of the Woozy Mop over top of the steak, spreading it evenly, and close lid, maintaining a closed grill temperature of about 450–550°F (230–290°C). Let the steak sit in there for 15–18 minutes, checking occasionally for medium-rare doneness. While you wait, have a shot of bourbon and an icy cold beer. It will help the time pass. Open the grill and test steak for doneness. Once cooked to your liking, remove steak from grill, cover loosely with a sheet of aluminum foil and let the steak rest for 5 minutes.

Get your steak knife and fork ready. Cut in. Take a bite. Big smile and repeat.

2 Kansas City strip steaks (approx. 20 to 24 oz/565 to 675 g each), cut 2 inches (5 cm) thick, well marbled and dry aged for approximately 35–42 days

WOOZY MOP

10 cloves garlic, minced

1 tsp (5 mL) freshly ground black pepper

1 tsp (5 mL) kosher salt

1 tbsp (15 mL) mirin

3 tbsp (45 mL) Worcestershire sauce

2 tbsp (30 mL) canola oil

Kosher salt and freshly ground black pepper

MY STEAK TIPS:

- Dry aged 35–42 days: Dry aging promotes tenderness and increases beef flavor.
- Cut about 2 inches (5 cm) thick: There's less chance of overcooking a thicker cut.
- Weighing approximately 16 oz (450 g) boneless and 20 to 22 oz (g) bone-in.
- Heavily marbled: Internal fat is the fat where the flavor is.

SKIRT STEAK WITH PORT WINE SYRUP & SMOKED WALNUT-CRUSTED GOAT'S CHEESE

Skirt steak is a pretty tough cut of meat and requires a lot of marinating, a recommended 2–3 days. That's a pretty long time, especially if you are gastro busy. So go buy yourself this fancy little kitchen gadget that chefs like to use to make meat relatively tender, quickly. It's called a Jaccard Meat Tenderizer or Super Meat Tenderizer, made in Buffalo, NY. This meat tenderizer is a press with about 48 very sharp, spiky blades so that when you press down on the meat with it, it cuts into the meat and tenderizes it. This means that you don't have to marinate and yet you will get a full-flavored tender steak. In my humble opinion, this gadget actually works better than marinating. **SERVES 4**

WHAT YOU NEED: Jaccard Super Meat Tenderizer; Oak or maple grilling plank (12 × 8 × ½ inches/30 × 20 × 1 cm), soaked in water for a minimum of 1 hour

1 + 1 cups (500 mL) port
1½ lb (625 g) skirt steaks, trimmed of silver skin
3 tbsp (45 mL) brown sugar
1 tbsp (15 mL) grainy mustard
4 cloves garlic, minced
2 tbsp (30 mL) chopped fresh oregano
Drizzle of walnut oil
Freshly ground black pepper to taste
½ cup (125 mL) panko breadcrumbs
½ cup (125 mL) crushed walnuts
2 tbsp (30 mL) chopped fresh parsley
9 oz (250 g) soft goat's cheese
Salt and pepper to taste

Take a cup (250 mL) of port and put it in small saucepot. Bring to a boil, reduce heat and simmer for 10–15 minutes, until it reduces in volume by about three-quarters, leaving you with a port wine syrup. Set aside, keeping warm.

Lay the skirt steaks onto a flat work surface. Pat dry with paper towels. Press the Jaccard up and down the steak every inch (2.5 cm) so that it pierces the meat all the way through. Flip the steak over and do it again. Flip the steak over another time and do it again. And, last, flip it one last time and press it again. That's two times on both sides.

In a bowl, combine another cup (250 mL) of port, brown sugar, grainy mustard, garlic and oregano. Drizzle in a little walnut oil and season with a little black pepper. Pour over the steaks and marinate for 20–30 minutes.

Remove the steak from marinade, discarding leftover marinade.

In a bowl, combine the breadcrumbs, walnuts and parsley. Set aside.

Divide the goat's cheese into eight equal parts. Shape into 1-inch (2.5 cm) thick discs and roll the goat's cheese in the nut mixture, pressing firmly so that it adheres. Place in refrigerator to rest.

Fire up your grill to 550–650°F (290–345°C). Set grill for both direct and indirect grilling.

continued...

Season the steak liberally on both sides with kosher salt and black pepper, rubbing the seasoning into the meat.

Place the nut-crusted goat's cheese medallions onto the grilling plank and place on the grill. These won't take long to heat up and get nice and gooey, about 8–10 minutes. Set aside, keeping warm.

Grill skirt steaks for 1–3 minutes per side for rare to medium-rare doneness, basting with reserved port wine syrup. Remove from grill. Allow the steak to rest for 5 minutes.

Cut each skirt steak into four equal portions and serve with a warm walnut-crusted medallion of goat's cheese. Drizzle with a little extra walnut oil and port wine syrup.

STEAK OSCAR WITH CRAB BRIE COMPOUND BUTTER & GRILLED ASPARAGUS

Classic steak house fare, with the addition of Brie. Like the steak wasn't rich enough already topped with asparagus and crabmeat, now add that Brie! **SERVES 6**

WHAT YOU NEED: Eight 6-inch (15 cm) bamboo skewers soaked in cold water for a minimum of 1 hour

Trim the ends off the asparagus spears (asparagus spears should be approx. 4 to 5 inches/10 to 12 cm long after trimming) and place in a large bowl or pan. Cover with cold water and let stand for 1 hour. This will allow the asparagus to absorb a little moisture and stay crisp and moist when grilling.

Drain asparagus and drizzle with a little olive oil and balsamic vinegar — not too much, just a little — and season to taste with black pepper. Gently mix to evenly coat the asparagus. Line up asparagus spears and skewer the spears together, two skewers per group of 6 asparagus. This will make it easier to grill the asparagus. Repeat until you have four skewers. They should look similar to a raft. Set aside.

Slice the Brie cheese into thin slices. Julienne the slices of cheese and place the cheese in a small bowl. Add the softened butter, lump crabmeat, shallots, garlic and dill. Add a splash of brandy and a squeeze of fresh lemon juice and season to taste with kosher salt and black pepper. Gently mix to incorporate. Easy does it so that you keep the crab lumps as big as possible. Transfer to a smaller dish, cover and refrigerate until needed. Note: Remove the crab and Brie compound butter from the refrigerator about 30 minutes prior to grilling your steaks to allow the butter to slightly soften.

Season steaks with the Steak Spice, pressing the seasoning into the meat.

24 spears fresh asparagus (approx. 1½ lb/675 g)
Drizzle of olive oil (approx. 2 to 3 tsp/10 to 15 mL)
Drizzle of balsamic vinegar (approx. 2 to 3 tsp/10 to 15 mL)
Freshly ground black pepper to taste
1 small wheel Brie cheese (4½ oz/125 g)
¼ cup (60 mL) butter, softened
1 cup (250 mL) lump crabmeat
2 shallots, minced (approx. ¼ cup/60 mL)
2 cloves garlic, minced
1 tbsp (15 mL) chopped fresh dill
Splash of brandy
1 tsp (5 mL) freshly squeezed lemon juice
Kosher salt

4 New York strip loin steaks (approx. 8 oz/225 g each), cut 1½ inches (4 cm) thick
¼ cup (60 mL) Steak Spice (page 169)

continued . . .

Fire up your grill to 450–550°F (230–290°C).

Grill the steaks directly over the fire for 3–5 minutes per side for medium-rare doneness.

At the same time as you are grilling the steaks, grill the asparagus until lightly charred and crisp but still bright green, about 5 minutes. Top the steaks with a big dollop of crab and Brie compound butter and close the grill lid. Allow to melt over the steaks, about a minute or two maximum. Remove steaks and asparagus from grill.

Lay asparagus onto a plate, remove skewers and spread a little crab and Brie compound butter over top. Slice the steak into 1-inch (2.5 cm) thick strips and lay across the asparagus. Add a dollop or two of extra crab and Brie butter and serve immediately.

TED'S TIP
For this recipe, use asparagus spears that are not too small but yet not too large — ones that have a stalk that is about ½ inch (1 cm) thick.

STEAK ROLL-UPS WITH PORCINI MUSHROOM RUB, ROASTED GARLIC & PORTOBELLO MUSHROOMS

If you are having a dinner party and you want to make a good impression, this recipe will show your grill prowess. So tender and flavorful and really not that difficult to do! SERVES 4

WHAT YOU NEED: Coffee grinder or spice mill

2 heads garlic

Olive oil

Kosher salt and freshly ground
   black pepper to taste

2 portobello mushroom caps, soaked
   in warm water for 10 minutes

1 medium red onion, sliced into
   ½-inch (1 cm) thick rings

½ cup (125 mL) dried porcini
   mushroom caps

4 beef tenderloin steaks (approx.
   8 oz/225 g each), cut 2 inches
   (5 cm) thick

¼ cup (60 mL) fresh rosemary,
   chopped

4 strips bacon

4½ tsp (22 mL) butter

Fire up your grill to 450–550°F (230–290°C).

Cut the tops off the garlic heads, exposing the cloves on the inside. Drizzle with olive oil and season with kosher salt and black pepper. Wrap them in a little bit of aluminum foil and roast for 30–45 minutes, until the cloves are tender. Remove from grill and allow to cool for a few minutes. Squeeze the hot roasted garlic cloves from the heads. Set aside.

At the same time as you are roasting the garlic, grill the portobello mushrooms and red onions for 10–15 minutes, until lightly charred and tender. Remove from grill and allow to cool. Pat the mushrooms with paper towels to remove excess moisture. Thinly slice and set aside.

In a coffee grinder or spice mill, grind the porcini mushroom caps into a coarse powder.

Take a steak and stand it up on its side. Starting at the bottom of the steak, make an incision across the steak about ¼ to ½ inch (0.5 to 1 cm) thick and 6 to 8 inches (15 to 20 cm) long. Next slice the steak across and roll it at the same time to cut the beef tenderloin into a long strip of meat about ½ inch (1 cm) thick. Repeat with remaining steaks.

Mash the roasted cloves of garlic, mix with a little drizzle of olive oil and season with salt and pepper. Set aside.

Lay a strip of steak onto a flat work surface. Season both sides lightly with a little salt and black pepper and a liberal amount of porcini mushroom powder. Spread a little of the roasted garlic mixture across

continued . . .

the entire surface of the steak. Sprinkle with some chopped rosemary leaves. Lay a few slices of grilled portobello mushroom and red onion across the entire surface of the steak. Starting at one end, roll up the steak into a tight pinwheel. Take a strip of bacon and twist it up so it looks a little like a piece of bacon rope. Wrap the bacon around the steak roll-up, knot it and secure with a toothpick. Repeat.

Get that grill hot again.

Grill roll-ups for 3–5 minutes per side, until the bacon is crisp and the meat is medium-rare. This is tenderloin, so it won't take too long. Just when the steaks are about done, place a little knob of butter on top of each steak, close lid and let it melt. Remove from grill, remove tooth-picks and serve immediately.

STEAKS ON A HOT BED OF COALS

I love steak. I have cooked steaks in a variety of different ways. There's steak done on a gas grill; these I do when I am rushed for time. There's steak grilled over charcoal, which is my preferred method of cooking up a steak. The flavor a steak gets from the hot coals is so much tastier than on a gas grill. Then there's when I'm feeling a little crazy and want to get the full fire experience with my steaks; I bury it in the hot coals.

Yes, I said bury it in the hot charcoal. This is a pretty amazing way to grill your steak. For a taste of the wild side, read on and fire up your coals. Note: When you do this for your friends, you may get a lot of questioning looks from onlookers. But it's okay because you will blow them out of the water! **SERVES 2-4**

WHAT YOU NEED: Steak turner or a very long pair of tongs; Barbeque gloves; Small shovel or scoop or rake

2 New York strip loin steaks (approx. 1 lb/450 g each), cut 2 inches (5 cm) thick
Salt and freshly ground black pepper to taste

GRILL TIMES
- 8–10 minutes for rare
- 10–15 minutes for medium-rare
- 15–18 minutes for medium
- 18–20 minutes for medium-well
- 20+ for well-done

Prepare your fire by bringing it up to 750°F (400°C). If you are working with a hardwood bonfire, then you will need to have patience, as you'll need to burn the wood down to hot coals. I recommend, if you are doing this, using hickory wood because it has incredible flavor. If you are using a charcoal fire in a grill, then heat the coals to white hot. White hot means the charcoal is no longer black and is covered with a thin layer of ash.

Season steaks with salt and black pepper to taste.

Using a long pair of tongs and barbeque gloves, place the steaks directly onto the hot coals and grill for 1–2 minutes. It won't take long. Turn the steak over and, using a small shovel or scoop, cover steaks with hot charcoal. When you do this, make sure to bury the entire steak with hot coals. If you leave any part of the steak exposed, it will burn, but completely buried it will roast nicely in the hot coals.

Now get yourself a cold beverage and watch the steaks cook. It doesn't get much more rustic than this!

When steaks are cooked to your liking, carefully move the hot coals from the steaks. Remove steaks from coals, making sure to brush off any hot coals and excess ash. Allow steaks to rest for 5 minutes. Season with a little extra salt and black pepper.

Slice each steak into ½-inch (1 cm) thick slices and serve immediately.

If you want to add a dollop of Garlic Chive Butter (page 66) or Espresso Gorgonzola Butter (page 177), go ahead. Live it up!

TERIYAKI FLANK STEAK

I like my teriyaki marinade to have a bit of a bite. For this I add Asian chili sauce and a bit of prepared horseradish. If you think that my recipe might be too spicy for you, cut back on these two ingredients and spice it up the way you like. Flank steak is quite lean and thus it is recommended not to overcook it. Rare to medium-rare is when it is at its best for tenderness. SERVES 4

Using the tip of a sharp knife, score both sides of the flank steak in a diamond pattern about ¼ inch (5 mm) deep. Make your cuts about an inch (2.5 cm) apart. This will allow for the marinade to penetrate into the meat. Place the steak into a self-sealing storage bag and set aside.

To make the Teriyaki Marinade, in a bowl, combine the sherry, soy sauce, brown sugar, mirin, rice wine vinegar, ginger, horseradish, garlic, chili sauce, star anise, black pepper, green onions and cilantro. Drizzle in a little sesame oil and whisk until the sugar has dissolved. Reserve ½ cup (125 mL) of the Teriyaki Marinade for basting and set aside. Pour remaining marinade over flank steak and seal bag, removing as much air as possible. Marinate overnight, turning every few hours to marinate evenly.

In a bowl, combine brown sugar, Szechuan pepper, kosher salt and cinnamon. Set aside.

Fire up your grill to 550-650°F (290–345°C).

Remove flank steak from marinade, discarding leftover marinade. Rub the flank steak with the Szechuan pepper mixture, pressing the spices into the meat.

Grill flank steak for 2–3 minutes per side, lid open, until lightly charred and the meat is tender and rare. Remove from grill and allow the steak to rest for 5 minutes. Sprinkle with toasted sesame seeds and thinly slice the steak on the bias into ¼-inch (5 mm) thick strips. Serve immediately.

1 flank steak (weighing approx. 1½ to 2 lb/675 to 900 g)

TERIYAKI MARINADE
½ cup (125 mL) dry sherry
¼ cup (60 mL) soy sauce
¼ cup (60 mL) brown sugar
¼ cup (60 mL) mirin
2 tbsp (30 mL) rice wine vinegar
2 tsp (10 mL) minced fresh ginger
1 tsp (5 mL) extra-hot prepared horseradish, squeezed of excess moisture
4 cloves garlic, minced
1 tsp (5 mL) Asian chili sauce
2 whole star anise
1 tsp (5 mL) freshly ground black pepper
2 green onions, finely chopped
1 tbsp (15 mL) chopped fresh cilantro
Drizzle of Asian sesame oil

1 tbsp (15 mL) brown sugar
1 tbsp (15 mL) cracked Szechuan peppercorns
1 tsp (5 mL) kosher salt
Pinch of ground cinnamon
Salt and freshly ground black pepper to taste
2 tsp (10 mL) toasted sesame seeds

SMOKED & GRILLED BEEF RIBS WITH BEER SCHMEER

This is an unusual way to make a barbeque sauce, but it's the best way to add real smoke flavor to your homemade sauces rather than using liquid smoke. In a hot, heavy pan you will dry roast wood chips over high heat until they begin to brown and smoke. The rest is easy. SERVES 2 TO 4

WHAT YOU NEED: Cast iron frying pan, about 3 inches (8 cm) deep; Hickory wood chips; Strainer; 1 large foil grill bag or heavy-duty aluminum foil

BEEF BACK RIBS

1 rack meaty beef back ribs (approx. 3 to 4 lb/1.4 to 1.8 kg), 6 to 7 bones

3 tbsp (45 mL) Steak Spice (page 169), plus extra for grilling

1 + 1 bottles (12 oz/341 mL each) Alexander Keith's Amber Ale

BEER SCHMEER

1 cup (250 mL) chili sauce

2 tbsp (30 mL) Worcestershire sauce

4 tbsp (60 mL) Dijon mustard

2 tbsp (30 mL) extra-hot prepared horseradish

½ cup (125 mL) molasses

8 cloves garlic, minced

¼ cup (60 mL) cold butter, cut into small cubes

Salt and freshly ground black pepper to taste

Cut the beef ribs into 1-bone segments. Season the beef ribs all over with Steak Spice, pressing the steak spice into the meat. Place the beef ribs in a self-sealing bag and pour in 1 bottle of beer. Seal bag, removing as much air as possible, and refrigerate to marinate for 4 hours.

Fire up your grill 350–450°F (180–230°C). Set grill for both direct and indirect grilling.

To make the Beer Schmeer, place cast iron frying pan onto the burner to get hot. When it is smoking hot, pour in the hickory wood chips and shake the pan to move the wood chips around to allow them to get hot and begin smoking and browning. This may take a few minutes. When the wood chips begin to brown and smoke, slowly pour the second bottle of beer into the pan. Allow the beer to boil and reduce by half with the wood chips in there. This will extract the smoky flavor from the wood and infuse it into the beer. Remove from direct heat and add the chili sauce, Worcestershire sauce, Dijon mustard, horseradish, molasses and garlic. Return to the fire and bring to a boil, stirring. Remove from heat and stir in the butter, one or two cubes at a time, until it is incorporated into the sauce. Strain, discarding wood chips, season to taste with salt and freshly ground pepper and set aside, keeping warm.

Reduce your grill to 250–350°F (120–180°C). Set grill for indirect smoking/grilling.

Remove beef ribs from marinade and season with a little extra Steak Spice. Rub it in. Place beef ribs in grill indirectly, add a handful of smoking chips and smoke ribs for 2 hours, basting with Beer Schmeer during the second hour of smoking and monitoring the temperature and adding more smoking chips as necessary. Remove beef ribs from grill, baste with a little extra Beer Schmeer and wrap 3–4 bones

continued…

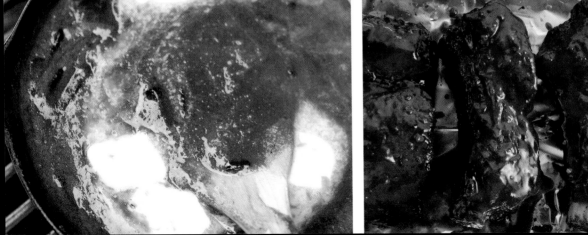

together in a double thickness of aluminum foil. Repeat with remaining beef ribs. Place on grill, close lid and cook for 45–60 minutes, turning the bag or foil package every 15 minutes, until ribs are fully cooked and tender. Remove the foil-wrapped beef ribs from the grill.

Now turn your grill up nice and hot, approx. 550–650°F (290–345°C).

Unwrap ribs and place on the grill. Allow ribs to char and baste with extra Beer Schmeer. Remove from grill and dig in.

BEER BUTTER-BASTED ROTISSERIE OF PRIME RIB

This is one of those recipes that is so simple and delicious, rotisserie of prime rib where the meat spins slowly over the fire, turning and basting itself with its natural juices. Low and slow on the spit is the way to go for this recipe. I like to add beer and butter plus lots of garlic. It's a way to impress friends and family for that big backyard gathering. After making this recipe, prime rib could easily become your favorite meat dish. **SERVES 8**

WHAT YOU NEED: 1 rotisserie rod with 2 rotisserie tines, 1 counterweight and 1 rotisserie motor; Pan for drippings; Meat thermometer; Fresh herb basting brush (page 22)

1 bone-in prime rib roast (approx. 12 lb/5.4 kg)

1 tbsp (15 mL) smoked salt

1 tbsp (15 mL) kosher salt

3 tbsp (45 mL) coarsely ground black pepper

2 bottles (12 oz/341 mL each) Hoegaarden

½ cup (125 mL) garlic, minced

¼ cup (60 mL) Worcestershire sauce

1 stick (4 oz/115 g) butter

TED'S TIP

For an added boost of grill flavor, take the sliced portions of prime rib and quickly grill directly over the fire for a minute or two.

Prepare your grill for rotisserie cooking as per manufacturer's instructions.

Fire up your grill to 450–550°F (230–290°C).

Run the rotisserie rod through the center of the roast and secure with tines.

In a bowl, combine both salts and black pepper. Rub prime rib roast all over with mixture, pressing the seasoning into the meat to adhere.

Place the rod into the rotisserie motor and turn it on. Monitor and ensure that roast turns easily and evenly. You may have to use the counterweight to even out the weight so the motor turns easily. Place a pan under the roast to catch any drippings. Pour a couple of bottles of beer, garlic, Worcestershire sauce and a stick of butter into the pan. This will be what you baste the prime rib with as it spins. Close grill lid and roast for 10 to 15 minutes to sear. Reduce heat to medium (about 350–375°F/180–190°C) and roast for approximately 1½–2 hours or to an internal temperature of 135°F (58°C) for medium-rare doneness. While cooking, be sure to baste frequently with beer mixture. Remove roast from grill and remove rotisserie rods and tines. Allow roast to rest for 10–15 minutes, covered, before carving.

Slice into 1-inch (2.5 cm) thick slices and serve.

MAUI SHORT RIBS

Ask your butcher to prepare your short ribs Maui style. These ribs will be about ½ inch (1 cm) thick and 1½ inches (4 cm) wide and have 5 rib bones. Marinate for at least 6 hours and then grill them quickly over high heat. You will love these succulent morsels of tender meat. **SERVES 4**

In a glass dish large enough to hold the ribs, combine the vegetable oil, brown sugar, sherry, vinegar, ginger, molasses, sesame oil, garlic, shallots, green onions, lemongrass, black pepper and salt. Add the ribs, turning to coat. Marinate, covered and refrigerated, for 4–6 hours or overnight.

Fire up your grill to 450–550°F (230–290°C).

Remove ribs from marinade, reserving marinade. Grill for 2–3 minutes per side, basting liberally with reserved marinade. Garnish with toasted sesame seeds.

¼ cup (60 mL) vegetable oil
¼ cup (60 mL) brown sugar
¼ cup (60 mL) dry sherry
¼ cup (60 mL) balsamic vinegar
2 tbsp (30 mL) chopped fresh ginger
2 tbsp (30 mL) molasses
1 tbsp (15 mL) Asian sesame oil
6 cloves garlic, minced
2 shallots, diced
4 green onions, finely chopped
1 stalk lemongrass, pale green part only, smashed and finely chopped
2 tsp (10 mL) cracked black pepper
1 tsp (5 mL) salt
2 lb (900 g) beef short ribs, cut across the bones ½ inch (1 cm) thick, approx. 15 to 20 pieces
2 tsp (10 mL) toasted sesame seeds

PLANKED MEATLOAF & MASHED POTATOES WITH BEER BBQ GRAVY

Who doesn't love meatloaf and mashed potatoes with gravy! My version is done on the grill. **SERVES 8**

WHAT YOU NEED: Maple grilling plank (12 × 8 × ½ inches/30 × 20 × 1 cm), soaked in water for a minimum of 1 hour

MASHED POTATOES

6 large gold-fleshed potatoes (approx. 1½ lb/675 g)

1 stick (4 oz/115 g) unsalted butter,
    at room temperature

3 tbsp (45 mL) sour cream

½ cup (125 mL) grated white cheddar cheese

2 green onions, minced

Salt and pepper to taste

MEATLOAF

2 lb (900 g) ground beef chuck

2 tbsp (30 mL) butter, softened

1 cup (250 mL) sweet onion, finely diced

6 cloves garlic, minced

½ cup (125 mL) crispy fried shallots (you can find this
    already prepared item in ethnic grocery stores)

1 tbsp (15 mL) Dijon mustard

¼ bunch fresh parsley, chopped

3 tbsp (45 mL) freshly grated Parmesan cheese

BEER BBQ GRAVY

4 tbsp (60 mL) butter

2 sweet onions, diced

1 tsp (5 mL) garlic, chopped

¼ cup (60 mL) all-purpose flour

½ cup (125 mL) Hoegaarden

1½ cups (375 mL) beef stock

½ cup (125 mL) your favorite gourmet-style barbeque
    sauce (I use my Beerlicious™ BBQ Sauce)

Salt and freshly ground black pepper to taste

Fire up your grill to 350–450°F (180–230°C).

To make mashed potatoes, place potatoes onto grill, close lid and roast for 45–60 minutes, until flesh is soft all the way through when pierced with a skewer. Remove the potatoes from grill and allow to cool slightly. Cut each potato in half, scoop out the hot flesh and place in a bowl. Mash the potatoes. Add butter, sour cream, cheddar cheese and green onion. Season to taste with salt and black pepper and mix well. Cool, cover and refrigerate for 4 hours or overnight.

To make meatloaf, in a large bowl, combine ground beef, butter, onions, garlic, crispy fried shallots, Dijon mustard, parsley and Parmesan cheese. Mix well.

To make the Beer BBQ Gravy, melt the butter over medium heat in a small saucepan. Sauté the onions and garlic for 2–3 minutes or until tender and transparent. Add the flour and cook, stirring constantly, for 4–5 minutes, being careful not to burn the flour. Add the beer and beef stock, ½ cup (125 mL) at a time, stirring constantly, until smooth and thickened. Stir in the barbeque sauce, salt and pepper. Reduce heat to low and simmer for 10–15 minutes, stirring occasionally. Strain and adjust seasoning. Set aside.

continued...

Remove grilling plank from water and pat dry with paper towels. Form a meatloaf log that runs the entire length of the plank on one side, leaving a 1-inch (2.5 cm) border from the edge of the plank. Make sure to pack the meat tightly together. It is important to keep it well packed so that it stays together and gives you a better bite when fully cooked.

Remove mashed potato mixture from refrigerator and allow it to come to room temperature. Mix it up and form it into a log beside the meatloaf, making sure it is about the same size and shape of the meat loaf. Cover and refrigerate to rest for 1 hour.

If you turned your grill off, fire it back up to 350–450°F (180–230°C).

Place planked meatloaf and mashed potatoes on the grill, close lid and plank for 10 minutes. The plank will start to smoke and crackle. Reduce heat to medium to medium-low and continue to cook meatloaf for 20–30 minutes longer, until the meatloaf is fully cooked (internal temperature 160°F/70°C) and the mashed potatoes are golden brown and hot on the inside and crispy on the outside. Remove from grill. Allow to rest for 10 minutes.

While the meatloaf and mashed potatoes are resting, reheat the Beer BBQ Gravy.

Slice the meatloaf and scoop the mashed potatoes onto plates and serve immediately. Top with Beer BBQ Gravy.

FIVE RIB RUBS

BONE DUST BBQ SPICE

I've been making my Bone Dust BBQ Spice for many years and have included the recipe in many of my cookbooks. I use it for a variety of recipes throughout this book too. Many fans have told me how much they love Bone Dust. I love it too! Use it on ribs and chicken, steaks and chops. Have fun and get sticky! **MAKES ABOUT 2½ CUPS (625 ML)**

½ cup (125 mL) paprika
¼ cup (60 mL) chili powder
3 tbsp (45 mL) salt
2 tbsp (30 mL) ground coriander
2 tbsp (30 mL) garlic powder
2 tbsp (30 mL) white sugar
2 tbsp (30 mL) curry powder

2 tbsp (30 mL) hot mustard powder
1 tbsp (15 mL) freshly ground black pepper
1 tbsp (15 mL) dried basil
1 tbsp (15 mL) dried thyme
1 tbsp (15 mL) ground cumin
1 tbsp (15 mL) cayenne pepper

Mix together the paprika, chili powder, salt, coriander, garlic powder, sugar, curry powder, mustard powder, black pepper, basil, thyme, cumin and cayenne. Store in an airtight container in a cool, dry place away from heat and light.

SWEET AND FIERY APPLE RUB

Everyone loves a good fruit rub. **MAKES ABOUT 1 CUP (250 ML)**

WHAT YOU NEED: Cookie sheet, lined with parchment paper

2 Granny Smith apples
¼ cup (60 mL) brown sugar
2 tbsp (30 mL) kosher salt
2 tbsp (30 mL) ground ginger
2 tbsp (30 mL) paprika
1 tbsp (15 mL) smoked paprika
2 tsp (10 mL) cayenne pepper

2 tsp (10 mL) dried ancho chile powder
2 tsp (10 mL) granulated garlic
2 tsp (10 mL) dried onion flakes
2 tsp (10 mL) ground cinnamon
2 tsp (10 mL) freshly ground black pepper
1 tsp (5 mL) ground fennel

Heat your oven to 200°F (100°C).

Using a mandoline or extremely sharp knife, slice the apples into extremely thin rounds. Lay the apples in a single layer on the prepared cookie sheet. Sprinkle a little sugar over the apple slices — not a lot, just a little. Place in the oven and dry the apples until they are dried and crisp.

Place the dried apple pieces into a food processor and pulse until you have small flakes and granules. Place apple into a large bowl, add brown sugar, kosher salt, ginger, paprika, smoked paprika, cayenne, chile powder, garlic, dried onion, cinnamon, black pepper and fennel. Mix well. Store, refrigerated, in a sealed container. Keeps up to 2 weeks.

CAJUN RUB

Try this rub on fish and chicken to give them that Louisiana kick. **MAKES ABOUT 1 CUP (250 ML)**

2 tbsp (30 mL) salt
2 tbsp (30 mL) paprika
2 tbsp (30 mL) cayenne pepper
1 tbsp (15 mL) white sugar
1 tbsp (15 mL) hot mustard powder
1 tbsp (15 mL) black pepper
1 tbsp (15 mL) white pepper
1 tbsp (15 mL) garlic powder

1 tbsp (15 mL) onion powder
2 tsp (10 mL) ground cumin
1 tsp (5 mL) dried oregano
1 tsp (5 mL) dried thyme
1 tsp (5 mL) dried sage
1 tsp (5 mL) ground coriander

Combine the salt, paprika, cayenne, sugar, mustard, black pepper, white pepper, garlic powder, onion powder, cumin, oregano, thyme, sage and coriander. Mix well. Store in an airtight container in a cool, dry place away from heat and light.

MEDITERRANEAN HERB & GARLIC RUB

I love this rubbed on pork or chicken. Rubbin' is lovin'. **MAKES ABOUT 1 CUP (250 ML)**

¼ cup (60 mL) dried minced garlic
¼ cup (60 mL) kosher salt
3 tbsp (45 mL) sugar
2 tbsp (30 mL) dried sweet red pepper flakes
2 tbsp (30 mL) chicken stock powder (with no MSG)
1 tbsp (15 mL) medium ground black pepper
2 tbsp (30 mL) dried minced onion

1 tbsp (15 mL) dried parsley flakes
1 tbsp (15 mL) dried basil
1 tbsp (15 mL) dried marjoram
1 tbsp (15 mL) fennel seeds, coarsely ground
2 tsp (10 mL) dried thyme
2 tsp (10 mL) cayenne pepper

In a large bowl, combine dried garlic, kosher salt, sugar, red pepper flakes, chicken stock powder, black pepper, dried onion, parsley, basil, marjoram, fennel, thyme and cayenne. Mix well. Store in an airtight container and use as needed.

continued . . .

BROWN SUGAR CHIPOTLE RUB

This is a fantastic rub for pork ribs and chops. Make sure to rub the spices into the meat so they adhere.

MAKES ABOUT 1½ CUPS (375 ML)

½ cup (125 mL) brown sugar

¼ cup (60 mL) kosher salt

¼ cup (60 mL) granulated
    garlic flakes

2 tbsp (30 mL) coarsely ground
    black pepper

1 tbsp (15 mL) hot red pepper flakes

2 tsp (10 mL) ground ginger

1 tbsp (15 mL) dried cilantro

1 tsp (5 mL) hot mustard powder

1 tsp (5 mL) chipotle powder

½ tsp (1 mL) cayenne pepper

1 tsp (5 mL) orange zest

Combine brown sugar, kosher salt, garlic flakes, black pepper, hot pepper flakes, ginger, cilantro, mustard, chipotle, cayenne and orange zest. Store in an airtight container in a cool, dry place away from heat and light.

FOUR BBQ SAUCE RECIPES FOR GRILLING, GLAZING, DIPPING & LICKING!

ROOT BEER BARBEQUE SAUCE

A great glaze for your chicken or ribs. **MAKES ABOUT 2 CUPS (500 ML)**

½ cup (125 mL) ketchup

½ cup (125 mL) sweet Thai
    chili sauce

½ cup (125 mL) brown sugar

½ cup (125 mL) root beer

1 tbsp (15 mL) chopped fresh sage

1 tsp (5 mL) Worcestershire sauce

Kosher salt to taste

Prepare the sauce by whisking together the ketchup, sweet Thai chili sauce, brown sugar, root beer, sage and Worcestershire sauce and season to taste with kosher salt. Transfer to a canning jar and refrigerate until baste is required.

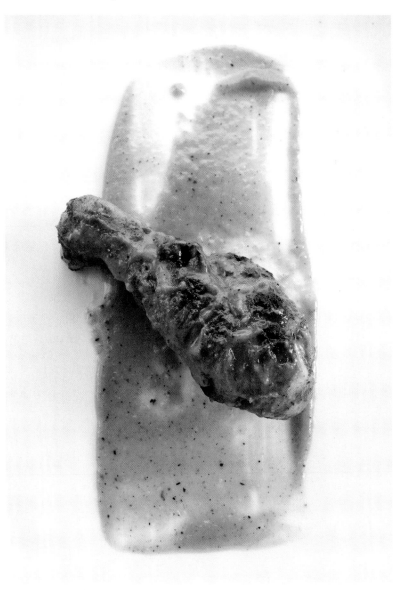

SOUTH CAROLINA YELLA BBQ MOP

They like their sauce yellow in South Carolina. These golden sauces are sweet and tangy, heavily flavored with prepared yellow mustard. For my version of this recipe, I like to fire-roast sweet yellow bell peppers and spicy hot yellow banana peppers. The banana peppers give the sauce a bit of kick. This yellow sauce will give your ribs a lovely sheen and complement the flavor of the meat. Mop it on and get sticky! MAKES ABOUT 2 CUPS

WHAT YOU NEED: Blender or hand-held blender

Fire up your grill to 450–550°F (230–290°C).

Place peppers and onion on the grill. Roast, moving around to avoid a full burn, until skins of peppers are well scorched and onion is softened when pressed on. Remove peppers from grill and rub scorched skins off and remove outer scorched skin from the onion as well.

Rough chop the peppers and onions.

In a saucepan, combine the chopped pepper and onion pieces. Add the garlic, mustard, vinegar, orange juice, honey, turmeric, cumin, black pepper and cayenne. Bring to a boil, whisking well to combine. Reduce heat to medium-low and simmer, stirring occasionally, for 20–30 minutes or until reduced by one-third.

In blender, purée the mixture until smooth. Let cool. Season to taste with salt and set aside until ready to use.

2 yellow bell peppers, seeded and halved

2 yellow hot banana peppers, seeded and halved

1 small yellow onion, peeled and halved

4 cloves garlic, minced

½ cup (125 mL) prepared mustard

¾ cup (175 mL) cider vinegar

¾ cup (175 mL) orange juice

½ cup (125 mL) honey

1 tsp (5 mL) ground turmeric

1 tsp (5 mL) ground cumin

1 tsp (5 mL) black pepper

½ teaspoon (2 mL) cayenne pepper

Salt to taste

TED'S TIP

To more easily remove skins from roasted peppers, place them in a sealed paper bag for 5–10 minutes. The skins will magically loosen and be easily rubbed away.

MAPLE BACON BARBEQUE SAUCE

These days you can just about guarantee a winner with the addition of maple syrup and bacon. MAKES ABOUT 2 CUPS (500 ML)

1 large onion

8 slices bacon, diced

6 cloves garlic, minced

¼ cup (60 mL) cider vinegar

2 oz (60 mL) spiced whiskey

¼ cup (60 mL) applesauce

½ cup (125 mL) pure maple syrup

2 tbsp (30 mL) TABASCO® brand Pepper Sauce

2 tbsp (30 mL) Worcestershire sauce

1 tsp (5 mL) Bone Dust BBQ Spice (page 212)

½ cup (125 mL) ketchup

Salt to taste

Fire up your grill to 450–550°F (230–290°C).

Cut the onion into ½-inch (1 cm) thick slices and grill for 4–5 minutes per side, until the onions are lightly charred and tender. Remove from grill and finely chop.

In a medium saucepan over medium heat, fry the bacon until it is half-cooked. Remove bacon and pat dry with paper towels to remove excess grease; coarsely chop.

Drain off all but 3 tbsp (45 mL) of the drippings. Add the garlic and grilled onions. Fry, stirring, until the onions are tender and golden brown, about 3 minutes. Deglaze with cider vinegar and spiced whiskey. Add the applesauce, maple syrup, a dash or two of TABASCO® brand Pepper Sauce, Worcestershire sauce, and Bone Dust BBQ Spice. Stir in the ketchup. Bring to a boil, whisking well to combine. Reduce heat to low and simmer, stirring occasionally, for 10 minutes. Season with salt to taste. Set aside until ready to use.

HONEY GARLIC BARBEQUE SAUCE

Garlic is literally the spice of life in my book. You can never have enough — especially when you roast it and develop all the sweet nutty goodness without the sharp acid. Hey, you don't get bad breath from roasted garlic! **MAKES APPROXIMATELY 2¼ CUPS (550 ML)**

In a small saucepan over medium heat, mix together the honey, pineapple juice, sesame seeds, soy sauce, vinegar, cinnamon and garlic. Season to taste with salt and black pepper. Bring to a boil, whisking well to combine. Remove from heat and keep warm until needed.

TED'S TIP
Before you measure the honey, rub the cup with oil and then the honey won't stick to the cup.

1 cup (250 mL) honey
½ cup (125 mL) pineapple juice
¼ cup (60 mL) sesame seeds
¼ cup (60 mL) soy sauce
¼ cup (60 mL) rice vinegar
1 tsp (5 mL) ground cinnamon
12 cloves roasted garlic, mashed
Salt and freshly ground black pepper

GRILLED RIBS

When it comes to cooking pork ribs, I would say that I know a thing or two about the subject, not only from the perspective of backyard grilling or smoking but through to the world of BBQ competitions and the industrial level of retail and food service product development. For many years I have been a consultant for retailers and food service operators and food processors on how to prepare ribs. I have developed recipes and formulas for a variety of companies. Whether my rib recipes and products end up on restaurant menus or on grocery store shelves, I spend a lot of time in the rib world. I have made presentations on fully cooked ribs to pretty much every major retailer in North America. I love ribs; I smoke 'em and grill 'em in my backyard as well as for you for your backyard. My life, in a nutshell, revolves around ribs.

So first things first, we need to learn a thing or two about ribs.

PORK BACK RIBS

Back ribs, or baby backs, are a premium rib. The back rib tends to be more tender than the side rib. Cut from the loin, the back rib is much leaner than spareribs and tends to have a higher meat-to-bone ratio. When prepared properly, these ribs provide the best eating.

A baby back rib should weigh 1¼ to 2 pounds (565 to 900 g) and meatier back ribs start at around 2 pounds (900 g) and run through to 2¾ pounds (1.3 kg). Back ribs are more expensive than spareribs but are the best quality. As the saying goes, "You get what you pay for." When shopping for your back ribs, look for ribs that are extra meaty, meaning that there is more loin meat left on the top side of the rib. You have to be careful with how much loin meat is left on the rib, as it will cook a little differently than the meat between the bones. Too much loin meat is not always a good thing. It gets dry and can be tough. Another thing to look for is too little loin meat. These are ribs where the butcher has taken away as much loin meat from the rib as possible, often leaving a rack of ribs with meat just in between the bones. This is not good. The rule of thumb that I use for ribs is that the thickness of meat between the bones should be the same as the thickness of the meat on top of the bones. That way you get a meaty, well-marbled, tender rib.

On the bone side of the rib, there is a thin membrane. Some folks cook ribs with the membrane on, while others take a sharp knife and score the membrane in a diamond pattern so that when it cooks the membrane loosens to allow the meat to relax. But the real gastro grillers peel the membrane completely from the back rib. The easiest way to remove the membrane is when the meat is cold. Take the tip of a sharp knife and cut under the membrane at one end of the rib to peel up a corner of the membrane. Next grab hold of the membrane using a kitchen towel and, while holding the rib with one hand, peel up the membrane with the other. This may take a few tries to perfect, but once you have it, you can be sure you are on the way to tender ribs. If you cannot remove the membrane, then at least score it.

PORK SIDE RIBS OR SPARERIBS

Spareribs are cut from the side, or underbelly, of the pig. These ribs are quite meaty but are also fattier than baby back ribs. Weighing usually between 3 and 5 pounds (1.4 to 2.25 kg), these ribs can serve several people. The term "St. Louis rib" means that the rib tip has been removed, which produces a rib that is more rectangular in look with a uniform width. The hard breast bone and the soft rib cartilage have been cut from the main portion of the side rib. Once the rib tip has been removed, the tip is cut to square up one end of the rack, and the end bone is often split and that too is removed. The skirt meat is also removed, along with the membrane (follow membrane removal method above, in back ribs section). All of these pieces are tough and make for an inconsistent cook. The St. Louis rib is a premium cut and is very meaty and with a higher fat level than back ribs. These are full-flavored ribs, and my favorite ones at that.

COOKING METHODS

Now that you have had a lesson in the varieties of ribs, the next is the method of cooking them. Some folks say to me, "Oh these ribs are so good; did you boil them?" and at that point I lose it, big time! So let me say this one last time. Never, ever boil your ribs. I don't care if your grandmother made the best ribs ever and she boiled them. It doesn't cut it. Not now, not ever. NO boiling! I hope that I have made my point. That goes for steaming ribs as well.

So if we are not allowed to boil them, then what can we do?

Well there are a couple of other methods that I can recommend. One is a little less BBQ than the other and it is the *oven braise, finish on the grill method*. Here is the basic method for cooking ribs this way:

- Choose your rib: Pork back, side or St. Louis.
- Remove the membrane from the bone side of the ribs.
- Rub the ribs liberally with barbeque seasoning (I have five recipes that you can try — see pages 212–216 — but make sure you try my Bone Dust BBQ Spice because it is my favorite). Be sure to rub the seasoning into the meat. I like to do approximately 3 to 4 tablespoons (46 to 60 mL) of spice rub per rack of ribs.
- Cover, refrigerate and allow ribs to marinate in the rub for 4–6 hours or overnight. The pork meat will pick up the flavors of the seasonings.
- Preheat oven to 225°F (110°C).
- Take a large roasting pan or lasagna pan and pour in a bottle of beer, add a chopped onion, a few cloves of smashed garlic and a chopped jalapeño.
- Lay the racks of ribs into the pan, meat side down.
- Cover pan with a sheet of plastic wrap, making sure to seal it well (no holes).
- Cover plastic wrap with aluminum foil.
- Place in oven and allow ribs to braise for 3–4 hours, until you can wiggle the bones between the meat.
- Remove from oven and let stand for 10 minutes to slightly cool.
- Peel back plastic wrap and foil and allow the ribs to cool completely.
- Fire up your gas or charcoal grill to 350–450°F (180–230°C).

- Spray ribs with a little nonstick cooking spray and sprinkle with a couple more tablespoons (30 mL) of rib spice.
- Grill ribs for 5–8 minutes per side, until heated through (remember to baste with your favorite barbeque sauce).

This is a pretty foolproof recipe for cooking ribs. It's not real BBQ or smoked ribs, but this method will give you tender, juicy ribs that pull cleanly from the bones but do not fall off. Be careful not to over-braise the ribs. The bones should just wiggle in the meat, not pull clean out. This will give you fall-apart and yet tender ribs, which is not what you want on the grill.

But for me, over all the years of cooking ribs, there really is only one method in my mind, and that is low and slow over hardwood coals, barbeque style, smoking your ribs.

Smoked ribs is the second method:

- Choose your rib: Pork back, side or St. Louis.
- Remove the membrane from the bone side of the ribs.
- Rub the ribs liberally with barbeque seasoning (I have five recipes that you can try — see pages 214–216 —but make sure you try my Bone Dust BBQ Spice because it is my favorite). Be sure to rub the seasoning into the meat. I like to do approximately 3 to 4 tablespoons (45 to 60 mL) of spice rub per rack of ribs.
- Cover, refrigerate and allow ribs to marinate in the rub for 4–6 hours or overnight. The pork meat will pick up the flavors of the seasonings.
- Now when it comes to smoking ribs, it's all about the low and slow. The easiest method to learn is the 3-2-1 method. This means 3 hours of smoke, 2 hours in foil and 1 hour again with smoke, and finish with sauce if desired.
- Set your smoker temperature or your grill at 225°F (110°C), but your temperature might drop or spike, so keep a working window of 200–235°F (100–115°C).
- Remove ribs from refrigerator and give them an extra shake of barbeque rub on both sides.
- Place in smoker or on a grill indirectly and smoke for 3 hours (3 hours is best for a full side rib, less for St. Louis or back rib). Look at it this way: for every pound of rib meat your rack of ribs weighs, smoke for 1 hour per pound. During the smoking cycle, make sure to keep your ribs moist with a spritz of some liquid. I tend to use apple juice mixed with water and bourbon (a 1-1-1 ratio), but you can create your own spritz.
- Smoke, maintaining temperature and replenishing with smoke source as required. I recommend a blend of hickory, apple and maple wood chips for smoking,
- Now, while the ribs are smoking, cream together ¼ cup (60 mL) softened butter (some barbeque competitors use butter-flavored margarine, but that's not for me) and ½ cup (125 mL) brown sugar. Set aside.
- After the ribs have been smoked, tear off two big double-layered sheets of heavy-duty aluminum foil, each long enough to wrap completely around the ribs. Transfer ribs to foil, meat side up, and give the ribs a good spritz of liquid. Next spread the butter and brown sugar mixture over the entire surface. Work fast; the butter sugar will melt. Drizzle with a little of your favorite barbeque sauce or one of my sauce recipes (pages 218–221).

- Now wrap the ribs up nice and tight, and it's always just one rack of ribs per foil packet. Place back in smoker and continue to cook the ribs for 2 hours, maintaining a temperature of 225°F (110°C).
- After 2 hours, remove ribs from smoker and unwrap. Carefully place the ribs back on the grill grate, reserving cooking liquids in the foil.
- Continue to cook ribs for another hour, basting with reserved cooking liquids and your favorite barbeque sauce or one of my recipes (pages 218–221).
- Remove ribs from smoker and serve.

This rib method is for you to use as a guide to making great ribs. Times may vary, but practice makes perfect. Use this as a reference to begin from:

Back ribs: 2-2-1: 2 hours smoke, 2 hours foil, 30 minutes smoke and baste
St. Louis ribs: 2-2-1: 2–3 hours smoke, 2 hours foil, 30 minutes to 1 hour smoke and baste
Side ribs: 3-2-1: 3 hours smoke, 2 hours foil, 1 hour smoke and baste

Now remember, most people think this is the best way to smoke ribs. For many people, a good rib has meat that is attached to the bone. In other words, the meat should pull away cleanly from the bone when you bite, but not fall off. Wrapping the ribs in foil for cooking causes steaming and the steaming loosens the meat from the bones. But if you didn't wrap the ribs, it means you run the risk of dry, tough ribs. If you want great-tasting ribs, invest in a smoker, or if working with a gas grill, you can make this happen by setting up your grill for indirect smoking and adding wood smoke. There are many accessories that you can use to create the smoke, but my preference is a foil pan scattered with wood chips sitting directly over the grate.

Cooking great ribs takes time and patience and with these methods I believe you can create delicious, mouth-watering, tender ribs.

PLANK-ROASTED RACK OF PORK STUFFED WITH GRILLED APRICOT & SHALLOT STUFFING

This is one of those Sunday night family dinners, but instead of turning on the oven you will roast this on your grill. It is impressively delicious. **SERVES 8**

WHAT YOU NEED: Nonstick cooking spray; Pastry bag or large self-sealing plastic bag with a hole cut out of one bottom corner; Maple grilling plank (12 × 8 × ½ inches/30 × 20 × 1 cm), soaked in water for a minimum of 1 hour

Fire up your grill to 350–450°F (180–230°C).

Lightly spray the rustic bread with nonstick spray. Place onto grill and grill-toast for 2–3 minutes per side, until lightly charred and golden brown. Remove from grill, dice into ½-inch (1 cm) chunks and place into a large bowl.

Spray apricots and shallots with nonstick spray. Place shallots on grill and grill-roast, turning occasionally, for 8–10 minutes, until lightly charred and tender. While the shallots grill-roast, place apricots onto grill, cut side down, and grill for 3–4 minutes, until charred and softened. Remove shallots and apricots from grill and allow to cool slightly.

Dice grilled apricots into ½-inch (1 cm) chunks and place into bowl with bread. Dice grilled shallots into ¼-inch (5 mm) chunks and add to bowl. Add parsley, salt and black pepper, a splash of beer and melted butter. Mix well until the stuffing is sticky but not too dry.

To make a hole for stuffing, start at one end of the pork loin by inserting a sharp, long, thin knife lengthwise toward the center of the loin. Repeat at opposite end, making an incision that runs throughout the middle of the loin. Using your hands, open up the incision, working from both ends, to create a 2-inch (5 cm) wide opening the length of the loin. You could also use a sharpening steel to help create the hole.

Fill a pastry bag (without tip) or self-sealing plastic bag with a corner cut off with stuffing. Insert end of pastry bag into one end of pork loin and squeeze bag while holding pork loin with your other hand. Squeeze half the stuffing into pork. Insert pastry bag into opposite

6 slices rustic bread

3 medium fresh apricots, cut in half and pits removed

4 large shallots, peeled

2 tbsp (30 mL) chopped fresh parsley

Salt and freshly cracked black pepper to taste

Big splash (approx. ¼ cup/60 mL) Alexander Keith's IPA

¼ cup (60 mL) melted butter

1 center-cut frenched rack of pork (approx. 4 to 5 lb/1.8 to 2.25 kg), 6 bones

2 tbsp (30 mL) Smoky Garlic & Herb Grilling Oil (page 170), plus extra for basting

½ tsp (2 mL) cracked black pepper

½ tsp (2 mL) kosher salt

continued...

end of pork loin and squeeze in remainder of the stuffing until pork loin is full. Ensure stuffing is tightly packed by pushing on filling from both ends with your hands.

Fire up your grill to 550–650°F (290–345°C).

Pat pork loin dry with paper towels. Rub outside of stuffed pork loin with 2 tbsp (30 mL) Smoky Garlic & Herb Grilling Oil and season with cracked black pepper and kosher salt on all sides. Place stuffed pork loin onto grill and sear for 2–3 minutes per side. Transfer pork loin to a thick maple plank and return it to the grill. Close lid and grill-roast stuffed pork loin for 50–60 minutes, basting occasionally with Smoky Garlic & Herb Grilling Oil. Close lid, reducing grill temperature to 350–450°F (180–230°C), and allow stuffed pork loin to grill-roast for an additional 10 minutes or until sauce is sticky and lightly caramelized and pork is cooked to a minimum internal temperature of 160°F (70°C). Remove planked pork from grill and transfer to a cutting board. Allow meat to rest for 5–10 minutes before slicing.

To serve, slice stuffed pork loin into 1-inch (2.5 cm) thick slices and serve with extra sauce for dipping, if desired. Serve with any extra grilled apricots.

GRILLED PORK CHOP WITH CANDIED CHILE GLAZE

This sticky, delicious sauce is modeled after Chinese orange sauce, but what I do is to fry the chiles in hot boiling sugar to bring out the heat and almost candy them. **SERVES 4**

Rub the pork chops with the Bone Dust BBQ Spice, pressing the seasoning into the meat. Marinate, covered and refrigerated, for 2 hours.

Meanwhile, prepare the candied chile glaze by heating the honey, sugar, water and mirin in a small heavy saucepan over medium heat, stirring occasionally with a wooden spoon, until it boils and bubbles. Add in the chopped hot peppers, orange peel, garlic and ginger and cook the chile mixture in the boiling sugar for 5–6 minutes, stirring occasionally, until the sauce is thick and a light golden brown. Immediately remove from heat. Whisking constantly, add the orange juice and soy sauce in a steady stream. Whisk in butter. Bring to a boil and simmer for 5 minutes. Remove from heat and set aside keeping warm.

Fire up your grill to 450–550°F (230–290°C).

Grill the pork chops for 6–8 minutes per side for medium doneness, internal temperature 145°F (63°C), glazing with reserved candied chile glaze. Serve chops with remaining glaze.

TED'S TIP
You'll find dried orange peel in Asian food stores.

4 pork loin chops (6 oz/170 g each), cut 1½-inches (4 cm) thick
2 tbsp (30 mL) Bone Dust BBQ Spice (page 212)
¼ cup (60 mL) honey
¼ cup (60 mL) white sugar
2 tbsp (30 mL) water
3 tbsp (45 mL) mirin
¼ cup (60 mL) red or yellow hot peppers, chopped
2 pieces dried orange peel (approx. 1 inch/2.5 cm long)
3 cloves garlic, minced
1 tbsp (15 mL) finely chopped fresh ginger
¼ cup (60 mL) freshly squeezed orange juice
1 tsp (5 mL) soy sauce
2 tbsp (30 mL) butter

BOURBON STREET GRILLED PORK TENDERLOIN WITH PRALINE BBQ SAUCE

This recipe comes from memories of good times in the French Quarter on Bourbon Street, NOLA. Festive nights and many tasty treats! SERVES 4

2 pork tenderloins (¾ to 1 lb/340 to 450 g each), trimmed

3 tbsp (45 mL) Bone Dust BBQ Spice (page 212)

2 + 2 tbsp (60 mL) butter

4 cloves garlic, minced

1 sweet onion, finely diced

1 cup (250 mL) brown sugar

2 oz (60 mL) Jim Beam

¼ cup (60 mL) pecans, chopped

Salt and freshly ground black pepper to taste

Rub the tenderloins with Bone Dust BBQ Spice, pressing the seasoning into the meat. Marinate, covered and refrigerated, for 4 hours.

In a medium saucepan, melt 2 tbsp (30 mL) butter over medium heat. Sauté the garlic and onion for 10–15 minutes, stirring, until lightly browned and tender. Stir in the brown sugar, bourbon whiskey and pecans. Bring to a boil, reduce heat to low and stir in another 2 tbsp (30 mL) butter a little bit at a time until incorporated. Season to taste with salt and black pepper and set aside, keeping warm.

Fire up your grill to 450–550°F (230–290°C).

Grill tenderloins for 6–8 minutes per side for medium doneness, basting liberally with praline barbeque sauce. Remove tenderloins from grill and let rest for 5 minutes.

Thinly slice and spoon praline barbeque sauce over the slices.

CINNAMON CHIPOTLE-RUBBED LEG OF LAMB WITH RAITA

My local butcher specializes in locally grown meats, and when the lamb is fresh, it's tender and oh so easy to prepare. The key to this recipe is a hot, fast sear and then a low and slow indirect cook. Once the meat is done, slice it thin and serve it with grill-toasted naan bread and this refreshing Raita. The rub is quite aromatic, with flavors from cinnamon, cumin and allspice and the heat of chipotle chile. **SERVES 4 TO 6**

WHAT YOU NEED: Wood chips (flavor of your choice); Fresh herb basting brush (page 22)

Rub the lamb with ¼ cup (60 mL) of the Brown Sugar Chipotle Rub, pressing the spices into the meat. Place the lamb leg into a large bowl. Cover with buttermilk, turning to coat evenly. Cover and refrigerate for 24 hours.

To prepare the Raita, combine the yogurt, lime juice, mint, tomatoes, garlic, red onion, cucumber and salt in a bowl. Cover and refrigerate for 1 hour to allow flavors to develop.

Fire up your grill to 350–450°F (180–230°C).

In a small bowl, combine the clarified butter, garlic and 2 tsp (10 mL) Brown Sugar Chipotle Rub; stir and set aside for basting.

Remove lamb from the buttermilk, scraping off and discarding the excess. Rub the lamb with a few tablespoons more of the Brown Sugar Chipotle Rub.

Sear the lamb for 5–6 minutes per side, brushing with the garlic butter mixture. Reduce heat to medium-low, add in a handful of wood chips to get a little smoke added and close the lid. Grill the lamb, turning once and brushing liberally with the garlic butter, for 15–18 minutes per side or until a meat thermometer inserted into the thickest part of the meat reads 140–145°F (60–63°C) for medium-rare doneness. Remove lamb from grill and let rest for 5 minutes, tented loosely with aluminum foil.

Thinly slice and serve with Raita and grilled naan bread.

1 boneless leg of lamb (approx. 4 to 5 lb/1.8 to 2.2.5 kg), butterflied
½ cup (125 mL) Brown Sugar Chipotle Rub (page 216)
2 cups (500 mL) buttermilk

RAITA

½ cup (125 mL) plain yogurt
Juice of 1 lime
1 tbsp (15 mL) chopped fresh mint
2 plum tomatoes, seeded and chopped
1 clove garlic, minced
½ small red onion, finely diced
½ seedless cucumber, peeled and thinly sliced into rounds
Salt to taste

¼ cup (60 mL) ghee or clarified butter
4 cloves garlic, minced
4 pieces naan bread

GRILLED LAMB CUTLETS WITH FIRE-ROASTED SHALLOT, MINT & GOAT'S CHEESE PESTO

This recipe is pretty easy for those "I want something delicious but I'm in a hurry" moments. You can buy frenched racks of lamb. Although pretty, they do not have as much flavor as an untrimmed lamb rack. Ask your butcher to trim the rack, removing the fat cap and slicing the rack into 1-bone chops about 1 inch (2.5 cm) thick. The pesto can be made a few days in advance and kept in the refrigerator until needed.

SERVES 4

WHAT YOU NEED: Food processor

FIRE-ROASTED SHALLOT, MINT & GOAT'S CHEESE PESTO

4 large shallots, unpeeled

¼ cup (60 mL) pine nuts

1 cup (250 mL) fresh mint leaves

2 tbsp (30 mL) fresh rosemary

4 cloves garlic

Pinch of kosher salt

Freshly ground black pepper to taste

Juice of 1 lime

3 tbsp (45 mL) olive oil

2 tbsp (30 mL) freshly grated
  Parmesan cheese

2 tbsp (30 mL) creamy goat's cheese

2 lamb racks, untrimmed and cut into
  1-inch (2.5 cm) chops

2 tbsp (30 mL) Steak Spice (page 169)

4 tbsp (60 mL) Smoky Garlic & Herb
  Grilling Oil (page 170)

Fire up your grill to 450–550°F (230–290°C).

Place the whole shallots onto the hot grill and roast, turning occasionally, until the skins are blackened and charred and the shallots are tender. Remove shallots, peel and then slice. Set aside.

While the shallots are roasting, toast the pine nuts in a hot dry heavy-bottomed pan until toasty brown. Remove from grill and allow to cool.

To make the pesto, in food processor, combine the mint, rosemary, 2 tbsp (30 mL) toasted pine nuts and garlic. Add a pinch of kosher salt and season to taste with black pepper. Pulse until smooth. Squeeze in lime juice and add the olive oil, Parmesan and goat's cheese. Pulse until smooth but still a little chunky. Transfer to a medium bowl and fold in the reserved sliced roasted shallots. You may need to add a little more oil or a teaspoon or two (5 to 10 mL) of water if the mixture is a little too dry. You want the pesto to be thick but a little loose at the same time. Transfer to a small dish, cover and refrigerate.

Season lamb chops with the Steak Spice, pressing seasoning into meat to adhere. Grill lamb with grill lid open for 2–4 minutes per side, turning once and basting with Smoky Garlic & Herb Grilling Oil, for medium-rare to medium doneness. Just before the chops are done, spread a teaspoon (5 mL) of Fire-Roasted Shallot, Mint & Goat's Cheese Pesto onto one side of each chop. Remove from grill and sprinkle with toasted pine nuts. Drizzle with a little Smoky Garlic & Herb Grilling Oil and serve immediately.

GRILLED LAMB KIDNEYS WITH PRUNES & PORT WINE REDUCTION

I enjoy the odd bits that come from a variety of animals, but one of my favorites is lamb kidneys. See your local butcher and request fresh lamb kidneys. They should have a sweet smell to them when fresh, and when a little old, well, the smell is not so nice. Served with grilled fresh prune (Italian) plums, this dish is quick and easy to prepare. **SERVES 4**

WHAT YOU NEED: 4 grapevines for skewers

Trim the fat from the lamb kidneys and cut each kidney in half lengthwise.

With a sharp paring knife, sharpen one end of each grapevine into a sharp point. Skewer 3 halves of kidney onto each skewer. Lay the skewered kidneys into a glass dish.

In a small bowl, combine garlic, 2 tsp (10 mL) rosemary, small pinch of black pepper, olive oil and ½ cup (125 mL) port wine. Mix and pour over the kidneys, turning to coat. Cover, refrigerate and marinate for 1 hour.

Cut the fresh plums in half and set aside. Pour 2 cups (500 mL) port wine into a medium saucepan and bring to a rolling boil. Reduce heat and simmer until the port is reduced by at least half and has a syrup-like consistency. Set aside, keeping warm.

Fire up your grill to 550-650°F (290–345°C).

Remove the kidneys from the marinade, discarding leftover marinade. Season kidneys with kosher salt and black pepper.

Place a few sprigs of fresh rosemary directly onto the grill and let the rosemary grill, char and smoke. This will add rosemary smokiness to the grilling kidneys.

Grill the kidneys for 4–5 minutes per side, basting with a little port wine reduction. Do not overcook, as the kidney will get dry and tough.

At the same time as you are grilling the kidneys, grill the prune plums for about the same amount of time. Remove from grill. Cut the prune halves in half and place in a bowl. Season with a little salt and pepper and drizzle with port wine reduction. Transfer skewers to a plate, spoon over grilled plums in port wine, garnish with a sprig of fresh rosemary and serve immediately.

6 fresh lamb kidneys

4 cloves garlic, minced

2 tsp (10 mL) chopped fresh rosemary

Small pinch of freshly ground black pepper

2 tsp (10 mL) olive oil

½ + 2 cups (625 mL) port wine

6 fresh ripe prune plums, halved and pitted

Kosher salt and freshly ground black pepper to taste

1 bunch fresh rosemary sprigs

GRILLED LAMB T-BONES WITH PINK PEPPERED POMEGRANATE GLAZE

This is a pretty sexy dish. Truly worth making for that special someone. My butcher at Black Angus Fine Meats & Game cuts my lamb T-bones nice and thick for me—about 2 inches. The thicker the chop, the less likely you'll overcook it! **SERVES 4**

8 lamb T-bone chops, cut approx.
    1½ to 2 inches (4 to 5 cm) thick
½ cup (125 mL) Red Stag by
    Jim Beam
2 cups (500 mL) pomegranate juice
¼ cup (60 mL) pomegranate
    molasses
2 tsp (10 mL) cold butter, cut
    into cubes
1 tsp (5 mL) cracked pink
    peppercorns
½ teaspoon (2 mL) fresh thyme
Himalayan pink salt and freshly
    ground black pepper to taste
3 to 4 tbsp (45 to 60 mL) Smoky
    Garlic & Herb Grilling Oil
    (page 170)
Fresh pomegranate seeds
    (if available)

Place the lamb T-bones into a self-sealing bag and pour in the Red Stag, seal bag, removing as much air as possible, and marinate, refrigerated, for 30 minutes.

While the chops lounge in the whiskey, prepare the pomegranate glaze. Pour the pomegranate juice into a medium saucepot and bring to a boil over high heat, reduce heat and let simmer until there is about ½ cup (125 mL) pomegranate juice left. Remove from heat and stir in a heaping tablespoon (15 mL) of pomegranate molasses. Add in the butter, a few pieces at a time, and stir until incorporated. Stir in the pink peppercorns and fresh thyme and season to taste with pink salt and black pepper. Set aside, keeping warm.

Fire up your grill to 450–550°F (230–290°C).

Remove lamb from marinade and pour whiskey into a cup; reserve, as you're going to flame the chops with it. Season lamb T-bones with pink salt and black pepper. Grill lamb T-bones over high heat for 3–5 minutes on one side, basting with Smoky Garlic & Herb Grilling Oil. Flip, baste with pink pepper pomegranate glaze and grill for a further 3–5 minutes. When the chops are just about finished grilling, open grill lid, stand back and drizzle the chops with reserved whiskey to flambé. Be careful as your chops will ignite. Allow the flambé to burn out. Remove from grill and serve lamb T-bones drizzled with extra sauce and, when in season, garnish with a few juicy pomegranate seeds. Serve immediately.

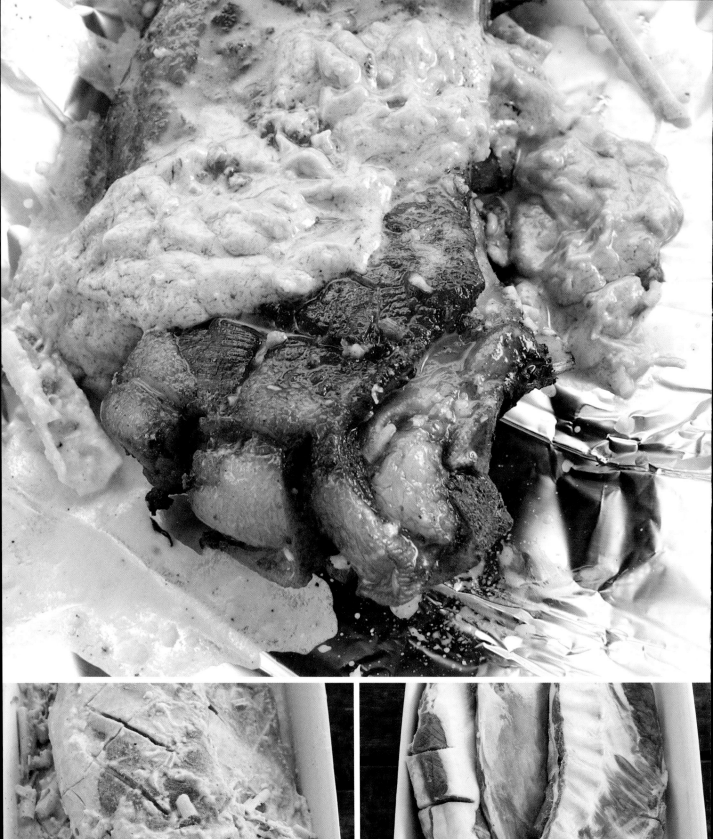

SMOKED LAMB RIBS WITH SPICY PEANUT SAUCE

Ask your butcher for lamb ribs; they are usually a by-product and the price should be pretty reasonable.

SERVES 4

WHAT YOU NEED: Oak or maple smoking chips, soaked in cold water

To make the marinade, in a glass dish large enough to hold the lamb, stir together well the coconut milk, lemongrass, lime juice, chiles, ginger, garlic, brown sugar, oil and black pepper.

With a sharp knife, score the lamb ribs on both sides, about ¼ inch (5 mm) deep, in a diamond pattern. Add ribs to marinade, turning to coat. Marinate, covered and refrigerated, for 4–6 hours or overnight.

Meanwhile, make the Spicy Peanut Sauce. Heat the vegetable oil in a medium saucepan over medium heat. Sauté the shallots, garlic and ginger, stirring, until tender. Add the peanut butter, coconut milk and sherry, stirring until smooth. Add the lime zest and juice, vinegar, chili sauce and cilantro. Bring just to a simmer, stirring to prevent sticking, and simmer for 5–10 minutes, stirring occasionally. Let cool.

Fire up your grill to 200–225°F° (100–110°C). Set grill for indirect grilling/smoking.

Remove ribs from marinade, reserving marinade. Smoke ribs for 1½–2 hours, basting with reserved marinade. Remove ribs from grill and brush the marinade over the ribs and pour in a few tablespoons (30 to 60 mL) of Spicy Peanut Sauce. Wrap each lamb rib in a double sheet of aluminum foil and return to grill. Cook indirectly for about 60 minutes, until the rib bone can wiggle easily in the meat. Remove ribs and unwrap.

Adjust your grill's temperature to 450–550°F (230–290°C).

Heat the Spicy Peanut Sauce.

Grill ribs for a couple of minutes per side on medium-high heat to get little char into the meat, basting with Spicy Peanut Sauce. Remove from grill and cut the ribs in 2-bone sections. Serve immediately with extra sauce.

COCONUT GREEN CHILE MARINADE

½ cup (125 mL) coconut milk

1 stalk lemongrass, pale green part only, smashed and chopped

Juice of 3 limes

2 small spicy Thai green chiles

1 tbsp (15 mL) chopped fresh ginger

6 cloves garlic, minced

2 tbsp (30 mL) brown sugar

2 tbsp (30 mL) vegetable oil

1 tsp (5 mL) cracked black pepper

8 racks of lamb ribs (8 to 10 oz/225 to 285 g each), trimmed

SPICY PEANUT SAUCE

2 tbsp (30 mL) vegetable oil

2 shallots, diced

2 cloves garlic, minced

1 tbsp (15 mL) minced fresh ginger

1 cup (250 mL) crunchy peanut butter

1 cup (250 mL) coconut milk

½ cup (125 mL) dry sherry

Zest and juice of 1 lime

¼ cup (60 mL) rice wine vinegar

1 tsp (5 mL) Asian chili sauce

1 tbsp (15 mL) chopped fresh cilantro

GASTRO GRILL ABCS: GRILLED APPLE, BACON & CALF'S LIVER WITH ICE SYRUP

Gastro Grilling ABCs, grilled crispy sweet and tart apple, double-smoked bacon and tender calf's liver. This is a quick and easy grill recipe full of delicious flavors. Once the ABCs are grilled, drizzle with ice syrup.

What is ice syrup, you say? Ice syrup is similar to maple syrup, only it is made from grapes — ice wine grapes. Grapes that have been frozen by Mother Nature and the sweet nectar turns to crystals, intensifying the sweetness of the grape. Ice syrup or grape syrup is the new gastro maple syrup of the syrup world. So sweet and tasty. For more information on ice syrup and how to get yourself some, visit icesyrup.com. **SERVES 2**

2 slices double-smoked bacon, cut
    ¼-inch (5 mm) thick
Dash of Bone Dust BBQ Spice
    (page 212)
1 slice calf's liver (approx. 8 oz/225 g),
    peeled of membrane, cut ½ inch
    (1 cm) thick
1 crisp firm tart-sweet apple, such as
    Fuji or Mutsu
1 cup (250 mL) spiced whiskey
1 cup (250 mL) cold water
Juice of ½ lemon
2 sprigs fresh thyme, plus extra
    for garnish
Kosher salt and freshly ground black
    pepper to taste
Drizzle of ice syrup
4 tbsp (60 mL) crumbled 4-year-old
    white cheddar cheese

TED'S TIP

- Ideal bacon for this recipe should be approximately 6 to 8 inches (15 to 20 cm) long and about 2 inches (5 cm) wide.
- Ideal liver for this recipe should be approximately 7 to 8 inches (18 to 20 cm) long and 3 to 4 inches (8 to 10 cm) wide.

Cut the bacon slices in half so that you have 4 equal-length pieces. Season the bacon slices with Bone Dust BBQ Spice and set aside.

Cut the calf's liver into 4 equally small slices. Set aside, refrigerated.

Slice the apple into ¼-inch (5 mm) thick slices across the middle to expose the core. Pick out any seeds and place apple slices in a bowl. Pour over the spiced whiskey, water and the juice of half a lemon. Throw the squeezed lemon half into the bowl. Add a sprig or two of thyme and set aside. This will flavor the apples. You need at least 6 slices of apple.

Fire up your grill to 450–550°F (230–290°C).

Drain the apples. Season the apples and calf's liver slices with kosher salt and black pepper. Put the apple slices on the grill first, followed by the bacon and then by the liver. When the apples are tender and the bacon is a little crispy, set them aside, keeping warm, and then grill the calf's liver. The apples and bacon will take 2–3 minutes per side and the liver will take about 30 seconds to a minute per side. Remove items from grill.

On a plate, lay a slice of grilled apple, top with a slice of grilled bacon, followed by a sliced of grilled calf's liver. Drizzle with a little ice syrup. Add another slice of grilled apple, followed by bacon and liver. Drizzle with ice syrup and finish with another slice of apple and some crumbled very old white cheddar cheese. Garnish with a sprig of thyme and drizzle again with a little syrup. Serve immediately.

GRILLED VEAL RACK CHOPS WITH BLACK OLIVE TAPENADE

Veal rack chops are extremely tender and there is really no need to marinate the meat. Prepare the tapenade a day in advance to allow for the flavors to fully develop. For an added boost of smoke flavor, add a bit of oak wood chips to your fire. **SERVES 4**

WHAT YOU NEED: Food processor; Oak wood chips, soaked in water

To make the tapenade, in a food processor, place the olives, garlic, anchovies, oregano, lemon juice, green onion and olive oil. Top with lid and pulse to chop. Purée until smooth. Transfer mixture to a bowl and season to taste with salt and black pepper. Cover and refrigerate until needed.

To make the baste, zest and juice the lemon and place in a small bowl. Add the minced garlic, oregano and season with good pinch of kosher salt and black pepper. Add in olive oil and stir to form a paste. Set aside.

Fire up your grill to 450–550°F (230–290°C). Set grill for both direct and indirect grilling.

Season chops with kosher salt and black pepper.

Throw a handful of soaked oak chips onto the grill fire.

Grill chops for 2–3 minutes on one side to sear. Flip them over. Continue to sear for another 2–3 minutes. Spoon the garlic and lemon juice mixture over the veal chops. Move chops to an indirect part of your grill and close lid. Grill-roast indirectly for 10–12 minutes for medium-rare doneness. Remove chops from grill and let rest for about 5 minutes.

Smear a spoonful of tapenade onto a plate and top with a grilled veal chop. Serve immediately.

BLACK OLIVE TAPENADE

1 cup (250 mL) pitted dry-cured black olives

3 cloves garlic, minced

2 anchovies

1 tbsp (15 mL) chopped fresh oregano

1 tbsp (15 mL) lemon juice

1 green onion, chopped

2 tbsp (30 mL) olive oil

Salt and freshly ground black pepper to taste

BASTE

1 juicy lemon

4 cloves garlic, minced

2 tbsp (30 mL) chopped fresh oregano

Pinch of kosher salt and freshly ground black pepper

2 tbsp (30 mL) olive oil

4 bone-in white veal rack chops (approx. 16 oz/450 g), cut 1½ inches (4 cm) thick

Kosher salt and freshly ground black pepper to taste

GRILLED VEAL SWEETBREADS WITH HORSERADISH GREMOLATA

You won't find sweetbreads on grocery store shelves; you will need to special order these from your local butcher or meat purveyor. It's worth the effort to have tender, rich deliciousness. **SERVES 4**

3 cups (750 mL) milk

1 to 1½ lb (450 to 675 g) whole veal sweetbreads

3 tbsp (45 mL) Steak Spice (page 169)

3 to 4 tbsp (30 to 46 mL) Smoky Garlic & Herb Grilling Oil (page 170)

HORSERADISH GREMOLATA

3 tbsp (45 mL) olive oil

3 cloves garlic, minced

1 juicy lemon

½ cup (125 mL) fresh Italian (flat-leaf) parsley leaves

¼ cup (60 mL) fresh dill

3 tbsp (45 mL) freshly grated horseradish

2 tbsp (30 mL) freshly grated Parmesan cheese

1 tsp (5 mL) cracked black pepper

Salt to taste

Drizzle of brandy

Bring the milk to a boil, reduce heat to medium-low and add in the veal sweetbreads. Simmer for 30–40 minutes to blanch. Peel the sweetbreads, removing the membrane and any veins that should pull easily from the meat. Allow to fully cool.

Wrap each sweetbread in plastic wrap and place a heavy weight on top to press the sweetbreads. Refrigerate for 1–2 hours to allow the sweetbreads to firm up.

Unwrap the sweetbreads and slice into 1-inch (2.5 cm) thick medallions. Season the sweetbreads with Steak Spice and brush with a little Smoky Garlic & Herb Grilling Oil. Set aside.

Fire up your grill to 450–550°F (230–290°C).

Next prepare the Horseradish Gremolata. In a small saucepan, heat the olive oil over medium heat. Cook the garlic until tender, 1–2 minutes. Remove from heat and let cool slightly. Zest and juice the lemon and add to the garlic. Add parsley, dill, horseradish, Parmesan cheese, black pepper and season to taste with a little salt. Add a drizzle of brandy.

Grill veal for 3–5 minutes per side, basting with a little Smoky Garlic & Herb Grilling Oil, until lightly charred and browned. Remove from grill. Spoon over the Horseradish Gremolata and serve immediately.

GRILLED VEAL T-BONES WITH CHANTERELLE FRICASSEE & BUFFALO MOZZARELLA

When I first made this recipe, I added butter-poached lobster meat to the Chanterelle Fricassee. It was over-the-top delicious. This version is a little easier on the pocketbook, but if you feel like taking it to the next level, add the lobster meat. **SERVES 4**

WHAT YOU NEED: Cast iron frying pan

Zest and juice the lemons and place in a glass dish large enough to hold the chops in one layer. Whisk together with the garlic, oil, rosemary and mustard. Season to taste with lots of pepper. Add the T-bone steaks, turning to coat. Marinate, covered and refrigerated, for 2 hours.

To prepare the Chanterelle Fricassee, heat the olive oil and truffle oil in a cast iron pan over medium-high heat. Sauté the shallots and mushrooms until tender, about 8–10 minutes. Drizzle with port and cook, stirring, for 1 minute. Stir in veal demi glace. Bring to a boil; reduce heat to low and set aside, keeping warm. Adjust seasoning with sea salt and black pepper.

Fire up your grill to 450–550°F (230–290°C).

Remove chops from marinade, reserving the marinade. Grill chops, basting with the reserved marinade, for 6–8 minutes per side for medium-rare doneness. When the chops are just done, move them to the side of the grill. Top each chop with one-quarter of the Chanterelle Fricassee and a slice of buffalo mozzarella. Close the lid and heat until the cheese is melted and bubbling. Serve immediately.

2 juicy lemons
4 cloves garlic, minced
¼ cup (60 mL) olive oil
2 tbsp (30 mL) chopped fresh
 rosemary
2 tbsp (30 mL) Dijon mustard
Cracked black pepper to taste
4 white veal T-bone steaks (approx.
 10 to 12 oz/285 to 340 g each)

CHANTERELLE FRICASSEE
¼ cup (60 mL) olive oil
Drizzle of truffle oil
4 shallots, finely chopped
1½ cups (375 mL) chanterelle
 mushrooms
Drizzle of port
¼ to ½ cup (60 to 125 mL)
 veal demi glace
Sea salt and freshly ground black
 pepper to taste

1 ball buffalo mozzarella cheese,
 cut into 4 slices

GRILLED BUFFALO STEAKS WITH HONEY DATE BUTTER

Buffalo meat is a little more full-flavored than beef. Grill the steak hot and fast for rare to medium-rare doneness; that is the best way to serve tender and moist buffalo. If you overcook buffalo, it will be dry and tough, and that is just not any fun. Foods should melt in your mouth and make you feel really good. **SERVES 4**

WHAT YOU NEED: Cast iron frying pan

HONEY DATE BUTTER
¼ cup (60 mL) butter, softened
1 shallot, minced
½ cup (125 mL) dried pitted
    honey dates (approx. 6),
    coarsely chopped
1 tbsp (15 mL) honey
1 tsp (5 mL) chopped fresh sage
Splash of cognac
Pinch of nutmeg
Kosher salt and freshly ground black
    pepper to taste

4 buffalo strip loin steaks (5 to
    6 oz/140 to 170 g each), cut
    1½ inches (4 cm) thick
2 tsp (10 mL) Steak Spice (page 169)
Drizzle of honey
½ cup (125 mL) sliced almonds

To prepare the Honey Date Butter, mix the softened butter with the shallot pieces, dates, honey and sage in a bowl. Add a splash of cognac and season to taste with a pinch of nutmeg, kosher salt and black pepper. Mix and set aside at room temperature.

Season buffalo steaks with the Steak Spice, pressing the seasoning into the meat.

Fire up your grill to 550-650°F (290–345°C).

Toast the sliced almonds over the hot fire in a dry cast iron frying pan, shaking the pan to keep them from sticking and burning. Remove once toasted and set aside, keeping warm.

Grill steaks directly over the fire with the lid open for 3–4 minutes per side for rare to medium-rare doneness. After the flip, spoon a small amount of the Honey Date Butter over the steaks and brush it into the meat. Remove buffalo steaks from grill and let rest for 5 minutes, tented loosely with a sheet of aluminum foil.

Slice the steaks on the bias and serve with a little extra dollop of Honey Date Butter. Garnish with toasted sliced almonds and a drizzle of honey.

GRILLED VENISON RACK CHOPS WITH PISTACHIO NUT CRUST & PARTRIDGE BERRY GLAZE

My friends at Black Angus Fine Meats and Game have been supplying me with all of my game meat requirements. The quality and variety of their different game meats is fantastic. When you want to get a little exotic, they are the ones you want to see: blackangusmeat.com. SERVES 4

WHAT YOU NEED: Hand-held blender or food processor

To make the Partridge Berry Glaze, heat the oil in a medium saucepot. Sauté the garlic and shallots for 2–3 minutes, until tender. Deglaze with balsamic vinegar and reduce liquid by half. Add partridge berries and continue to cook for 3 minutes, stirring and slightly mashing the berries to extract the juice. Add maple syrup, savory sprigs and black pepper. Bring to a low boil and reduce heat to medium. Let simmer for 10–15 minutes.

Using a hand blender or food processor, purée until smooth. Strain, season to taste with salt and let cool.

To prepare the venison chops, mix together the Dijon and grainy mustards, chopped savory, red wine and olive oil in a bowl. Set aside.

Pat racks of venison dry with paper towels to remove excess moisture. Using a sharp knife, cut each rack into three 3-inch (8 cm) thick chops (2 bones each). Place venison chops in a glass dish and pour mustard mixture over, turning to coat each chop evenly. Let marinate, covered, in the refrigerator for 3–4 hours.

Fire up your grill to 450–550°F (230–290°C).

Remove venison chops from marinade and scrape off the marinade.

In a bowl, combine Steak Spice and ½ cup (125 mL) chopped pistachio nuts. Rub the mixture into the chops, pressing the seasoning and nuts into the meat.

Grill the chops directly over the fire with the lid open for 3–5 minutes per side for medium-rare to medium doneness, basting 2 or 3 times with Partridge Berry Glaze. When venison chops are just done, glaze liberally with Partridge Berry Glaze and sprinkle with remaining ¼ cup (60 mL) pistachios. Remove chops from the grill, allow to rest for 5 minutes and serve.

PARTRIDGE BERRY GLAZE

2 tbsp (30 mL) olive oil

3 cloves garlic, minced

3 shallots, diced

½ cup (125 mL) balsamic vinegar

1½ cups (375 mL) frozen or fresh partridge berries (raspberries, blueberries or red currants are all acceptable alternatives if you can't find partridge berries)

1 cup (250 mL) pure maple syrup

2 sprigs fresh savory

Salt and freshly ground black pepper to taste

¼ cup (60 mL) Dijon mustard

2 tbsp (30 mL) grainy mustard

2 tbsp (30 mL) fresh savory, chopped

1 cup (250 mL) Creekside Estates Shiraz

2 tbsp (30 mL) olive oil

2 frenched venison racks (approx. 1 lb/450 g each), cut 1½ inches (4 cm) thick

¼ cup (60 mL) Steak Spice (page 169)

½ + ¼ cup (185 mL) pistachio nuts, coarsely chopped

GRILLED FIGS & FOIE GRAS

This sounds a lot harder than it really is. Grilled fresh figs and foie gras takes minutes and is very simple to do. Hot grill, fast hands and the desire for a truly delicious dinner. **SERVES 4**

4 plump ripe fresh figs, black or
    green, up to you
1 lobe foie gras (approx. 12 oz/340 g)
¼ cup (60 mL) honeycomb
Sea salt and freshly ground black
    pepper to taste
Drizzle of 40-, 50- or 100-year-old
    balsamic vinegar
4 sprigs fresh thyme

TED'S TIP
- Black figs tend to be sweeter.
  I prefer to use them.
- Use a balsamic vinegar that is old,
  sweet, fragrant and syrupy.

Cut the stem off each fig. Cut figs in half through the stem. Set aside.

Remove the foie gras from the refrigerator. Break apart the lobe and remove any veins. Be careful not to break it apart too much, as you want to be able to slice the lobe into ½-inch (1 cm) thick slices about 2 inches (5 cm) square, or as square as it can be. Set aside, refrigerated, to keep cold. You want the foie gras slices to be as cold as they can be without freezing when you start grilling. This will make it easier to grill, as the fat will not render as quickly.

Fire up your grill to 450–550°F (230–290°C).

Grill the fig halves for 1–2 minutes, cut side down, until lightly charred. Turn over and move the figs to a cooler part of the grill and continue to grill-roast. Spoon a little liquid honey from the honeycomb over the figs and season with sea salt and a little black pepper; let the figs roast for 5 minutes, until they are warm through and tender. Place two grill-roasted fig halves onto a plate, add a small chunk of honeycomb and set aside.

Season the foie gras with sea salt and black pepper. Grill foie gras slices for 30 seconds to 1 minute per side, until the foie gras is lightly charred. This will flare up while it grills, so you will need to be quick. Place two foie gras slices onto each plate of figs. Drizzle with very well-aged balsamic vinegar and garnish with a sprig of fresh thyme. Serve immediately.

POULTRY

BACON-WRAPPED CHICKEN CIGARS WITH SMOKED MOZZARELLA, PRUNE & BREAD STUFFING

Let's just say that anything wrapped in bacon is a good thing, and trust me, this is a good thing! **SERVES 6**

WHAT YOU NEED: 2 oak or maple grilling planks (12 × 8 × ½ inches/30 × 20 × 1 cm), soaked in water for a minimum of 1 hour; Sharp paring knife

Melt the 4 tbsp (60 mL) butter in a skillet over medium heat. Add the onions and sauté for 5–7 minutes, stirring frequently. Add the celery and garlic and continue slowly stirring and frying for 10 minutes, until very tender and beginning to brown.

In a bowl, combine the onion mixture with the 3 tbsp (45 mL) butter, smoked mozzarella, green onions, oregano, dried prunes and bread. Mix well and season with salt and black pepper. Set aside.

Using a sharp boning or paring knife, debone the chicken legs. First cut along the thigh bone from the outer edge to the joint. Using the tip of the knife, cut around the bone and peel back the meat, exposing the complete bone. Repeat with the drumstick portion of the leg. Now you have all the meat pulled back and the meat should only be attached at the joint. Cut the bones from the joint meat.

Lay one deboned chicken leg onto a flat work surface, skin side down. Spread it so that the leg takes on a square or rectangle shape. Season the meat with salt and black pepper. Take one-sixth of the stuffing mixture and spread it over the entire surface of the chicken leg to about 1-inch (2.5 cm) thickness. Starting from one end, roll up the chicken thigh into a cigar-like shape. Wrap tightly with 2 slices of bacon. Repeat with remaining legs, stuffing and bacon. Season with Bone Dust BBQ Spice.

Fire up your grill to 350–450°F (180–230°C).

Place chicken cigars onto the grilling planks, evenly spaced. Plank roast for 30–40 minutes or until the chicken is cooked, the bacon is crisp and a thermometer inserted into the stuffing registers 160°F (70°C). Remove from the grill, slice and serve.

4 tbsp (60 mL) butter
1 large onion, diced
1 stalk celery, diced
6 cloves fresh garlic, minced
3 tbsp (45 mL) butter, melted
6 oz (170 g) smoked mozzarella cheese, cut into ¼-inch (5 mm) cubes
3 green onions, chopped
2 tbsp (30 mL) chopped fresh oregano
½ cup (125 mL) dried prunes, apricots or dates, diced
3 cups (750 mL) day-old rustic bread, cut into 1-inch (2.5 cm) cubes
Salt and freshly ground pepper to taste
6 chicken legs
16 slices bacon
3 tbsp (45 mL) Bone Dust BBQ Spice (page 212)

TED'S TIP

Ask your butcher to debone the chicken legs for you, leaving the skin intact, if you do not want to do this step yourself.

CASA BBQ BEER CAN CHICKEN TACOS

Tacos are a great meal for the whole family to enjoy. Instead of grilling up chicken breasts for tacos or fajitas, try beer canning a whole chicken instead. It's so moist and juicy that the whole family will be asking you to make this a family staple. Mine did, and now beer can chicken taco night is a regular happening at Casa BBQ. It's fast and downright yummy! **SERVES 4**

WHAT YOU NEED: 4 aluminum foil or 2 metal pie plates; 2 beer can chicken holders

FIRE-ROASTED SALSA VERDE

6 tomatillos

2 poblano peppers

2 jalapeño peppers

1 small white onion, sliced into rings

4 cloves garlic

4 green onions, finely chopped

1 cup (250 mL) fresh cilantro leaves

2 tbsp (30 mL) cane vinegar

2 tbsp (30 mL) olive oil

Pinch of kosher salt

1 lime

GUACAMOLE

2 avocados, peeled and pitted

1 juicy lime

Drizzle of avocado oil

3 sprigs fresh cilantro, chopped

¼ cup (60 mL) white onion, diced

1 green onion, minced

Salt and freshly ground black pepper to taste

FIRE-ROASTED FOUR-PEPPER SALSA

2 red bell peppers, halved and seeded

1 yellow bell pepper, halved and seeded

1 green bell pepper, halved and seeded

1 red onion, peeled and quartered

2 tbsp (30 mL) olive oil

2 to 3 chipotle peppers in adobo sauce, puréed

2 cloves garlic minced

1 tbsp (15 mL) fresh cilantro, chopped

Juice of 1 lime

Salt and coarsely ground black pepper to taste

1 whole chicken (approx. 4 lb/1.8 kg)

¼ cup (60 mL) salt

2 tbsp (30 mL) honey

4 cups (1 L) cold water

2 + 1 cans (12 oz/341 mL) Stella Artois

4 cloves garlic

4 sprigs fresh sage

1 tsp (5 mL) black peppercorns

½ lime, cut into wedges

8 cloves garlic, minced

1 tsp (5 mL) ancho pepper powder

2 tsp (10 mL) Bone Dust BBQ Spice (page 212)

4 tbsp (60 mL) olive oil

Kosher salt and freshly ground black pepper to taste

GARNISH

12 flour or corn tortillas (5 to 6 inches/12 to 15 cm)

2 cups (500 mL) pepper jack cheese, shredded

1 cup (250 mL) Fire-Roasted Salsa Verde

1 cup (250 mL) guacamole

1 cup (250 mL) Fire-Roasted Four-Pepper Salsa

continued . . .

Fire up your grill to 350–450°F (180–230°C).

To make the Fire-Roasted Salsa Verde, fire-roast the tomatillos, poblano and jalapeño peppers and onions for 10–15 minutes, until lightly charred and tender. Place the tomatillos into a food processor. Peel and seed the poblano peppers and add roasted flesh to the tomatillos. Add the whole roasted jalapeño peppers. Chop the grilled onion and add it into the blender too. Add garlic, green onions, cilantro, cane vinegar and olive oil. Hit it with a good pinch of kosher salt and pulse until smooth. Add a squeeze of fresh lime juice and adjust seasoning. Transfer to a self-sealing container and refrigerate until needed.

To make the Guacamole, mash the avocados with a fork in a bowl. Squeeze the lime over the avocado and drizzle with a little avocado oil. Add cilantro, white and green onion and season to taste with a little salt and black pepper. Cover and refrigerate until needed.

To make the Fire-Roasted Four-Pepper Salsa, roast the red, yellow and green peppers and the red onion until lightly charred and tender. Peel any loose skin from the peppers. Dice the peppers and onion; place in a large bowl. Add the olive oil, puréed chipotle chiles, garlic, cilantro and lime juice and season to taste with salt and black pepper. Mix thoroughly, cover and refrigerate at least 1 hour.

To prepare the chicken, rinse the chicken under cold running water. Place chicken into a large self-sealing bag or small bucket.

In a bowl, combine the salt, honey, water and 2 cans of beer. Stir until salt and honey have dissolved. Add garlic cloves, fresh sage and peppercorns. Pour over chicken, cover and refrigerate for 24 hours.

Remove chicken from brine, discarding leftover brine. Pat chicken dry with paper towels.

Open the last can of beer; take a good-sized sip out of it. Quality assurance! Squish a couple of wedges of lime into the opening of the beer can. Put one pie plate inside another. Place beer can holder onto pie plate, then slide opened can into holder. Slide the chicken over the can so that the beer can is in the cavity of the bird and the bird is standing upright. Tuck the wings behind its back and pull the neck skin flap up over the opening. If there is not enough skin to seal it up, tuck a small lime or a small potato into the neck. This will help keep the steam and extra beer flavor in the chicken.

In a bowl, combine minced garlic, ancho pepper powder, Bone Dust BBQ Spice and salt and pepper. Drizzle with olive oil to make a slurry paste. Set aside.

Place the beer canned chicken and pie plate on the grill. Grill-roast chicken with the lid closed for 60–90 minutes (about 20 minutes per lb/450 g), until the chicken is fully cooked, basting during the last 20 minutes with the garlic and ancho paste.

Remove from grill and allow chicken to rest for a few minutes. Carefully remove the chicken from the beer can. Place beer can aside. Carve the meat from the chicken. Shred all of the chicken meat into a large bowl. Drizzle in a little of the hot beer from the can, just a little.

Warm the tortillas, place a mound of beer can chicken on the warm shell, sprinkle with shredded pepper jack cheese, spoon over guacamole and top with a little salsa. Serve immediately.

TED'S TIP
After I have beer canned my bird, I like to hot peel the meat from the bones. Shred the meat and chop up the skin and add it back in. Adding the chopped crispy garlicky skin back into the meat makes it taste like heaven.

DARK & STORMY CHICKEN WITH THREE-MELON SALSA

Boneless skinless chicken breasts might have lower fat content and are an easier cooking option, but bone-in and skin-on are the way to go. Believe me, there is no flavor comparison. This recipe is to die for! **SERVES 4**

To make the marinade, zest and juice the lemon, limes and orange and combine. Reserve ¼ cup (60 mL) juice and zest for the salsa. Add the ginger beer, rum, garlic, jalapeño pepper, ginger, cilantro, mint and olive oil. Season with a little black pepper and stir. Set aside.

Place chicken breasts into a glass dish or a self-sealing food storage bag. Pour over the marinade, turning the chicken to coat evenly, and marinate for 6–8 hours, turning occasionally to marinate evenly.

Meanwhile, prepare the Three-Melon Salsa. Place the cantaloupe, honeydew melon, watermelon, shallots and jalapeño into a medium bowl and set aside. Just before serving the salsa with the grilled chicken, add cilantro, mint and a splash of rum. Season to taste with salt and black pepper.

Fire up your grill to 350–450°F (180–230°C). Set grill for both direct and indirect grilling.

Remove chicken breasts from marinade, discarding leftover marinade, and season with salt. Grill chicken breasts, skin side down, for 3–5 minutes to lightly char the skin. Flip the chicken breasts over to the bone side and continue to cook for another 3–5 minutes. Move chicken breasts to indirect part of the grill and close lid. Grill indirectly for 25–20 minutes, keeping the temperature at about 350°F (180°C), until the chicken is fully cooked (minimum internal temperature of 160°F/70°C). Drizzle the chicken breasts with honey and add a squeeze of fresh orange.

Remove chicken from grill and season with a little black pepper. Serve immediately with Three-Melon Salsa.

DARK & STORMY MARINADE

1 lemon

2 limes

1 orange

1 cup (250 mL) ginger beer

2 oz (60 mL) spiced rum

3 cloves garlic, minced

1 jalapeño pepper, thinly sliced

1 tbsp (15 mL) chopped fresh ginger

1 tbsp (15 mL) chopped fresh cilantro

1 tbsp (15 mL) chopped fresh mint

2 tbsp (30 mL) olive oil

Freshly ground black pepper to taste

4 plump chicken breasts (approx. 8 to 10 oz/225 to 285 g each), bone in and skin on

THREE-MELON SALSA

1 cup (250 mL) cantaloupe, cut in ¼-inch (5 mm) dice

1 cup (250 mL) honeydew melon, cut in ¼-inch (5 mm) dice

1 cup (250 mL) watermelon, cut in ¼-inch (5 mm) dice

2 shallots, minced

½ jalapeño pepper, seeded and finely chopped

1 tbsp (15 mL) chopped fresh cilantro

1 tbsp (15 mL) chopped fresh mint

Drizzle of spiced rum

Salt and freshly ground black pepper to taste

Drizzle of honey

Squeeze of orange juice

GRILLED CHICKEN ROULADE

It may seem like a lot of work to put this recipe together. Well, it is! But trust me when I say that after all of your hard work to make this recipe, you will be rewarded with satisfaction. Give it a go. I know you can do it.
SERVES 4

WHAT YOU NEED: Meat mallet; Butcher twine

MUSHROOM SPINACH STUFFING
1 tbsp (15 mL) butter
4 cups (1 L) assorted exotic
mushrooms (a blend of oyster,
shiitake, white or brown field
mushrooms, portobello,
chanterelle and morel)
6 cloves garlic, minced
1 medium sweet onion, finely diced
2 cups (500 mL) fresh baby
spinach leaves
½ lb (225 g) ground chicken
8 oz (225 g) Fontina cheese, cut into
½-inch (1 cm) cubes
¼ cup (60 mL) freshly grated
Parmesan cheese

4 boneless skin-on chicken breasts
Salt and freshly ground black pepper

To prepare the Mushroom Spinach Stuffing, in a sauté pan, heat butter over medium-high heat. Add mushrooms and sauté for 3–4 minutes, until tender. Add garlic and onion and fry for 1–2 minutes, until softened. Add spinach and cook for another 1–2 minutes, until limp. Remove from heat and allow to cool fully.

Place the ground chicken into a large bowl, add Fontina and Parmesan cheese and the cooled mushroom mixture. Mix well. Set aside, keeping cold.

Peel the skin from the boneless chicken breasts and reserve the skin.

To flatten the chicken breasts, place breast between two pieces of plastic wrap and flatten with a meat mallet to a uniform thickness. Lay two chicken breasts beside each other, yin-yang-like, so that you get a square of chicken breast meat. Season with a little salt and black pepper. Spread half the mushroom mixture over top of the flattened chicken breasts, patting it down to about 1 inch (2.5 cm) thick. Roll the chicken up like a cigar into a pinwheel. Lay two pieces of reserved chicken skin over the roll. Tie it up with butcher twine to secure. Repeat with remaining two chicken breasts and stuffing. Season chicken roulades with salt and pepper.

Fire up your grill to 350–450°F (180–230°C).

Place chicken roulades onto grill and grill over moderate heat for 25–30 minutes, turning every 5–6 minutes for even grill marks and even cooking. Because the chicken is very thin, it won't take long to grill, so be careful not to overcook. Internal temperature of the chicken should be a minimum of 160°F (70°C). Remove chicken roulades from grill. Remove butcher twine, slice and serve.

GRILLED CHICKEN STUFFED WITH HAVARTI, DATES & HAM

A great way to jazz up chicken breasts is with a flavorful stuffing of Havarti cheese, honey dates and speck ham. Create your own stuffing with a variety of fillings, such as goat's cheese, roasted red pepper and oregano or bacon and cheddar or fig jam and butter. Be the artist of your own flavor combination.

If you wish to use skinless breasts for this recipe, be my guest. I just find that you get a more flavorful and juicy chicken breast with the skin on. Besides that, the crispy skin is so tasty! **SERVES 8**

4 boneless skin-on chicken breasts
   (approx. 6 oz/170 g each)
12 fresh sage leaves
Salt and freshly ground black pepper to taste
½ cup (125 mL) grated Havarti cheese

4 pitted dried dates, chopped
4 slices speck ham
Kosher salt
Drizzle of honey

Lay the chicken breasts skin side down. Remove the tenderloins. Lightly pound the tenderloins flat. Set aside.

Peel up a little edge of the chicken skin. It usually lifts easiest from the thicker portion of the breast. Run your finger under the skin to make a little pocket between the meat and skin. Tuck a few sage leaves under the skin. Pull the skin tight and seal.

Flip the breast over, meat side up. Using a sharp knife, cut a pocket about 1 inch (2.5 cm) deep from the top of the breast to the bottom. Using your fingers, carefully push the meat aside to make a large pocket. Season the chicken inside and out with salt and black pepper. Set aside.

Put the grated Havarti cheese and chopped dates into a bowl. Season with a little black pepper. Mash together to get the mixture to form a sticky cheesy paste.

Divide the stuffing into four equal portions and shape each portion into a firmly packed oval. Wrap each portion in a slice of speck ham. Place one stuffing portion into each chicken cavity. Place flattened tenderloin over the cavity and tuck the tenderloin into the opening, firmly pressing the edges to make a tight seal. Refrigerate for 1 hour to allow the chicken to firm up and cool.

Fire up your grill to 350–450°F (180–230°C). Set grill for both direct and indirect grilling.

Season the outside of the chicken with kosher salt and black pepper. Grill chicken, skin side down, for 3–5 minutes, then carefully turn over and grill for another 3–5 minutes. Move the stuffed chicken breasts to the indirect part of your grill, drizzle with honey and close lid. Grill indirectly with the grill temperature still around 350–450°F (180–230°C) for 10–12 minutes longer or until the chicken is fully cooked and the stuffing is hot, internal temperature minimum 160°F (70°C).

Remove from grill and drizzle with a little extra honey. Slice chicken breasts into two or three pieces and serve.

GRILLED HALF CHICKEN WITH KICK O'HONEY BBQ GLAZE

This has got to be one of my favorite recipes because it consists of crispy skin, a little white meat, a little dark meat, all moist and juicy with a sweet kick and NO bones!

Ask your butcher to split and debone a whole chicken; this will make your job a lot easier. For the glaze, make sure to use a really good full-flavored honey. I recommend orange blossom or buckwheat honey for this recipe. **SERVES 2 TO 4**

4 boneless skin-on half-chickens, skin intact
2 tbsp (30 mL) Bone Dust BBQ Spice (page 212)

KICK O'HONEY BBQ GLAZE
½ cup (125 mL) honey
¼ cup (60 mL) ketchup
2 tsp (10 mL) lemon juice
1 tbsp (15 mL) chopped fresh rosemary
1 tsp (5 mL) Worcestershire sauce
4 cloves garlic, minced
Dash or two of TABASCO® brand Pepper Sauce
Salt and freshly ground black pepper to taste

Season the chicken with Bone Dust BBQ Spice, pressing the seasoning into the meat. Refrigerate, uncovered, for 6–8 hours to allow the seasoning to penetrate the meat and the chicken to air dry. This will make it easier to grill.

To prepare the Kick O'Honey BBQ Glaze, in a small saucepan, whisk together the honey, ketchup, lemon juice, rosemary, Worcestershire sauce, garlic and TABASCO® brand Pepper Sauce. Over medium heat, stirring occasionally, bring the sauce to a boil. Reduce heat to low and simmer for 10 minutes, stirring occasionally. Season with salt and black pepper. Let cool.

Fire up your grill to 350–450°F (180–230°C). Set grill for both direct and indirect grilling.

Grill the chicken, skin side down, for 3–5 minutes, until the skin is lightly charred. Flip it over and continue to grill for another 3–5 minutes. Move the chicken to the indirect part of your grill and close lid. Let it grill-roast for 10–15 minutes, until fully cooked, basting every 5 minutes with the Kick O' Honey BBQ Glaze. Remove chicken from grill.

Slice the chicken into 1-inch (2.5 cm) thick strips or chunks, drizzle with extra glaze and serve immediately.

GRILLED MOJO CHICKEN

I love grilling Cuban style with spiced rum, citrus, garlic and oregano. The key to full flavor is the marinating, firing it over hot coals and basting it with Mojo. It's like living in the islands. Simple and tasty! **SERVES 2 TO 4**

WHAT YOU NEED: Kitchen shears

Zest and juice the oranges, lemon and limes into a large bowl. Throw in the juiced fruit rinds too. It's all flavor! Add the garlic, spiced rum, oregano, salt, cumin and black pepper. Add a pinch of cinnamon and mix. Divide the mixture into two equal parts. Set aside.

Using a pair of kitchen shears, cut the chicken in half and remove the backbone. Place the two halves into a large self-sealing bag. Pour in half of the marinade and seal bag. Refrigerate for 24 hours, turning occasionally to marinate evenly.

Fire up your grill to 350–450°F (180–230°C). Set grill for both direct and indirect grilling.

Take the other half of the marinade and add the honey, whisk and set aside.

Remove the chicken from the marinade, discarding leftover marinade. Pat chicken halves dry with paper towels. Season chickens with a little salt and black pepper. Place the chicken halves onto the grill, cavity side down, and grill for 15–18 minutes, lid open; watch it grill nice and easy. Not too hot. No basting yet. Flip chicken halves over onto the skin side and continue grilling for 10–15 minutes longer, basting liberally with the Mojo Marinade. Baste away and watch the sizzle. Enjoy the smell of sweetness from the grill. This is the fun part of cooking. When the chicken is fully cooked, internal temperature of 160°F (70°C) and the skin is sticky and crisp, remove from grill and allow it to rest for 5 minutes. Portion and serve immediately.

MOJO MARINADE

6 juicy oranges, approx. 2 cups (500 mL) juice

1 juicy lemon, approx. ½ cup (125 mL) juice

4 juicy limes, approx. ½ cup (125 mL) juice

24 cloves garlic, minced

¼ cup (60 mL) spiced rum

¼ cup (60 mL) fresh oregano, chopped

1 tsp (5 mL) kosher salt

½ teaspoon (2 mL) ground cumin

½ teaspoon (2 mL) freshly ground black pepper

Pinch of ground cinnamon

4 tbsp (60 mL) honey

1 whole chicken (approx. 4 lb/1.8 g)

Salt and freshly ground black pepper to taste

SLASH & GRILL CHICKEN DRUMS

This is an at-the-beach favorite for my family. Slash the drumsticks with a blade, rub 'em with Bone Dust BBQ Spice, grill 'em with love, glaze 'em for the sticky and toss 'em in crushed BBQ potato chips for the crunch. This makes these drumsticks rock and roll. **SERVES 6**

12 chicken drumsticks, nice and
    plump and meaty
2 tbsp (30 mL) Bone Dust BBQ
    Spice (page 212)
2 tbsp (30 mL) TABASCO®
    Chipotle Sauce
2 tbsp (30 mL) icing sugar
2 tbsp (30 mL) your favorite
    gourmet-style barbeque sauce
    (I use my Crazy Canuck Sticky
    Chicken and Rib BBQ Sauce)
1 oz (30 mL) Red Stag by Jim Beam
3 tbsp (45 mL) butter
2 cups (500 ml) coarsely crushed
    BBQ-flavored potato chips

Take a sharp knife and slash the outside of the chicken drumsticks, about ¼ to ½ inch (0.5 to 1 cm) deep at most. Rub Bone Dust BBQ Spice into the drums, making sure to rub it into the slashes. Let marinate in the rub for at least an hour. If you can go overnight, the flavor intensifies.

Fire up your grill to 350–450°F (180–230°C).

In a small bowl, whisk together the TABASCO® Chipotle Sauce, icing sugar, barbeque sauce and black cherry bourbon. Stir it until the sugar is dissolved and set aside.

Grill chicken drums for 20–25 minutes, turning frequently, until the drums are nicely charred and fully cooked but still moist and tender. Minimum internal temperature of 160°F (70°C) should be reached.

Place all the drumsticks into a large bowl. Add the butter and chipotle–black cherry bourbon mixture. Toss. Add the crushed BBQ potato chips and toss again. Serve immediately.

WASABI HONEY TERIYAKI GRILLED CHICKEN THIGHS

This is a pretty quick and easy recipe to do. It's perfect for that in-a-hurry weeknight dinner. Serve this over a bowl of rice with some steamed broccoli and you can feed the clan in no time at all. **SERVES 6**

2 tsp (10 mL) wasabi powder
2 tsp (10 mL) freshly squeezed
    lemon juice
1 oz (30 mL) sake
½ cup (125 mL) honey
1 tbsp (15 mL) soy sauce
3 tbsp (45 mL) hoisin sauce
1 tsp (5 mL) prepared horseradish,
    drained of excess moisture
1 tsp (5 mL) minced ginger
1 green onion, minced
12 boneless skinless chicken thighs
Kosher salt and freshly ground black
    pepper to taste
Pinch of cinnamon
¼ cup (60 mL) crushed wasabi peas
1 tsp (5 mL) toasted sesame seeds
1 tbsp (15 mL) chopped fresh cilantro

Place the wasabi powder into a small bowl and drizzle with the lemon juice and sake. Stir in honey, soy sauce, hoisin sauce, horseradish, ginger and green onion.

Fire up your grill to 450–550°F (230–290°C).

Season both sides of the thighs with kosher salt, black pepper and a pinch of cinnamon.

Grill the thighs for 6–8 minutes on one side, turn the thighs over and begin to baste with the wasabi honey baste. Continue to cook for another 6–8 minutes, basting with the sauce until fully cooked, minimum internal temperature 160°F (70°C). Remove from grill.

Sprinkle with crushed wasabi peas, toasted sesame seeds and fresh cilantro. Serve immediately.

X FACTOR CHICKEN STEAKS WITH WHISKEY GRILLED ONIONS

"X Factor" is for the skewers that you use to add stability to the chicken thighs while they grill. It makes them easier to flip. **SERVES 6**

WHAT YOU NEED: Twenty-four 6-inch (15 cm) bamboo skewers, soaked in water for a minimum of 1 hour, or metal skewers

8 boneless chicken thighs

3 + 2 tbsp (90 mL) Bone Dust BBQ Spice (page 212)

1 large red onion, sliced into rings

1 large white onion

1 large sweet yellow onion (Vidalia or Maui or Texas Sweets)

Drizzle of olive oil

Drizzle of Maker's Mark bourbon

1 cup (250 mL) your favorite gourmet-style barbeque sauce (I use my Crazy Canuck Sticky Chicken and Rib BBQ Sauce).

2 cups (500 mL) kettle-cooked sour cream and onion potato chips

2 tbsp (30 mL) chopped fresh chives

Rub chicken with about 3 tbsp (60 mL) Bone Dust BBQ Spice, pressing the spices into the meat. Skewer each thigh with two skewers in an X pattern. This will keep the chicken flat during grilling. Set aside, keeping refrigerated.

Fire up your grill to 450–550°F (230–290°C).

Slice the onions into rings and place in a large bowl. Season with about 2 tbsp (30 mL) Bone Dust BBQ Spice, olive oil and a drizzle of bourbon. Mix.

Grill onions for 6–8 minutes per side, until lightly charred and tender. Put the onions in a bowl. Drizzle with a little more bourbon. Drizzle in a little bit of your favorite barbeque sauce and set aside, keeping warm.

Brush the chicken steaks with a little oil. Grill steaks, starting skin side down, for 6–8 minutes per side, until fully cooked (internal temperature minimum 160°F/70°C) and the skin is crisp. Baste with your favorite barbeque sauce after the flip. Remove chicken steaks from the grill. Remove X skewers and set aside until needed.

Crush the sour cream and onion potato chips and sprinkle over the grilled onions, add chives and mix it up. Place a mound of grilled onions on top of each grilled chicken thigh and serve.

GRILL-BLACKENED TURKEY TENDERLOINS WITH CELERY BLUE CHEESE SALAD

When it comes to turkey, I tend to think a whole turkey is a lot of meat to grill. But I do crave turkey every so often, and instead of a whole bird, I have found turkey tenderloin. The tenderloins from a turkey can be as large as a whole chicken breast and grill just as easily and quickly. No more having to wait 5 hours for a roasted turkey; you can have it hot off the grill in about 20 minutes. **SERVES 4**

WHAT YOU NEED: Injection syringe; Cookie sheet, lined with parchment paper

In a small pot, melt the butter. Add TABASCO® brand Pepper Sauce to taste and stir. Place the needle of the injection syringe into the melted butter mixture. Pull up on the plunger to fill the chamber. Take the needle of the syringe and insert into the middle of a turkey tenderloin. Inject about 1 oz (30 mL) of hot butter into each tenderloin. Brush each tenderloin with melted butter mixture and roll in Cajun Rub, making sure to cover the entire tenderloin. Place on prepared cookie sheet and refrigerate to allow the butter to harden.

Meanwhile, make the Celery Blue Cheese Salad by combining chopped celery, red onion, crumbled blue cheese, mayonnaise and parsley in a bowl. Season to taste with a little lemon juice, salt and black pepper. Set aside, keeping cool.

Fire up your grill to 450–550°F (230–290°C).

Place the spiced injected tenderloins directly onto the hot grill and char the outside to blacken the spices, about 6–8 minutes. Watch for flare-ups as the butter injection melts and oozes. Flip the tenderloins over and continue to grill for another 6–8 minutes, until the tenderloins are fully cooked, internal temperature of 160°F (70°C).

At the same time as you are grilling the turkey, grill the apple wedges for about 10 minutes, turning occasionally, until lightly charred yet still a little bit firm. Drizzle with honey and season with salt and black pepper. Remove both the tenderloins and the apples from the grill.

Slice the turkey tenderloins on the bias and serve with a spoonful of Celery Blue Cheese Salad and couple of wedges of grilled apple.

1 cup (250 mL) melted butter
1 to 2 tsp (5 to 10 mL) TABASCO® brand Pepper Sauce
4 turkey breast tenderloins
½ cup (125 mL) Cajun Rub (page 213)

CELERY BLUE CHEESE SALAD
2 stalks crisp celery, chopped
½ cup (125 mL) red onion, diced
½ cup (125 mL) blue cheese, crumbled
2 tbsp (30 mL) mayonnaise
¼ cup (60 mL) Italian (flat-leaf) parsley leaves
1 tsp (5 mL) freshly squeezed lemon juice
Salt and freshly ground black pepper to taste

2 tart crisp apples, quartered
Drizzle of honey

TED'S TIP
Keep the tenderloins icy cold so that when the butter is injected into the meat it begins to harden.

GRILLED DUCK BREASTS WITH STRAWBERRY RHUBARB ICE WINE JAM

I buy my duck at Black Angus Fine Meats & Game — the breasts are always nice and plump. Duck is best served rare or medium-rare. Be careful not to overcook it, or it will be tough. **SERVES 4**

2 fresh duck breasts (approx. 8 to 10 oz/225 to 285 g each)
2 tbsp (30 mL) Steak Spice (page 169)

STRAWBERRY RHUBARB ICE WINE JAM
2 tbsp (30 mL) grapeseed oil
¼ cup (60 mL) finely chopped sweet onion
1 tbsp (15 mL) minced fresh ginger
3 stalks rhubarb
1 cup (250 mL) fresh strawberries, hulled and chopped
½ cup (125 mL) ice wine
1 vanilla bean, split lengthwise
¼ cup (60 mL) white sugar
¼ cup (60 mL) honey
¼ cup (60 mL) champagne vinegar
1 tsp (5 mL) cold butter

TED'S TIP
While grilling the duck, if flare-ups occur, reduce grill heat and move duck so it is not directly over the flames.

Using a sharp knife, score the skin side of the duck breasts in a diamond pattern, slicing about ¼ inch (5 mm) deep into the fat. Season the duck breasts with the Steak Spice, pressing the seasoning into the meat. Set aside.

To prepare the Strawberry Rhubarb Ice Wine Jam, heat the grapeseed oil in a medium frying pan over medium-high heat until hot but not smoking. Add the onion and ginger; sauté for 1–2 minutes, stirring, until tender. Add the rhubarb and cook, stirring, until the rhubarb is a bit browned and smoky. Add in the strawberries. Deglaze with the ice wine. Add the vanilla bean, sugar, honey and vinegar. Bring to a boil, stirring. Reduce heat to low and simmer for 5–10 minutes, stirring occasionally, until the mixture is a little thick and sticky. Remove from heat, stir in the cold butter and set aside, keeping warm.

Fire up your grill to 350–450°F (180–230°C). You will need to have your grill set for direct and then indirect grilling.

Take a sheet of aluminum foil and fold it in half. Fold over the edges to secure the folded sheet together. Place square of foil onto your grill directly over the fire and poke a few holes in it, not too many, 8 or 9 should do. Use a wooden skewer or toothpick to do this.

Remove duck from marinade, discarding leftover marinade. Pat the duck breast with paper towels to remove excess moisture. Place the duck skin side down onto the sheet of foil, with the lid open, and sear the duck breast for 2–4 minutes, until the skin gets a little crispy and the knife slits open up and begin to blister. Turn the duck breasts over, close lid and allow the breasts to roast for about 5 minutes. Not too long, as you do not want to overcook them. Remove duck from the grill and allow it to rest, lightly tented with aluminum foil, for 5 minutes.

Using a sharp knife, slice across the breast in thin slices. The duck should be medium-rare. Spoon over the Strawberry Rhubarb Ice Wine Jam and serve.

X FACTOR GAME HENS WITH ORANGE BUTTER BASTE

Butterflying a game hen allows for quick and easy grilling. The "X Factor" skewers make it easy to flip and provide even grilling. **SERVES 2 TO 4**

WHAT YOU NEED: Poultry shears; 4 long hardwood skewers (approx. 8 to 10 inches/20 to 25 cm long); 1 bunch fresh rosemary, for basting (optional)

Using poultry shears, split each Cornish hen down the middle on each side of the backbone to remove the backbone. Using a sharp knife, carefully debone the breast and legs. Lay the flattened chicken skin side down. Skewer the hens in an X pattern. This will give stability to your hens when grilling and make them easier to flip.

In a glass dish large enough to hold the hens, combine the oranges, onion, olive oil, rosemary, ginger, mustard seeds, black pepper, white wine and the first 2 oz (60 mL) of orange liqueur. Add the X factor hens, turning to coat. Refrigerate, meat side down, and marinate for 4 hours.

Fire up your grill to 350–450°F (180–230°C). You will need to have your grill set for direct and then indirect grilling.

In a bowl, whisk together the other 2 oz (60 mL) of orange liqueur, melted butter and icing sugar. Set aside.

Remove hens from the marinade, discarding marinade and patting dry of excess marinade with paper towels. Season on both sides with kosher salt and black pepper. Grill hens, skin side down, for a few minutes, until the skin is lightly charred but not burned. Turn hens over and continue to grill for a few minutes more to sear. Move the hens to an indirect part of the grill and close lid. Maintaining a temperature of about 350–450°F (180–230°C), roast the hens for 25–30 minutes, basting every 5 minutes with the orange butter glaze, until the hens are fully cooked (minimal internal temperature of 160°F/70°C). When the hens are just finished, squeeze a fresh orange over top and garnish with leaves of fresh rosemary. Remove hens from grill and serve immediately.

2 Cornish game hens
2 oranges, thinly sliced
¼ cup (60 mL) onion, thinly sliced
2 tbsp (30 mL) olive oil
1 tbsp (15 mL) chopped fresh rosemary
2 tsp (10 mL) chopped fresh ginger
1 tbsp (15 mL) mustard seeds
1 tbsp (15 mL) cracked black pepper
½ cup (125 mL) white wine
2 + 2 oz (120 mL) orange liqueur
¼ cup (60 mL) melted butter
2 tbsp (30 mL) icing sugar
Kosher salt and freshly ground black pepper to taste

GARNISH

1 orange, halved
Fresh rosemary leaves

TED'S TIP
Use a bunch of rosemary as your basting brush for a burst of flavor.

X FACTOR PEPPERED QUAIL WITH RASPBERRY SYRUP

Ask your butcher to butterfly and remove the backbone of the quail. Quails are small; one is fine as an appetizer, but allow two per person for a main course. The syrup is also delicious drizzled on the Grilled Pound Cake (page 360). **SERVES 2 TO 6**

WHAT YOU NEED: 12 metal or bamboo skewers (approx. 8 inches/20 cm long)

RASPBERRY SYRUP

1 pint (2 cups/500 mL) raspberries

½ cup (125 mL) white sugar

¼ cup (60 mL) pure maple syrup

3 tbsp (45 mL) water

2 tsp (10 mL) balsamic syrup or glaze

2 tsp (10 mL) raspberry wine vinegar

2 to 3 tsp (10 to 15 mL) cold butter

6 quails, butterflied

Drizzle of walnut oil

Kosher salt and freshly ground black pepper to taste

¼ cup (60 mL) crushed toasted walnuts

1 tbsp (15 mL) chopped fresh sage

To make the Raspberry Syrup, combine the raspberries, sugar, maple syrup, water, balsamic glaze and raspberry vinegar in a small saucepan. Bring to a boil, stirring, reduce heat to low and simmer for 10 minutes. Purée mixture in a blender. Strain through a fine-mesh sieve to remove seeds. Return syrup to pot and over low heat stir in the cold butter a teaspoon (5 mL) at a time until combined. Set aside, keeping warm.

Skewer the butterflied quails in an X pattern. Brush with a little walnut oil. Rub quails on both sides with kosher salt and black pepper.

Fire up your grill to 550–650°F (290–345°C).

Grill quails for 2–3 minutes per side, until the quails are just cooked, basting after the first turn with Raspberry Syrup. Don't overcook the quail, as it will be very dry. A little more medium to medium-rare doneness is preferred. Remove quail from grill. Brush with a little extra Raspberry Syrup. Sprinkle with crushed toasted walnuts and fresh sage. Serve immediately.

FISH & SHELLFISH

CHAR-GRILLED SALMON WITH GRAPEFRUIT MAPLE BUTTER SAUCE

Be careful not to overcook the salmon. I find it cooked to an internal temperature of 145–150°F (63–65°C) is perfect. It's gastrolicious! **SERVES 4**

WHAT YOU NEED: Sharp-edged spatula

Fire up your grill to 450–550°F (230–290°C).

To make the marinade, zest one of the red grapefruit and place zest into a bowl. Set aside.

Cut all red grapefruit in half and place on hot grill cut side down. Grill for 8–10 minutes, until the cut side is charred and the grapefruit is hot. Remove from grill and allow the char-grilled grapefruit halves to cool slightly, cut side up so you don't lose those precious juices. Squeeze the juice into the bowl with the zest. You need about 1 cup (250 mL) juice. Add maple syrup, a big splash of wine, shallots, dill and mustard. Add a little drizzle of olive oil and season to taste with a little bit of black pepper. Stir to combine.

Place the salmon evenly in a shallow dish large enough to hold it in one layer. Pour half of the marinade over the salmon, turning to coat. Marinate for 30 minutes, turning once to promote even marinating.

Place the remaining marinade in a small saucepan and warm it over medium-low heat. Stir in the maple butter and continue to heat. Peel 1 grapefruit, cut the segments from the membranes and place segments into pot. Set aside, keeping warm.

Remove salmon from marinade, discarding leftover marinade. Pat dry with paper towels. Brush salmon all over with a little bit of olive oil. Season salmon all over with black pepper. On a well-seasoned grill, grill the salmon for 4–5 minutes per side or until just cooked through and the salmon easily flakes with a fork.

While the salmon is grilling, cut the last grapefruit in half and grill it cut side down. When the salmon is cooked, squeeze the char-grilled grapefruit halves over the salmon. Add butter to grapefruit maple sauce, stirring until the butter is melted and combined. Spoon sauce over salmon. Serve immediately.

GRAPEFRUIT MAPLE MARINADE

4 ruby red juicy grapefruit
½ cup (125 mL) pure maple syrup
Big splash of Creekside Estates Riesling (approx. ¼ cup/60 mL)
2 shallots, minced
2 tbsp (30 mL) chopped fresh dill
2 tbsp (30 mL) whole-grain mustard
Drizzle of olive oil
Freshly ground black pepper to taste

4 fresh salmon fillets (approx. 6 oz/170 g each), skinned
1 tbsp (15 mL) maple butter
2 ruby red grapefruit
2 tsp (10 mL) cold butter

TED'S TIP
Maple butter can be found in specialty food stores and farmer's markets.

CINNAMON-SKEWERED SCALLOPS WITH BROWN SUGAR BASTING BUTTER

A recipe like this, made for the right mate, could turn an evening dinner into an all-night love affair. **SERVES 4**

WHAT YOU NEED: 4 cinnamon sticks (approx. 4 to 6 inches/10 to 15 cm long)

BROWN SUGAR BASTING BUTTER

½ cup (125 mL) butter, softened

2 tbsp (30 mL) brown sugar

2 tbsp (30 mL) orange juice

3 tbsp (45 mL) chopped golden raisins

½ tsp (1 mL) chopped fresh thyme

2 drizzles of spiced rum

Sea salt and freshly ground black pepper to taste

12 jumbo diver scallops, U10 size

2 ripe peaches

TED'S TIP

- When using cinnamon sticks as skewers, you want to use a stick where the cinnamon bark is tightly rolled and hard.
- Large plump scallops that are thick through the middle are best for this recipe.

In a small saucepot, combine the butter, brown sugar, orange juice, raisins and thyme. Add a splash of spiced rum and season to taste with a little sea salt and black pepper. Warm over low heat, stirring occasionally, until the butter is melted. Keep warm.

Take a paring knife and whittle one end of the cinnamon stick into a bit of a point. Repeat with remaining sticks. Skewer 3 scallops onto each cinnamon stick. Season with sea salt and black pepper on both sides, brush with a little melted butter mixture and refrigerate to keep cool and allow the butter to firm up.

Fire up your grill to 550–650°F (290–345°C).

Cut the peaches in half and remove the pit. Slash the flesh of each peach half about ½ inch (1 cm) deep. Drizzle the cuts with spiced rum and season with a little salt and pepper to taste. Grill peaches, cut side down, for 4–6 minutes, until lightly charred. Turn them over and continue to grill until the skin is lightly charred and it looks like it is separating from the flesh. Remove, peel and set aside, keeping warm.

When the peaches are just about ready, grill the scallops directly over the fire for 3–5 minutes per side, basting after the flip with warm brown sugar butter. Cook until the scallops are lightly charred, opaque and just cooked through. Remove from grill and drizzle with a little more of the brown sugar butter. Serve immediately with grilled peach halves.

CRAZY LOBSTER TAILS

I call this recipe Crazy Lobster Tails because I'm crazy for lobster! Warm water lobster tails stuffed with crab and artichoke dip, wrapped in a chicken tenderloin and then in bacon . . . Yum! Yes, double meat wrapped and stuffed with seafood. Two shellfish, two meats . . . how bad can it be! It's pure decadence and worth every penny. Make these superstars for your next backyard blitz. **SERVES 4**

WHAT YOU NEED: Kitchen shears; Meat mallet; Maple grilling plank (12 × 8 × ½ inches/30 × 20 × 1 cm), soaked in water for a minimum of 1 hour

Using a pair of kitchen shears, cut the shell of the lobster tail. Peel the shell away from the flesh. Discard shells and rinse lobster tails under cold water. Pat dry with paper towels. Butterfly the lobster tail meat by using a sharp knife to cut down the middle of the tail lengthwise, about three-quarters of the way through. Using your fingers, spread the tail apart to flatten slightly. Take the tip of the knife and, starting at the top of one side of the tail, cut a pocket into the side walls of the tail to make a pocket for stuffing.

To make the stuffing, mix together the crabmeat, cream cheese, mozzarella cheese, artichoke hearts, breadcrumbs, shallots, cilantro and lemon juice and season to taste with sea salt and black pepper. Scoop about one-quarter of the stuffing mixture into the cavity of each lobster tail, pressing the stuffing gently but firmly.

In between two sheets of plastic wrap, gently pound the chicken tenderloins until flat. Lay two chicken tenderloins over top of the stuffing, tip to tail.

Next take a slice of smoked bacon and lay it flat on a cutting board. Run your fingers along the surface of the bacon, stretching to increase its length by about 50%. Starting at the tail end, wrap the entire stuffed tail in bacon, overlapping slightly with each pass around the tail. You may need a couple of slices of bacon. Repeat with remaining stuffed tails and bacon. Place tails on soaked grilling plank.

Fire up your grill to 350–450°F (180–230°C).

Place plank onto grill and close lid. When plank starts to crackle, turn heat down to medium-low. Plank stuffed lobster tails for 20–30 minutes, until the bacon is crisp and the stuffing hot. Remove plank from grill and serve immediately.

4 warm-water lobster tails (approx. 4 oz/115 g each), thawed and drained

LOBSTER STUFFING

½ cup (125 mL) lump crabmeat

¼ cup (60 mL) cream cheese, softened

¼ cup (60 mL) mozzarella cheese

½ cup (125 mL) artichoke hearts, drained and coarsely chopped

¼ cup (60 mL) panko breadcrumbs

2 small shallots, minced

1 tbsp (15 mL) chopped fresh cilantro

1 tsp (5 mL) freshly squeezed lemon juice

Sea salt and freshly ground black pepper to taste

8 chicken tenderloins

8 to 12 slices smoked bacon

GRILLED BACON-WRAPPED SARDINES

If you make this recipe, you will feel as though you are on vacation in Italy, eating items that you may not always have a chance to. It's about romancing your grill. Buy fresh sardines about 6 inches (15 cm) in length for this recipe. You can also substitute young herring or sprat. **SERVES 4**

8 fresh whole sardines, cleaned

1 tbsp (15 mL) olive oil

Sea salt and freshly ground black pepper to taste

8 slices double-smoked bacon, thinly sliced

8 large sprigs fresh rosemary

8 slices rustic bread

2 to 3 cloves garlic

Drizzle of extra virgin olive oil

1 juicy lemon, halved

Drizzle of aged balsamic vinegar

Rinse sardines under cold water and pat dry with paper towels. Brush both sides of sardines with a little olive oil and season with sea salt and black pepper. Tightly wrap 1 slice of double-smoked bacon around each sardine, leaving head and tail exposed. Repeat with remaining sardines and double-smoked bacon.

Fire up your grill to 450–550°F (230–290°C).

Place the sardines onto the grill and cover each sardine with a sprig of fresh rosemary. This will smoke and burn as the sardines grill and add rosemary essence into the sardines. Grill for 8–10 minutes per side, until bacon is crisp and the sardines are hot and cooked through.

At the same time as the sardines are grilling, toast the rustic bread on the grill until browned on both sides. Rub a raw clove of garlic over the surface of the toasted bread, drizzle with olive oil and set aside.

Grill the lemon halves, cut side down. Squeeze the grilled lemon over top of the grilling sardines. Remove from grill; drizzle sardines with olive oil and aged balsamic vinegar.

To eat, unwrap the bacon from the grilled sardine. Carefully remove the grilled flesh from the bones and place on toast with the bacon and munch on!

GRILLED FOIL-POUCHED PICKEREL WITH BLUEBERRY PEPPER BUTTER

A quick and easy way to grill delicate fish is inside an aluminum foil pouch. Guaranteed never to have your fish stick to your grill. **SERVES 6**

WHAT YOU NEED: 6 sheets (12 × 24 inches/30 × 60 cm each) heavy-duty aluminum foil

Place the soft butter, blueberries, pepper and thyme in a bowl. Drizzle over a little bourbon. Mix until well combined. Set aside.

Season each pickerel fillet with sea salt and black pepper.

Divide blueberry mixture into 2 equal portions. Reserve one half for garnish.

Fold each sheet of aluminum foil in half to make a 12-inch (30 cm) square. Smear about 2 tsp (10 mL) of blueberry mixture onto the center, leaving a good margin around the edges of each square of foil. Fold over the foil and crimp the edges to seal very tight. Keep the butter side down and the fish side up. Repeat with remaining ingredients.

Fire up your grill to 350–450°F (180–230°C).

Place pouches butter side down onto the grill. Grill pouches for 12–15 minutes. Do not flip. Transfer pouches to plates and carefully open. Garnish with another dollop of warm blueberry butter and serve immediately.

1 stick (4 oz/115 g) unsalted butter, softened
½ cup (125 mL) fresh or frozen wild blueberries
1 tsp (5 mL) cracked black pepper
1 tsp (5 mL) chopped fresh thyme
Drizzle of Red Stag by Jim Beam
6 pickerel fillets (approx. 6 oz/170 g each)
Sea salt and freshly ground black pepper to taste

TED'S TIP
Mashed potatoes and some grilled asparagus are the perfect side dishes to serve alongside this delicious fish dish.

GRILLED FROG LEGS WITH FROG SAUCE

I am lucky enough to be able to find fresh frog legs in the seafood section of an Asian specialty food store. But when you can't find fresh, seek out frozen frogs legs. They do taste a bit like chicken, and they grill similarly too. This recipe is loaded with garlic, butter, Dijon mustard, fresh tarragon and of course my favorite — beer! It's all in the Frog Sauce, baby! **SERVES 4**

8 cloves garlic, minced

¼ tsp (1 mL) freshly ground black pepper

¼ tsp (1 mL) sea salt

1 tbsp (15 mL) chopped fresh tarragon

1 tbsp (15 mL) honey

¼ cup (60 mL) Dijon mustard

¼ cup (60 mL) Leffe Blonde

1 tbsp (15 mL) olive oil

¼ cup (60 mL) melted butter

8 pairs fresh or thawed frozen frog legs

Sea salt and freshly ground pepper to taste

Sprinkle of freshly grated Parmesan cheese

In a small saucepot, whisk together the garlic, ¼ tsp (1 mL) black pepper, ¼ tsp (1 mL) salt, tarragon, honey, mustard, beer, olive oil and melted butter. Set aside, keeping warm.

Rinse the frog legs under cold running water and pat dry with paper towels. Season the frog legs with sea salt and black pepper on all sides.

Fire up your grill to 450–550°F (230–290°C).

Grill frog legs, basting with sauce, until meat is firm and opaque, about 5–6 minutes per side. Before removing from the grill, baste one more time with Dijon-beer baste and sprinkle with Parmesan cheese. Remove from grill. Grab a leg with each hand and pull apart.

This recipe is definitely meant to be eaten with your hands.

GRILLED HALIBUT STEAKS WITH GREEN GRAPE & AVOCADO BUTTER SAUCE

When I visit my local fishmonger, I look to see what looks freshest and tastiest. I want to be inspired by the atmosphere of the fish shop. It's a chef thing. I shop with my eyes fueled by my passion for food. **SERVES 4**

WHAT YOU NEED: Sharp-edged spatula

In a glass dish large enough to hold the fish, whisk together the grape juice, olive oil, parsley, black pepper, mustard powder, shallots, green onions, jalapeño and sea salt. Add halibut, turning to coat. Cover and marinate at room temperature for about 30 minutes.

Fire up your grill to 450–550°F (230–290°C).

Remove halibut from marinade, discarding leftover marinade. Brush halibut with a little olive oil on both sides. Season with salt and black pepper.

Grill halibut for 6–8 minutes per side, until just cooked through and the fish easily flakes with a fork.

While the halibut is grilling, prepare the Green Grape & Avocado Butter Sauce. In a small saucepan over medium-high heat, melt 2 tbsp (30 mL) of the butter. Sauté the shallots and garlic for 2 minutes or until tender. Add the grape juice and wine. Bring to a boil and reduce the liquid by half. Gently stir in the grapes and heat, stirring, for a couple of minutes. Add avocado and parsley. Reduce heat to low and stir in the cubed butter until melted and incorporated. Remove from heat and season to taste with a little sea salt and black pepper.

When the halibut is cooked, squeeze a little lemon over top. Serve with Green Grape & Avocado Butter Sauce.

1 cup (250 mL) white grape juice
2 tbsp (30 mL) olive oil
2 tbsp (30 mL) chopped
    fresh parsley
1 tsp (5 mL) cracked black pepper
1 tsp (5 mL) mustard powder
2 shallots, finely chopped
2 green onions, finely chopped
1 jalapeño pepper, finely chopped
Sea salt to taste
4 halibut fillets (approx.
    6 oz/170 g each)
1 lemon, halved
Salt and freshly ground pepper
    to taste

GREEN GRAPE & AVOCADO BUTTER SAUCE

2 + 4 tbsp (90 mL) cold butter,
    4 tbsp (60 mL) cut into cubes
4 shallots, chopped
2 cloves garlic, chopped
½ cup (125 mL) white grape juice
¼ cup (60 mL) Creekside Estates
    Riesling
1 cup (250 mL) seedless green
    grapes, cut in half
1 avocado, diced
1 tbsp (15 mL) chopped fresh parsley
Sea salt and freshly ground black
    pepper to taste

Lemon wedges

GRILL-ROASTED ARCTIC CHAR WITH ONION, PEAR & SAGE STUFFING

If you have important guests coming for dinner, this recipe will give them the wow factor. **SERVES 4**

WHAT YOU NEED: Butcher twine

2 leeks, trimmed, leaves separated and washed
  (16 leaves needed)
1 pear
1 sweet onion, thinly sliced into rings
½ cup (125 mL) fresh sage leaves
Pinch of ground cinnamon

Pinch of cayenne pepper
Sea salt and freshly ground black pepper to taste
1 orange, halved
1 tbsp (15 mL) melted butter
2 arctic char fillets (approx. 8 oz/225 g each), skin on
4 to 5 slices bacon

In a pot of boiling water, blanch the leek leaves for 1 minute or until tender and bright. Cool in ice water. Drain on paper towels.

Using a sharp knife, slice the pear into thin slices, cutting from the top of the pear to the bottom so that you get a cross-section of pear. Remove seeds. Place in a bowl. Add sliced onions and sage leaves and season with a little pinch of cinnamon, cayenne pepper, sea salt and black pepper. Squeeze the orange halves over top. Add melted butter and mix well. Set aside.

Using a sheet of plastic wrap a little longer than each of the fish fillets, lay 6 to 8 pieces of blanched leek onto the plastic, slightly overlapping. Place 1 fillet of arctic char, skin side down, crosswise across the middle of the leeks. Season the char fillet with a little salt and black pepper. Spread the stuffing mixture over the entire surface of the char.

Season the second fillet of arctic char with a little salt and black pepper. Lay fillet skin side up on the onion-pear stuffing. Starting on the edge closest to you, roll the leeks around the fish to make a tight leek wrap.

Next run your fingers along the top side of the bacon, pressing firmly to stretch the slice of bacon by about 25%. Wrap the bacon around the leek in three separate bands, leaving a swatch of leek in between. Cut 3 to 5 strips of butcher twine, each about 10 to 12 inches (25 to 30 cm) in length. Wrap one string around one strip of bacon and tie tightly around the fish bundle. Repeat with other strips of bacon and add a couple more if necessary. You don't want this bundle to fall apart. Cover and refrigerate to rest for 1 hour.

Fire up your grill to 350–450°F (180–230°C).

Place the fish bundle onto the grill directly over the heat. Grill for 10–12 minutes with the lid open, watching for flare-ups, until the bacon starts to crisp and you can see some juices come from the fish. Using spatula, carefully turn fish over. Reduce grill heat and close lid. Continue to grill for another 10–15 minutes, until the bacon is crisp and the fish is just cooked through; ensure the stuffing is hot. Use a small metal skewer to test for doneness. Poke it in, and if it comes out hot, it's ready to go!

Remove from grill. Remove butcher twine. Slice stuffed char into 2-inch (5 cm) thick slices. Serve immediately.

GRILLED SKATE WING WITH BAY SCALLOPS & CAPERS

One of my favorite things about skate besides its delicate flavor is that it has no bones. The pectoral wings are made up of cartilage. Do not fillet the skate wings before grilling, as it makes it harder to grill. Reminds me of what my mom says, "House guests are like fish, they begin to smell after three days." With fish, my rule is buy it today, grill it today. **SERVES 2 TO 4**

WHAT YOU NEED: Grill basket; Nonstick cooking spray; Sharp-edged, flexible spatula

Rinse the skate wing under cold running water and pat dry with paper towels. Mix the olive oil, garlic and sea salt to taste and rub all over the skate wing. Refrigerate for 20 minutes.

Fire up your grill to 450–550°F (230–290°C).

Spray your grill basket with nonstick cooking spray. Lay the skate wing into the grill basket and close basket lid. Grill for 5–6 minutes per side, until the flesh is opaque but still moist and juicy. The flesh should flake easily from the cartilage.

While the skate is grilling, heat a frying pan over medium-high heat. Use a side burner or stovetop or even the grill, but get that pan hot. Add the 2 tbsp (30 mL) butter and fry the scallops for 1–2 minutes, shaking the pan to keep the scallops from sticking. Grate a little lemon zest over the scallops as they fry, and while you are at it, a little over the skate as it grills too. Squeeze the lemon juice into the pan, and don't forget about half a lemon for the skate. Add a few teaspoons (10 to 15 mL) cold butter and the capers and stir until melted. Season scallops to taste with sea salt and black pepper and the fresh chives. Set aside, keeping warm.

Remove skate from grill. Carefully open grill basket and lift the skate out. Carefully cut the cooked skate flesh from the cartilage. You'll need to be careful, as it will be a little delicate. Use the sharp-edged, flexible spatula to help lift the skate from the cartilage. Transfer to a serving platter. Spoon bay scallop lemon butter over top and serve.

1 skinless fresh skate wing (approx. 2 lb/900 g), not filleted

1 tbsp (15 mL) olive oil

4 cloves garlic, minced

Sea salt and freshly ground black pepper to taste

2 tbsp (30 mL) butter

1 to 1½ lb (450 to 675 g) fresh bay scallops, drained of excess moisture and patted dry with paper towels

2 juicy lemons

3 tsp (15 ml) butter, cold and cut into pieces

2 tsp (10 mL) capers

¼ cup (60 mL) chopped fresh chives

TED'S TIP

When shopping for skate wing, if it smells like ammonia, it's not that fresh. Remember, fresh fish has no odor.

GRILLED SQUID WITH GRILLED PROSCIUTTO-WRAPPED RADICCHIO & CAPER BALSAMIC SAUCE

There is more time here in the preparation of the squid than in the actual grilling. For me, the key to making squid taste not so rubber band–like is to first marinate the fresh squid in buttermilk and then second to grill it quickly. High heat, grill lid open, direct heat, fast grilling time and take it to the plate. **SERVES 6**

6 fresh squid (approx. 6 to 8 oz/170 to 225 g each)
1 cup (250 mL) buttermilk
Sea salt and freshly ground black pepper to taste

SQUID MARINADE

4 cloves garlic, minced
2 tbsp (30 mL) olive oil
¼ cup (60 mL) aged balsamic vinegar
2 tbsp (30 mL) roughly chopped fresh oregano

PROSCIUTTO-WRAPPED RADICCHIO

1 medium head radicchio
Drizzle of olive oil
Drizzle of aged balsamic vinegar
Salt and freshly ground black pepper to taste
6 slices prosciutto

CAPER BALSAMIC SAUCE

5 tbsp (75 mL) butter
4 cloves garlic, minced
4 shallots, finely diced
½ cup (125 mL) balsamic vinegar
Salt and freshly ground black pepper to taste

2 slices rustic Italian bread
Drizzle of olive oil
Drizzle of balsamic vinegar
Salt and freshly ground black pepper to taste
2 tbsp (30 mL) freshly grated Parmesan cheese
1 tbsp (15 mL) chopped fresh oregano

Pull the mantle (body) from the tentacles on the squid. Remove and discard the hard transparent pen (backbone) and other inner matter from the body. Rinse under cold water and peel off the outer membrane. Cut the eye section away from the tentacles and remove the hard bone (beak) from the center of the tentacles. Rinse under cold water and pat dry with paper towels. Using a sharp knife, score the body of the squid every ½ inch (1 cm), cutting about two-thirds of the way into the flesh. Place body and tentacles in a glass dish and cover with buttermilk, turning to coat. Marinate, covered and refrigerated, for 4–6 hours.

Discard buttermilk and pat squid dry with paper towels. Season the squid inside and out with a little sea salt and black pepper.

To make the marinade, in the glass dish, whisk together the garlic, oil, vinegar and oregano. Add squid, turning to coat. Marinate for 20 minutes.

Meanwhile, prepare the Prosciutto-Wrapped Radicchio by cutting the radicchio into 6 wedges. Place radicchio in a large bowl with icy cold water and let soak for 10–20 minutes so that the radicchio leaves crisp

continued . . .

a little and absorb a little moisture. Drain; drizzle radicchio wedges with a little olive oil and balsamic vinegar. Season to taste with a little salt and pepper. Fold each slice of prosciutto in half lengthwise and wrap 1 slice around the middle of each radicchio wedge. Set aside.

Prepare the Caper Balsamic Sauce by melting 2 tbsp (30 mL) butter in a small saucepan over medium-high heat. Sauté the garlic and shallots until tender, 2–3 minutes, then add in the balsamic vinegar. Bring to a boil and reduce vinegar by half. Remove from heat and whisk in the remaining 3 tbsp (45 mL) butter, 1 tablespoon (15 mL) at a time, whisking until incorporated. Season to taste with salt and pepper. Set aside, keeping warm.

Remove squid from marinade, reserving leftover marinade for basting.

Fire up your grill to 550–650°F (290–345°C).

Grill the rustic bread slices on both sides for a few minutes, until grill-toasted crisp. Remove from grill and, using a sharp knife, chop the bread into coarse crumbs. Place in a bowl and season with a little drizzle of olive oil, balsamic vinegar and salt and pepper. Add Parmesan cheese and 1 tbsp (15 mL) chopped fresh oregano and set aside.

Grill Prosciutto-Wrapped Radicchio for 4–5 minutes per side, until the lettuce is lightly charred and the prosciutto a little crisp.

Grill squid until just cooked through, 1–3 minutes per side, basting with reserved marinade. After the first flip of the squid, give it a liberal baste with the marinade and sprinkle with grill-toasted bread crumbs.

To serve, place a wedge of grilled Prosciutto-Wrapped Radicchio on a plate in the center. Lay a grilled squid over top, spoon the Caper Balsamic Sauce over top and serve immediately.

GRILLED STUFFED SQUID WITH TOMATO OLIVE SALSA

A trio of seafood in one nice bundle of fire-grilled goodness. **SERVES 4**

WHAT YOU NEED: Food processor; Piping bag (optional); Toothpicks

12 medium fresh squid tubes (approx. 4 to 6 oz/115 to 170 g each)
1 cup (250 mL) buttermilk

SQUID STUFFING

1 tbsp (15 mL) freshly squeezed lemon juice
1 cup (250 mL) bay scallops
1 cup (250 mL) raw baby shrimp
1 egg white
Pinch of salt
2 tbsp (30 mL) freshly grated Parmesan cheese
1 green onion, thinly sliced
2 tbsp (30 mL) chopped fresh parsley
1 cup (250 mL) lump crabmeat
Salt and freshly ground black pepper to taste
Dash of cayenne pepper

TOMATO OLIVE SALSA

2 tbsp (30 mL) olive oil
1 cup (250 mL) grape tomatoes, halved
½ cup (125 mL) onion, sliced
¼ cup (60 mL) Niçoise black olives
2 small green hot peppers, sliced
4 cloves garlic, minced
1 cup (250 mL) tomato sauce
Salt and freshly ground black pepper to taste
1 tbsp (15 mL) chopped fresh basil

Soak squid tubes in buttermilk for 4 hours, covered and refrigerated.

In food processor, combine lemon juice, scallops and shrimp. Purée until smooth. Add egg white and a pinch of salt. Pulse until incorporated. Transfer to a bowl. Stir in Parmesan cheese, green onion, parsley and crabmeat. Season to taste with salt, black pepper and a dash of cayenne pepper. Cover and refrigerate; allow mixture to chill for 45 minutes.

Remove squid tubes from buttermilk, discarding buttermilk. Pat squid tubes dry with paper towels. Using a piping bag or a spoon, stuff each tube with 2 to 3 oz (57 to 85 g) of scallop crab stuffing. Do not overstuff the squid. Secure open end of stuffed squid with one or two toothpicks. Cover and refrigerate to set for 30 minutes.

Meanwhile, prepare the Tomato Olive Salsa by taking a heavy pan and heating the olive oil over high heat until oil begins to smoke. Add grape tomatoes and onions and sauté quickly, stirring, until lightly charred, about 1 to 2 minutes. Add olives, chiles and garlic and sauté for about 30 seconds. Add tomato sauce, stir and bring to a quick boil. Remove from heat and season with salt, pepper and fresh basil. Set aside and keep warm.

Fire up your grill to 350–450°F (180–230°C).

Brush stuffed squid with a little olive oil and season with salt and pepper to taste. Grill stuffed squid for 8–10 minutes per side, until fully cooked and heated through. Place grilled stuffed squid on a platter. Spoon over Tomato Olive Salsa and serve immediately.

GRILLED SUGAR CANE TUNA STICKS WITH GRILLED PINEAPPLE GINGER COMPOTE

The natural sweetness of sugar cane blends well with the firm texture of tuna. You can find fresh sugar cane in most grocery stores and specialty food markets. Change this up by switching the tuna to a variety of other seafood — scallops, shrimp, grouper, salmon and halibut all work extremely well too. **SERVES 4**

WHAT YOU NEED: Hand-held blender; Sharp-edged spatula

Using a sharp knife, peel the sugar cane. This might be a bit of work, but you want to expose the sweet inner flesh. Once you have it peeled, cut the cane into 4 equal skewers, each about ¼ to ½ inch (0.5 to 1 cm) square and about 6 to 8 inches (15 to 20 cm) long. Cut a point at one end of each of the skewers. Place skewers into self-sealing storage bag. Pour in the rum and add the cinnamon stick. Seal and let stand to marinate for 1 hour. The cane will suck up the rum and cinnamon flavors, giving you deliciously flavored sticks.

Cut the tuna into sixteen 1½-inch (4 cm) square chunks. Skewer 4 chunks of tuna onto each rum-soaked sugar cane skewer. Don't throw that rum marinade out. You can enjoy it in a beverage or use in your Grilled Pineapple Ginger Compote.

Fire up your grill to 550–650°F (290–345°C).

Slice the pineapple into ten or twelve ¼-inch (0.5 cm) thick slices. Grill the slices for 2–3 minutes per side, until lightly charred and tender. Remove from grill. Count out 4 slices of grilled pineapple and set aside for garnish. Coarsely chop the remaining slices of grilled pineapple and place in medium pot. Over medium heat, drizzle the grilled slices of pineapple with honey, add a splash of dark rum and minced ginger and stir. Add the lemon juice and season with a pinch of kosher salt and black pepper. Continue to cook for 5 minutes, until just bubbling. Remove from heat and, using blender, purée the grilled pineapple mixture until it is almost smooth but still a little chunky. Stir in the hot pepper flakes and set aside, keeping warm.

Season the tuna skewers with a little kosher salt and black pepper. Grill the sugar cane tuna skewers for 1–2 minutes per side for rare to medium-rare doneness. Remove from grill.

Stir the fresh cilantro into the warm Grilled Pineapple Ginger Compote and spoon over the grilled tuna skewers. Garnish dish with a sprinkling of crushed peanuts and serve immediately.

1 stick fresh sugar cane (approx. 6 to 8 inches/15 to 20 cm long)
1 cup (250 mL) dark rum
1 cinnamon stick (approx. 2 inches/10 cm long)

1½ lb (675 g) fresh tuna loin

GRILLED PINEAPPLE GINGER COMPOTE

1 fresh ripe pineapple, peeled
¼ cup (60 mL) honey
Splash of dark rum (approx. 1 oz/30 mL)
1 tsp (5 mL) minced fresh ginger
Juice of ½ lemon
Kosher salt and freshly ground black pepper to taste
Pinch of hot red pepper flakes
1 tbsp (15 mL) chopped fresh cilantro

¼ cup (60 mL) crushed peanuts

HAY MACKEREL!

This recipe is not for the amateur. It is for the serious experienced griller. This is a hot, fast way to infuse smoke into the fish and grill it at the same time. There will be flames. Do not do this on a covered patio. Do not do this on a windy day. And most of all, be careful and have fun. **SERVES 4**

WHAT YOU NEED: Green hay (fresh all-natural farmer's hay)

1 whole mackerel, cleaned and scaled
2 cups (500 mL) kosher salt
2 cups (500 mL) white sugar
¼ cup (60 mL) chopped fresh thyme
¼ cup (60 mL) chopped fresh
    rosemary
1 cup (250 mL) spiced whiskey
4 to 6 large handfuls of hay
3 to 4 bottles (12 oz/341 mL each)
    Alexander Keith's Amber Ale
Cracked black pepper to taste

BACON CRUMBLE TOPPING
½ cup (125 mL) double-smoked
    bacon, diced
2 white onions, diced
2 cups (500 mL) French bread,
    cubed
1 tbsp (15 mL) chopped fresh thyme
Salt and freshly ground black pepper
    to taste

Using a sharp knife, slash the mackerel on both sides of the fish about ½ to 1 inch (1 to 2.5 cm) deep.

In a bowl, mix together kosher salt, sugar, thyme and rosemary. Set aside.

Rub the mackerel inside and out with the salt mixture, making sure to get the cure into the slashes. In a pan long enough to hold the mackerel, pour in half of the remaining salt mixture. Lay the rubbed mackerel on top. Sprinkle mackerel with remaining salt mixture. Drizzle mackerel with approximately 1 cup (250 mL) spiced whiskey. Cover with plastic wrap and refrigerate for 2 days to cure, turning every 6 hours and spooning the cure mixture over top of the fish.

Soak hay in beer for at least 1 hour.

Remove mackerel from cure and rinse under cold water to remove excess salt, sugar and herbs. Pat dry with paper towels and season with cracked pepper.

Shake off excess liquid from hay and place a few handfuls onto a flat work surface. Try to have all the strands of hay going in the same direction; it's easier for rolling. Lay the cured mackerel onto hay and roll it up like a cigar, wrapping the entire mackerel in hay. You want enough hay to cover the fish but still see little parts of it through the hay. Take a single strand of hay and tie it around the fish. Repeat 2 to 3 more times so that the hay is held in place. Set aside.

Prepare the Bacon Crumble Topping by heating a frying pan to medium-high heat. Add bacon and sauté until golden brown, about 3–4 minutes. Add onions to pan and cook until soft, about 3–4 minutes. Add diced French bread and cook for an additional 4–5 minutes. Season with fresh thyme and salt and black pepper to taste. Set aside, keeping warm.

Fire up your grill to 450–550°F (230–290°C).

continued . . .

Place the mackerel bundles directly over the fire and close lid. Let hay-wrapped mackerel cook away in the grill for about 20 minutes; do not open lid. You will see a fair bit of smoke happening, but unless you see flames, keep that lid closed and let the mackerel smoke on the grill. After 20 minutes, open lid and stand back; as the air rushes in, the dry hay will ignite and burn. Let it burn and as the hay burns it will char the outside of the mackerel. Carefully turn the mackerel over and continue to grill for another 5–10 minutes, until the mackerel is fully cooked. Carefully remove hay from the top of mackerel. Discard hay into a galvanized bucket filled with water. Remove fish from grill with two spatulas, leaving fish intact.

To serve, cut fillets off the hay-smoked mackerel and place onto platter. Top with Bacon Crumble Topping. Serve immediately.

TED'S TIP
Be sure to keep a spray bottle filled with water onsite in case of a fire or flare-ups.

PLANK-SMOKED SALMON WITH SAKE BRINE & WASABI MAYONNAISE

For me, the art of plank grilling started with planking salmon. Classically delicious! **SERVES 6**

WHAT YOU NEED: Cedar grilling plank (12 × 8 × ½ inches/30 × 20 × 1 cm), soaked in water for a minimum of 1 hour

1½ cups (375 mL) brewed soy sauce (such as Kikkoman)
½ cup (125 mL) sake
¼ cup (60 mL) mirin
1 cup (250 mL) firmly packed brown sugar, plus extra for grilling
12 thin slices peeled fresh ginger
6 cloves fresh garlic, minced
½ tsp (2 mL) Asian chili sauce
1 tbsp (15 mL) coarse kosher salt
2 lb (900 g) side of salmon, skin on, pin bones removed
Freshly ground black pepper to taste

WASABI MAYONNAISE
1 cup (250 mL) mayonnaise
1 tbsp (15 mL) wasabi paste
1 tsp (5 mL) fresh ginger, minced
1 clove fresh garlic, minced

Fresh sage leaves, lightly chopped

In a bowl, combine the soy sauce, sake, mirin, brown sugar, sliced ginger, garlic, chili sauce and kosher salt. Whisk together until the sugar and salt have dissolved.

Place the salmon fillet, skin side down, in a shallow glass dish large enough for the fillet to lie flat. Pour the marinade over. Cover and place in the refrigerator for at least 12 hours. Turn the fillet every few hours to allow the marinade to penetrate all over.

Remove fillet from marinade and set, skin side down, on the grilling plank. Refrigerate for 2 hours to allow the remaining marinade to set on the surface of the salmon. Season salmon with a little black pepper — not a lot, just a little. Sprinkle with a little extra brown sugar.

Fire up your grill to 350–450°F (180–230°C).

Place the salmon plank on the grill and sprinkle salmon with the sage. Close grill lid and plank smoke for 25–35 minutes, until the salmon is just done and can easily flake with a fork. Remove salmon from grill. Sprinkle surface of salmon with chopped fresh sage.

To make the Wasabi Mayonnaise, whisk together the mayonnaise, wasabi paste, minced ginger and garlic. Set aside.

Slice salmon into six equal portions and serve with a dollop of Wasabi Mayonnaise.

PLANKED BLACK COD WITH CRAB, PRAWN & SPINACH STUFFING

This recipe is inspired by the many wonderful trips I have had to the Pacific Northwest. Fresh, line-caught black cod stuffed with Dungeness crab and spot prawns. **SERVES 4**

WHAT YOU NEED: Maple or oak grilling plank (12 × 8 × ½ inches/30 × 20 × 1 cm), soaked in water for a minimum of 1 hour

Blanch the spinach leaves for a second or two to soften. Drain, rinse under cold running water and squeeze to remove excess moisture. Coarsely chop and place in a large bowl. Set aside.

In another bowl, combine the crabmeat, shrimp, cream cheese, mozzarella cheese, mayonnaise, dill, lemon juice, shallots and green onion. Season to taste with sea salt and black pepper and mix thoroughly.

Fire up your grill to 350–450°F (180–230°C).

With a sharp knife, cut an incision lengthwise in the top of each fillet, cutting about three-quarters of the way through the fish. Using your fingers, open the incision to make a large pocket. Season the fillets with a little sea salt and black pepper. Divide the stuffing into 4 equal portions. Pack the crab, shrimp and spinach stuffing into each of the pockets. It does not matter if some stuffing is on top of the fish. Mix the breadcrumbs and Parmesan cheese. Sprinkle the top of the fillet with the breadcrumb Parmesan mix.

Place grilling planks on the grill and close the lid. Let the plank heat for 3–4 minutes or until it starts to crackle and smoke. Carefully open the lid and place the stuffed fillets on the plank. Close the lid and bake the stuffed black cod for 15–18 minutes or until it flakes easily with a fork. Periodically check the plank; if it is burning, spray it with water and reduce heat.

Carefully remove the planks from the grill and serve immediately.

4 cups (1 L) fresh spinach leaves

1 cup (250 mL) lump crabmeat

½ lb (225 g) fresh shrimp (approx. 12 pieces), peeled, deveined and cut in half lengthwise

¼ cup (60 mL) cream cheese, softened

½ cup (125 mL) shredded mozzarella cheese

2 tbsp (30 mL) mayonnaise

1 tbsp (15 mL) chopped fresh dill

2 tsp (10 mL) freshly squeezed lemon juice

2 shallots, finely chopped

1 green onion, finely chopped

Sea salt and freshly ground black pepper to taste

4 fresh black cod fillets (approx. 4 to 6 oz/115 to 170 g each)

½ cup (125 mL) panko breadcrumbs

¼ cup (60 mL) freshly grated Parmesan cheese

SHRIMP & GRITS

Fire grilled Devil's Cut bourbon and butter–injected colossal shrimp with Pimento Cheese Grits. **SERVES 4**

WHAT YOU NEED: Injection syringe; Cookie sheet, lined with parchment paper; Maple or oak grilling plank (12 × 8 × ½ inches/30 × 20 × 1 cm), soaked in water for a minimum of 1 hour

DEVIL'S CUT GRILLED SHRIMP

8 jumbo shrimp (XXL, approx. 3 to 5 pieces per lb/450 g)
½ cup (125 mL) butter
¼ cup (60 mL) TABASCO® Chipotle Sauce
½ cup (125 mL) Devil's Cut by Jim Beam, plus extra to flambé
⅓ cup (75 mL) Bone Dust BBQ Spice (page 212)

PIMENTO CHEESE GRITS

1 sweet onion, sliced into rings
2 red bell peppers
2 cups (500 ml) chicken stock
1 tsp (5 mL) salt
1 cup (250 mL) white cornmeal grits
2 tbsp (30 mL) butter
4 tbsp (60 mL) cream cheese, softened
4 oz (115 g) Muenster cheese, shredded
Pinch of smoked paprika
Sea salt and freshly ground pepper to taste

To prepare the Devil's Cut Grilled Shrimp, peel the shrimp, leaving the tail shell intact. Using a sharp knife, cut the top of each shrimp from head to tail about a quarter of the way into the flesh to expose the vein. Remove the vein. Rinse the shrimp under cold running water. Pat dry with paper towels. Refrigerate to keep cold.

In a small saucepan, melt the butter over medium-low heat. Add the TABASCO® Chipotle Sauce and bourbon. Stir. Using injection syringe, fill the chamber with Devil's Cut mixture. Insert the needle into a shrimp once or twice and inject about a tablespoon (15 mL) of the hot whiskey butter into the shrimp. Repeat with remaining shrimp. Brush the outside of each shrimp with any leftover butter whiskey mixture. Roll each butter-glazed shrimp in Bone Dust BBQ Spice, place on prepared cookie sheet and refrigerate.

Fire up your grill to 550–650°F (290–345°C).

Grill the onion until lightly charred, tender yet crispy. Set aside.

Grill-roast the bell peppers until charred black and blistered. Place peppers into a bowl, cover with a sheet of plastic wrap and let stand for 10 minutes. This will steam the peppers and help the skin peel easily from the roasted flesh. Remove peppers from bowl and peel away charred skin, seed and cut into 1-inch (2.5 cm) strips. Set aside.

In a large saucepan, bring the chicken stock to a boil over high heat. Add 1 tsp (5 mL) salt. Reduce heat to medium-low and add white cornmeal grits in a steady stream while whisking constantly. Using a wooden spoon, stir constantly for 15–20 minutes, until grits are thick and smooth. Remove from heat. Stir in the butter, cream cheese, Muenster cheese, grill-roasted onions and peppers. Season to taste with a little smoked paprika, sea salt and black pepper. Let cool in the pot for about 5 minutes.

Spoon Pimento Cheese Grits onto a grilling plank, piling it high and leaving a 1-inch (2.5 cm) border around the edge of the plank. Place on grill, keeping warm.

Grill the shrimp until just cooked through, about 4–5 minutes a side or until just opaque, pink and firm to the touch. Do not overcook the shrimp. Remove from grill and stand the shrimp tail up in the Pimento Cheese Grits. Drizzle the whole thing with a little Devil's Cut and light with a match to flambé. Serve immediately.

SLASH & GRILL SEA BASS

The aroma in your backyard will be off the hook with this recipe, grill-smoked sea bass, wrapped in cedar boughs and a selection of fresh herbs. It doesn't get much more rustic than this. It's the art of grilling. Bring on the flavor! **SERVES 6 TO 8**

WHAT YOU NEED: Cedar boughs; Butcher twine; 1 handful fresh rosemary sprigs; 1 handful fresh sage sprigs; 1 handful fresh thyme sprigs; 1 handful fresh oregano sprigs

Cut the cedar boughs into small sprigs about 6 to 8 inches (15 to 20 cm) in length, just a little bigger than the fresh herbs. Soak the cedar boughs and fresh herbs in a large bowl of ice water. This will freshen them up and let them absorb a little bit of extra moisture so they stay moist when grilling. Cut the butcher's twine into eight 12-inch (30 cm) lengths and soak in the cold water with the fresh herbs. This will help keep the string from burning while on the grill.

Take a sharp knife and slash the flesh on both sides of the fish every 1 to 2 inches (2.5 to 5 cm), about ½ inch (1 cm) deep.

Season the fish on all sides, inside and outside, with sea salt and black pepper.

Lay a few sprigs of each herb as well as a sprig or two of cedar bough on both sides of the bass. Wrap it up and tie the cedar and herbs to the sea bass with 3 to 4 pieces of butcher twine. Ensure it is nice and tight. You don't want to completely hide the fish with the herbs, as you want the hot grill flavor to get into the flesh. A sprig or two of each herb and cedar on both sides is plenty.

Fire up your grill to 350–450°F (180–230°C).

Cut the lemons in half across the middle. Sprinkle the sugar evenly over the cut side of each lemon half. Set aside.

Place the cedar and herb–wrapped sea bass onto the grill directly over the fire and grill for 10–15 minutes per side. Place the lemons, sugar-coated side down, and grill for 3–5 minutes, until the sugar caramelizes and burns a little. Set aside.

While the sea bass is grilling, squeeze a little caramelized lemon juice over the fish. Fish is done when the flesh flakes easily with a fork. Remove from grill. Cut string and remove cedar herbs. Squeeze a little grilled lemon over top and serve immediately.

2 fresh whole sea bass (approx. 2 to 2½ lb/0.9 to 1.125 kg each)
Sea salt and freshly ground black pepper to taste
2 juicy lemons
6 tbsp (90 mL) white sugar

TED'S TIP

- If you don't have your own herb garden, the next best thing is to take a trip to your local market and grab 4 to 5 bunches of different fresh herbs — rosemary, thyme, oregano, sage and parsley. You need a fair amount of herbs for this recipe.
- Head to your local fish market and purchase a couple of whole sea bass. Have your fishmonger scale, cut and trim the fins.
- If the grilled lemons are too hot for your hands to squeeze, use your tongs.

TUNA PEPPER STEAK WITH SMASHED GREEN ONION BUTTER

When it comes to grilling seafood, sometimes extremely hot and very fast is best. With tuna, that rule certainly applies. Keep your tuna icy cold prior to grilling; this will keep the firm flesh and your fish fresh!

SERVES 4

WHAT YOU NEED: Sharp-edged spatula

FIVE-PEPPER RUB

1 tbsp (15 mL) cracked black peppercorns
1 tbsp (15 mL) cracked Szechuan peppercorns
2 tsp (10 mL) cracked green peppercorns
2 tsp (10 mL) cracked white peppercorns
2 tsp (10 mL) cracked coriander seeds
1 tsp (5 mL) hot pepper flakes
1 tsp (5 mL) kosher salt
1 tsp (5 mL) brown sugar
4 cloves garlic, minced
1 tbsp (15 mL) soy sauce
4 tbsp (60 mL) olive oil

SMASHED GREEN ONION BUTTER

4 green onions
Kosher salt to taste
Juice of ½ lemon
1 shallot, finely chopped
3 tbsp (45 mL) chopped fresh cilantro
1 stick (4 oz/115 g) unsalted butter, softened

4 tuna steaks (approx. 6 oz/170 g each), cut 1½ inches (4 cm) thick
1 to 2 bunches green onions, trimmed and soaked in cold water for 30 minutes prior to grilling
Salt and freshly ground black pepper to taste

In a bowl, mix together the four peppercorns, coriander, hot pepper flakes, kosher salt and brown sugar. Add the minced garlic, soy sauce and olive oil. Stir to make a pepper slurry and set aside.

To prepare the Smashed Green Onion Butter, place the 4 green onions onto a cutting board. Take a heavy-bottomed frying pan and smash the green onions. You want them to split apart and extract the juices. Roughly chop them up and place in a bowl. Season the smashed green onions with a little kosher salt and the lemon juice. Add the shallot, cilantro and softened butter. Mix it up with a spoon to incorporate. Transfer to a small bowl and set aside.

Fire up your grill to 550–650°F (290–345°C).

Rub the tuna steaks with the Five-Pepper Rub, pressing the seasoning into the flesh so that it adheres.

Grill the tuna steaks for 1–2 minutes per side directly over the hot flame for rare. It won't take long. Remember that the more done the tuna is, the dryer it becomes. Rare to medium is my recommendation.

At the same time as you are grilling the tuna, grill the green onions for 2–3 minutes, turning until lightly charred and tender yet still bright green. Season with a little salt and pepper. Remove onions from grill.

Remove tuna from grill. Serve immediately with a dollop of Smashed Green Onion Butter and grilled green onions on the side.

DRINKS

BLACK SPICED LEMONADE   337

DECONSTRUCTED FIRE-ROASTED BOURBON CAESAR
WITH TOMATO BOURBON BURSTS   338

MAPLE BOURBON CARROT ICED TEA   342

WEISS BIER COCKTAIL WITH CHARRED ORANGE & BOURBON   345

BLACK SPICED LEMONADE

This lemonade is what I'd serve on my yacht. That is, if I ever get a yacht. Maybe someone will invite me on their yacht and make it for me! It is incredibly delicious. **SERVES 2, WITH EXTRA BLACKBERRY LEMONADE CONCENTRATE**

Fire up your grill to 450–550°F (230–290°C).

Slice the lemons in half and grill them for 4–5 minutes, cut side down, until nicely charred and blackened. Remove from grill and squeeze the hot juice from the lemons into a pitcher. You should end up with approximately 1 cup (250 mL) hot lemon juice. Add 4 heaping tbsp (60 mL) honey, stir to dissolve and set aside. Add in a pint of fresh plump sweet blackberries and mash with a wooden spoon. Stir well and let it steep for at least 30 minutes.

Strain to remove the seeds.

Fill a couple of glasses with ice. Pour 2 oz (60 mL) of spiced whiskey into each glass. Add in ¼ cup (60 mL) blackberry lemonade syrup to each. Add a good pour of club soda and garnish with a few blackberries and a sprig of mint. Serve immediately.

4 juicy lemons

4 tbsp (60 mL) honey

1 pint (2 cups/500 ml) fresh blackberries, reserving a few for garnish

4 oz (120 mL) spiced whiskey

1 can (12 oz/355 mL) club soda

2 sprigs fresh mint

DECONSTRUCTED FIRE-ROASTED BOURBON CAESAR WITH TOMATO BOURBON BURSTS

I made this with my buddy Olaf while at my friend Tim's LuvLuv BBQ Festival in Winston-Salem, North Carolina. All I can say is that it was yummy. **MAKES 8 SHOTS**

WHAT YOU NEED: Blender; Cheesecloth, cut into 4 sheets about 24 inches (60 cm) square; 4 shot glasses (2 oz/60 mL each); Injection syringe; Martini shaker

1 small sweet onion

2 lb (900 g) juicy red vine-ripened tomatoes, plump and full of water

1 clove garlic, minced

1 hot red chile pepper, minced

1 tsp (5 mL) chopped fresh thyme

Kosher salt and freshly ground black pepper to taste

2 + 4 oz (180 mL) bourbon whiskey

¼ cup (60 mL) Bone Dust BBQ Spice (page 212)

4 slices lemon

12 small heirloom tomatoes (such as small grape, teardrop or cluster tomatoes)

4 tsp (20 mL) clam juice

Fire up your grill to 550–650°F (290–345°C).

Slice the onion into wedges. Grill the onions for 5–6 minutes per side, until lightly charred and tender.

At the same time as you are grilling the onions, fire-roast the vine-ripened tomatoes until the skin is blackened and blistered and the tomatoes are soft. This takes about 10–15 minutes, turning the tomatoes so they roast evenly.

Remove onions and tomatoes from the grill, transfer to a bowl and cool. Peel the charred skins from the tomatoes, discarding skins. Coarsely chop the tomatoes and finely chop the onions and place in blender. Add garlic, fresh chile and thyme. Season with a little kosher salt and black pepper, drizzle with a little bourbon, about 2 oz (60 mL) and pulse for 30 seconds to 1 minute.

Line a bowl with layers of cheesecloth, making sure the cheesecloth overhangs the edge of the bowl by about 4 to 6 inches (10 to 15 cm). Pour in the fire-roasted tomato mixture and bring the ends of the cheesecloth up to form a bundle. Tie the ends into a tight knot around the middle of a wooden spoon. Hang the fire-roasted tomato bundle over a deep pot or bowl and allow the tomato mixture to hang and drip its smoky tomato onion water into the pot. Do this at room temperature. Let drip slowly for 3–5 hours or until nothing more is dripping.

Transfer tomato water to a small container and refrigerate. You should end up with about 1 to 2 cups (250 to 500 mL). It depends based on how juicy the tomatoes are.

continued . . .

Pour the Bone Dust BBQ Spice onto a small plate.

Rub a slice of lemon around the rim of a shot glass. Dip the rim into the Bone Dust BBQ Spice to coat. Place glasses into the freezer for 1 hour to chill.

Using the injection syringe, suck up a couple of ounces (60 mL) of bourbon whiskey. Take a small tomato and hold it between your thumb and forefinger with the stem end facing you. Push the needle of the syringe into the tomato through the stem end. Inject a little bourbon into the tomato by pushing the plunger on the syringe slowly so you don't burst the tomato. Easy does it so all the bourbon stays inside the tomatoes. Repeat with remaining tomatoes, refilling the syringe as needed. Set aside, keeping cold.

Measure 1 cup (250 mL) tomato water into a martini shaker filled with ice. Add a teaspoon (5 mL) of chilled clam juice and shake. Strain into rimmed shot glasses. To serve, pop a whole chilled bourbon-injected tomato into your mouth, take a bite, it explodes. Shoot the fire-roasted tomato water. Repeat.

MAPLE BOURBON CARROT ICED TEA

Carrots have a natural sweetness that is ideal for this summertime drink, especially when you add in a little bourbon. I'll eat or drink my carrots any day of the week with bourbon added. **SERVES 2**

1 lemon

2 oranges

4 cups (1 L) water

½ cup (125 mL) pure maple syrup

6 fresh sweet orange carrots

1 green apple, peeled and sliced

4 black peppercorns

4 sprigs fresh thyme

Drizzle of honey

4 oz (120 mL) Maker's Mark

Fire up your grill to 550–650°F (290–345°C).

Slice the lemon and oranges in half. Grill lemon and oranges for 10 minutes, cut side down, to char. Squeeze the warm juices into a pitcher and set aside. You should end up with about approximately 1 cup (250 mL) juice.

In a large saucepan, bring the water and maple syrup to a boil. Add the carrots, apple, orange juice, lemon juice and peppercorns. Return to a boil. Remove from the heat and let steep for 30 minutes. Strain, discarding the solids, and chill.

Fill a couple of glasses with ice. Add a couple sprigs of thyme and a drizzle of honey, just a little drizzle. Pour a couple of ounces (60 mL) of bourbon into each glass. Top with carrot iced tea. Serve immediately.

WEISS BIER COCKTAIL WITH CHARRED ORANGE & BOURBON

Serve this beer cocktail with Molten Brie (page 77) and fresh baked baguette. **SERVES 2**

WHAT YOU NEED: Cocktail shaker and strainer; 2 wide-mouthed beer glasses, chilled

Fire up your grill to 450–550°F (230–290°C).

Zest the orange and reserve zest in a small bowl. Drizzle with a little bourbon whiskey to keep the zest moist and add flavor.

Slice the orange into eight ¼-inch (5 mm) thick rounds and place in a bowl. Drizzle slices with a little bourbon and honey, about an ounce (30 mL) of each. Season with black pepper and thyme and gently mix. Marinate orange slices for 10 minutes.

Grill orange slices for 2–3 minutes on both sides, until lightly charred and tender. Set aside to cool.

Coarsely chop a couple of slices of charred orange and place in a cocktail shaker. Add the 2 tsp (10 mL) honey, 3 oz (120 mL) bourbon and a drizzle of orange liqueur. Mash with a wooden spoon, then add ice. Put lid on shaker and shake it up to cool. Strain charred orange-infused bourbon into a chilled wide-mouthed beer glass. Add a slice of charred orange and fill glass with ice. Pour in the chilled wheat beer and serve immediately.

1 juicy seedless orange
Drizzles + 3 oz (approx. 100 mL) Jim Beam
Drizzles + 2 tsp (approx. 12 mL) honey
Freshly ground black pepper to taste
½ teaspoon (2 mL) fresh thyme
Drizzle of orange liqueur
2 bottles (12 oz/341 mL each) Shock Top, chilled

DESSERTS

ANGRY BLUEBERRIES WITH COLD CREAM

Okay, sometimes things can get a little carried away in my brain and I end up with a fun little crazy recipe. This one might be a bit foolish, but it is not anything if not fun! **SERVES 4**

WHAT YOU NEED: Medical syringe; Grilling stone; Rectangular wok-style grill basket, rimmed cookie sheet or heavy cast iron frying pan; Flat-edged spatula; Grilling gloves

Rinse the blueberries in cold running water, drain and pick through, removing any unwanted stems and leaves. Set aside.

Pour the spiced whiskey into a rocks glass. Insert the needle end of the syringe into the whiskey. Pull up on the plunger to suck the whiskey into the chamber. Yes, this is what excessive gastro grillers do!

Next carefully pick up one blueberry at a time, holding the blueberry between thumb and forefinger. Carefully insert the needle into the center of the blueberry, being careful not to stick yourself on the sharp needle. Inject the blueberry with a little squirt of spiced whiskey. Repeat with remaining blueberries. Place injected blueberries into a bowl. Cover with a paper towel dampened with cold water and squeezed of excess moisture. Add a couple of ice cubes to the top and refrigerate, allowing to marinate for a minimum of 30 minutes.

Place the grilling stone in the center of the rectangular wok-style grill basket or, barring that, rimmed cookie sheet or frying pan. Set aside.

In a bowl, whip the cream with an electric mixer or wire whisk until soft peaks form. Add the icing sugar and vanilla and continue beating until stiff peaks form. Using a rasp, zest a little rind from the orange over the whipped cream, fold it in, cover and refrigerate. Best to make this right before you are ready to have dessert.

Fire up your grill to 450–550°F (230–290°C).

Place grill basket with grilling stone onto the hot grill, close lid and let it heat for about 15 minutes, until the stone is hot. When you drop a drop of water onto the stone, it bursts and sputters and almost instantaneously evaporates.

Remove drunken blueberries from refrigerator, drain and place back in a bowl. Drizzle with grapeseed oil, about 2 tsp (10 mL), not a lot, just a little so that the berries have a fine coating of oil. Season with a little black pepper and a pinch of ancho chile powder. Add a small pinch of salt and gently mix to evenly coat.

1 + 2 cups (750 mL) fresh plump wild blueberries

½ cup (125 mL) spiced whiskey

1½ cups (375 mL) whipping cream (35% MF)

1 tbsp (15 mL) icing sugar

¼ tsp (1 mL) pure vanilla extract

1 orange

Drizzle of grapeseed oil

Freshly ground black pepper to taste

Pinch of ground ancho or cayenne or chipotle pepper

Small pinch of salt

4 scoops really good-quality vanilla ice cream

4 sprigs fresh oregano, sage or thyme

continued…

If you think that injecting each blueberry with a medical syringe full of spiced whiskey is too difficult or if you are unable to find a medical syringe, you can always take a sharp toothpick and poke a hole in each blueberry, place them in a bowl and cover with spiced whiskey.

Working in small batches, place a handful or so of seasoned drunken blueberries onto the hot grilling stone. If the stone is hot enough, they will begin to dance about on the hot stone, scorching their skins on all sides. Some will roll or bounce right off your hot stone; that's why the grill pan or cookie sheet is under and around the stone so they don't fall through the grill. Squeeze a little drizzle of fresh orange juice over top of the dancing blueberries and remove from stone. Using the flat-edged spatula, guide the angry blueberries to the edge of the stone and push them off into the safety of a waiting spoon.

Place a scoop of ice cream into a martini-style glass. Spoon over the angry blueberries. Add a dollop of whipping cream. Add a sprig of fresh oregano or sage or thyme — but NO mint! Drizzle with a little extra spiced whiskey and serve immediately.

BANANAS ON TOAST

You have to make this! The pictures alone are oozing deliciousness. **SERVES 2 TO 4**

WHAT YOU NEED: Injection syringe

Pour the bourbon into a canning jar. Split vanilla bean in two and scrape out the seeds, cut the pod into 1-inch (2.5 cm) sections and add both the seeds and the pod into the bourbon. Add in the honey and seal jar. Give it a shake to dissolve the honey in the bourbon. Set aside to infuse for 24 hours.

Cut the bacon into ½-inch (1 cm) thick lardons, or strips, across the width of the bacon. In a pan, fry the bacon lardons over medium heat for 5–8 minutes, stirring occasionally, until browned and crisp. Remove from heat and drain. Pat with paper towels to remove excess bacon grease. Place bacon in small bowl. Spoon over the condensed milk and drizzle with a little vanilla-infused bourbon. Stir to combine and keep warm.

Fire up your grill to 450–550°F (230–290°C).

Suck up the bourbon mixture into an injection syringe. Set aside.

Grill the bananas for 5–8 minutes per side, until the banana skin is darkened and begins to split. The flesh of the banana should be warm and soft. Inject each banana with a little squirt of infused bourbon. Be careful, as the bourbon will more than likely ignite as it drips out of the banana.

At the same time as you are grilling the bananas, grill the raisin bread until golden brown and crisp.

Remove bananas from grill and carefully open the peel to expose the hot, tender banana. Spread the warm grill-roasted banana over the raisin toast. Drizzle with crispy bacon condensed milk. Garnish with a little fresh chopped sage. Serve immediately.

2 cups (500 mL) Devil's Cut by Jim Beam
1 vanilla bean
¼ cup (60 mL) honey
2 slices double-smoked thick-cut bacon
½ cup (125 mL) condensed milk
4 ripe bananas, unpeeled
4 to 8 slices raisin bread
1 tsp (5 mL) chopped fresh sage

GRILL-BAKED CHOCOLATE PEANUT BUTTER COFFEE CAKE

Grill-baked coffee cake with all things good: peanut butter, chocolate and jam. **MAKES 1 LOAF**

WHAT YOU NEED: 9- × 5-inch (2 L) loaf pan; Heavy-duty aluminum foil; Nonstick spray; Cooling rack

1¼ cups (300 mL) all-purpose flour
1 cup (250 mL) brown sugar, packed
¼ tsp (1 mL) salt
¼ cup (60 mL) butter
¼ cup (60 mL) peanut butter
¼ cup (60 mL) peanuts, chopped
¼ + ¼ cup (120 mL) chocolate chips
½ tsp (2 mL) baking powder
1 tsp (5 mL) baking soda
1 egg
½ cup (125 mL) sour cream

GARNISH
Butter
Grape jelly (homemade or market-bought is always best)

TED'S TIP

- You want to maintain an even constant temperature, keeping the heat directly under the cake pan to a minimum to keep the bottom of the cake from scorching.
- If you want to bake this cake on the grill, grill it indirectly with the lid closed, with the grill temperature running about 325–375°F (160–190°C), turning the pan once for even baking.

Fire up your grill to 350–450°F (180–230°C). Set grill for indirect grilling/baking.

Line the outside of loaf pan with heavy-duty aluminum foil, leaving excess foil hanging over lip of pan. Grease the foil with nonstick spray and set aside.

In a large bowl, mix together the flour, brown sugar and salt. Using a pastry blender, cut in the butter and peanut butter until the mixture resembles coarse crumbs. Set one-quarter of the peanut butter and flour mixture aside and to it add chopped peanuts and ¼ cup chocolate chips.

To the remaining peanut butter mixture, add the baking powder and baking soda. Mix well to completely combine.

In a small bowl, beat the egg and stir in the sour cream. Add the sour cream and egg mixture to the peanut butter and baking soda mixture. Add remaining ¼ cup (60 mL) chocolate chips to the mixture and stir until just moistened. Spoon into prepared pan and spread evenly. Sprinkle with reserved peanut butter and flour crumb mixture and swirl the crumb mixture into the top of the batter (just a little to keep the crumb in place).

Place loaf pan on the top grill rack but not over direct heat. Close grill lid and bake for 45–60 minutes or until a wooden toothpick inserted near the center of the cake comes out clean. Cool in pan or on a wire rack for 30–40 minutes.

Using sides of foil, pull coffee cake out of pan and place onto a cooling rack. Let coffee cake cool for 5 minutes longer.

Slice, lightly butter and grill for 1–2 minutes per side, until lightly toasted. Spread with grape jelly and serve. Serve with a cup of espresso and a snifter of whiskey.

GRILLED APRICOT CHEESECAKE QUESADILLA WITH LAVENDER HONEY

For this recipe, you don't have to go through all the trouble of baking a cheesecake — you can buy a small whole plain cheesecake or, if possible, a couple of slices instead. **MAKES 8 SMALL QUESADILLAS**

WHAT YOU NEED: 4-inch (10 cm) round cookie cutter; Nonstick cooking spray

LAVENDER HONEY
½ cup (125 mL) honey
2 tsp (10 mL) dried lavender or 1 tsp (5 mL) chopped fresh sage

GRILLED APRICOTS
6 apricots
2 oz (60 mL) Canadian Club Small Batch
1 tbsp (15 mL) white sugar

CHEESECAKE QUESADILLA
2 slices plain NY-style cheesecake (approx. 1½ cups/375 mL)
½ cup (125 mL) cream cheese, softened
8 small flour tortillas, 5 to 6 inches (12 to 15 cm) in diameter

In a small saucepot, combine honey and lavender and warm over low heat, stirring occasionally, for 1 hour. Remove from heat and let stand at room temperature overnight. Strain and set aside for later drizzling.

Cut apricots in half and remove pit. Drizzle apricots with whiskey and add sugar. Set aside.

Fire up your grill to 350–450°F (180–230°C). Grill the apricots, cut side down to start, for 3–5 minutes per side, until the flesh is tender and the skins are coming away from the flesh. Remove from grill and peel skins from the hot flesh. Set aside to cool.

Slice each apricot into four slices. Set aside.

Remove cheesecake from the packaging. As best you can, separate the crumb crust from the cheesecake. Crumble the mixture. Set aside.

Place the cheesecake into a bowl, add cream cheese and smash together with the back of a wooden spoon to make it spreadable.

Lay a flour tortilla onto a flat work surface. Take the cookie cutter or a paring knife and cut a tortilla into a small round 4 inches (10 cm) in diameter so that you can make smaller dessert quesadillas. Repeat with remaining flour tortillas.

Spread about 1 to 2 tbsp (15 to 30 mL) cheesecake and cream cheese mixture over the entire surface of a tortilla. Lay a couple of slices of apricots onto one half of the cheesecake-spread tortilla. Drizzle apricots with a little Lavender Honey. Fold tortilla over to form a half-moon shape. Press down on tortilla so that the filling sticks to the shell. Spray outside of quesadilla with nonstick cooking spray on both sides. Repeat with remaining flour tortillas. Cover with plastic wrap and refrigerate for up to 1 hour.

Get your grill hot again. Grill quesadillas on preheated seasoned grill for 2–3 minutes per side, until lightly charred and crisp (but not burned) and the cheesecake mixture is warm. Remove from grill and rest for 2–3 minutes prior to cutting so that filling will set. After quesadillas have rested, cut each in half and serve with an extra drizzling of Lavender Honey.

GRILLED PEACHES WITH BOURBON HONEY BUTTER & FRESH RICOTTA

Fresh sweet peaches are meant for the grill. Lightly warmed and charred, then drizzled with bourbon-infused honey, they're a real summer treat. Served with fresh ricotta cheese, this will be a summertime favorite.

SERVES 4

4 ripe peaches

2 tbsp (30 mL) grapeseed oil

Freshly grated nutmeg to taste

Cracked black pepper to taste

¼ cup (60 mL) honey

¼ cup (60 mL) bourbon

2 tsp (10 mL) cold butter

4 tbsp (60 mL) fresh ricotta, crumbled

4 tsp (20 mL) toasted slivered almonds

TED'S TIP

When buying the ricotta cheese, find a cheesemaker who makes fresh ricotta. It is the key to this recipe.

Fire up your grill to 450–550°F (230–290°C).

Slice the peaches in half and remove the pit. Using the tip of a small sharp knife, score the cut side of each of the peach halves in a small diamond pattern. Brush the peach halves lightly with grapeseed oil. Season with freshly grated nutmeg and black pepper to taste. Set aside.

In a small saucepan over low heat, warm the honey and bourbon, stirring, until blended. Add the butter, ½ tsp (2 mL) at a time, and whisk to incorporate into the honey and bourbon. Remove from heat and set aside, keeping warm.

Grill the peach halves, cut side down, for 5–6 minutes or until lightly charred and warm. Turn, baste with bourbon honey mixture and grill for 5 more minutes or until fully cooked and tender and the skin peels easily from the flesh. Remove peaches from grill. Peel skins.

Arrange two grilled peach halves on a plate. Spoon over some crumbled ricotta cheese. Drizzle with a little extra bourbon honey butter and toasted slivered almonds.

GRILLED POUND CAKE WITH RED WINE STEWED BERRIES

You can make this recipe from scratch, or you can purchase a pound cake. **SERVES 4 TO 8**

WHAT YOU NEED: 8- × 4-inch (1.5 L) loaf pan, greased and floured; Food processor

ORANGE POUND CAKE

3 cups (750 mL) all-purpose flour

½ tsp (2 mL) baking powder

1 cup + 3 tbsp (295 mL) butter, softened

½ cup (125 mL) shortening

3 cups (750 mL) white sugar

6 medium eggs

½ cup (125 mL) sour cream

½ cup (125 mL) milk

1½ tsp (7 mL) vanilla

1 tsp (5 mL) orange zest

2 tbsp (30 mL) freshly squeezed orange juice

4 tsp (20 mL) butter, softened

RED WINE STEWED BERRIES

4 cups (1 L) assorted fresh in-season berries (raspberries, blackberries, blueberries, strawberries, red currants)

1 cup (250 mL) zinfandel

1½ cups (375 mL) white grape juice

⅓ cup (75 mL) white sugar

1 stick of cinnamon, 1 inch (2.5 cm) long

1 juicy orange

1 to 1½ tbsp (15 to 30 mL) quick-cooking tapioca

1½ cups (375 mL) whipping cream (35% BF)

Fire up your grill to 250–350°F (120–180°C) and set for indirect baking.

To prepare the cake, sift the flour and baking powder into a bowl.

In another mixing bowl, cream the 1 cup (250 mL) butter, shortening and sugar until smooth. Add the eggs and beat well. Mix in the flour and baking soda mixture, alternating with the sour cream and milk. Stir in the vanilla, orange zest and orange juice.

Place batter into prepared loaf pan. Grill-bake for 1–1¼ hours, maintaining a grill temperature of about 300–350°F (150–180°C), until a toothpick inserted in the center comes out clean. Let cool on a wire rack.

While the pound cake is grill-baking, prepare the Red Wine Stewed Berries. In a mixing bowl, gently toss together the berries. Transfer half the berry mixture to a food processor and purée until smooth.

In a large saucepan, mix the berry purée with the red wine, white grape juice, sugar and cinnamon stick. Zest and juice the orange and add to the berry mixture. Bring to a boil, stirring. Reduce heat and simmer, stirring occasionally, for about 10 minutes. Stir in the tapioca and return to a boil, stirring, until thick. Strain the berry mixture through a fine-mesh sieve, set over a bowl to remove the seeds, reserving the liquid. Pour the hot liquid over the fresh berries and gently fold together; let stand to cool.

Whip the whipping cream until it forms fluffy peaks. Set aside, keeping cool.

Run a knife around the edge of the pan, invert and remove pound cake. Slice the cake into 1-inch (2.5 cm) thick slices. Lightly butter both sides. Grill for 1–2 minutes per side or until lightly golden.

To serve, place a couple of slices of grilled orange pound cake onto a plate. Spoon over the Red Wine Stewed Berries. Garnish with a dollop of whipping cream and serve immediately.

RED STAG TWICE-GRILLED PEARS

I am always happy when my father-in-law brings me some freshly picked pears from his trees. Their flavor is so sweet and they always have a nice crunch to them. I normally like to cut them in halves or quarters and grill directly on the hot coals, but sometimes I just want it a little fancier. So I will peel the pears and wrap them up in thick aluminum foil and let them slowly roast, steaming in a foil pouch, so that the flesh infuses with flavor and gets tender. When you open the hot parcels of pears, it will bring a smile to your face. **SERVES 4**

WHAT YOU NEED: 8 sheets aluminum foil, cut into 12-inch (30 cm) squares

Place the dried cherries in a small bowl and cover with bourbon. Let stand for a couple of hours so that the cherries plump and absorb the whiskey. Set aside.

Using a sharp paring knife or vegetable peeler, peel the pears.

Drain the cherries, reserving the bourbon for drizzling, and coarsely chop.

Lay two sheets of foil (one on top of the other) on a flat surface. Place a tablespoon (15 mL) of brown sugar in the center of the foil. Place a peeled pear on top of the sugar. Draw the corners up slightly to form a bowl shape. Top each pear with 1 tsp (5 mL) soaked chopped cherries and drizzle with approximately 1 tbsp (15 mL) whiskey and 1 tbsp (15 mL) honey. Add a sprig of sage and a little freshly ground black pepper. Draw the corners of the foil up around each pear and crimp the edges to form a tightly sealed bundle. Repeat with remaining pear.

Fire up your grill to 350–450°F (180–230°C).

Place bundles on one side of the grill and turn the burner under that side off. Close the lid. Grill-roast pouches for 30–45 minutes or until the pears are tender. Remove from the grill.

You can either serve this immediately or you can take it to the next level if you are up for it. Carefully open each pouch, let the steam escape and remove the pears, reserving the juices in the foil for later drizzling. Cut each pear in half from top to bottom. Take a small spoon and carefully scoop out the seeds on either side of the cut pear, to make a little divot. Drizzle the pear halves with a little extra bourbon.

Grill the pear halves on both sides for 1–2 minutes to lightly char.

Garnish with fresh cherry halves and Greek-style vanilla-flavored yogurt. If you wish, add an additional fresh sage sprig and drizzle with the reserved syrup. Serve immediately.

¼ cup (60 mL) dried cherries
A couple drizzles (about 4 tbsp/60 mL) Red Stag by Jim Beam
4 ripe Anjou or Bartlett pears, firm yet juicy
4 tbsp (60 mL) brown sugar
4 tbsp (60 mL) honey
½ bunch fresh sage
Freshly ground black pepper

GARNISH

Fresh cherries, halved and pitted
4 tbsp (60 mL) Greek-style vanilla-flavored yogurt
Fresh sage leaves (optional)

ROTISSERIE OF RUM-INJECTED PINEAPPLE WITH BONE DUST BBQ SPICE

I love pineapple because it makes everything a little sweeter. I like it sliced in a variety of thicknesses, but my preferred method of cooking a pineapple is whole on a spit. The natural sweetness slowly bastes itself as the pineapple slowly spins over the hot fire. **MAKES 1 JUICY PINEAPPLE**

WHAT YOU NEED: 1 rotisserie rod with 2 rotisserie tines, 1 counterweight and 1 rotisserie motor; Injection syringe; 1 pan, for drippings; Fresh herb basting brush (page 22)

1 ripe pineapple
½ cup + 2 oz (185 mL) spiced rum
½ cup (125 mL) brown sugar
¼ cup (60 mL) molasses
1 juicy orange
2 tsp (10 mL) cold butter
Bone Dust BBQ Spice (page 212)
    to taste

Set up rotisserie as per manufacturer's instructions.

Using a sharp knife, cut top and bottom off the pineapple. With the help of a friend, one holding the pineapple and one holding the rotisserie rod, push the rotisserie rod through the center of the pineapple, starting at either the top or bottom. The core of a pineapple is pretty firm, so you will need a little muscle to push it through. A few taps with a rubber mallet on the end of the rotisserie rod can help make this easier. You want to push carefully so that you don't spit the pineapple in half. I leave the rind on to help keep you from squishing the pineapple and losing all those sweet tasty juices. The thinner the rotisserie rod, the easier it is to do.

Next, suck up the spiced rum with the injection syringe. Inject the pineapple through the rind with the rum. Plunge it in, give it a push and pull it out. Repeat. This will get the rum marinade deep inside the pineapple. Set aside to marinate for 30 minutes.

Fire up your grill to 450–550°F (230–290°C).

In a small saucepot over low heat, warm the brown sugar, molasses and 2 oz (60 mL) rum until the sugar has dissolved. Cut the orange in half and squeeze as much of the juice out of it as you can. Remove from heat and stir in butter, ½ tsp (2 mL) at a time, stirring to incorporate. Set aside, keeping warm.

Using a sharp knife, carefully cut the rind from the pineapple, removing the "eyes" as well.

Slide the rotisserie tines over the end of the rotisserie rod, one on either end, and press the spikes firmly into the pineapple; push it in as far as you can. Tighten fly nuts to secure. Place pineapple onto rotisserie motor and place a drip pan underneath to catch the juices and basting sauce. Turn on the motor and cook pineapple for 30–45 minutes, basting occasionally with the brown sugar rum butter baste and sprinkling with a little Bone Dust BBQ Spice every now and then until the pineapple is hot and tender throughout. Remove from grill.

Carefully remove hot tines and slide hot juicy pineapple off the rotisserie rod. Using a sharp knife, hot shave the rotisserie of pineapple into thin strips. Pile the hot juicy strips of pineapple onto a platter. Drizzle with any reserved spiced rum butter sauce and serve immediately.

ACKNOWLEDGMENTS

PAMELA: You are my heart and soul and the foundation of our family. You are the very best. I love you!

LAYLA AND JORDAN, MY WICKEDLY DELICIOUS LITTLE EATERS: Your smiles bring sunshine and inspiration.

GREG COSWAY AND LES MURRAY, MY PARTNERS IN TED'S WORLD FAMOUS BBQ AND CHEF EVENTS: You have worked very hard on rebuilding Ted Reader and my world of BBQ. T2 (as you like to say) is on the right track and I am proud to be in business with you and love that your passion for me and my barbeque world is so strong and focused. Thanks for taking care of business and allowing me to do what I do best. Cook!
tedreader.com

CAITI MCLELLAND: WOW! Thank you for all your hard work. This book would not have happened without your true expertise and dedicated hard work. Thanks for the continued "pushes" to keep me on track. Thank you so much!

WENDY BASKERVILLE: My dearest friend Wendy, thank you for coming to my rescue and helping me with this book. We have shared many great times together. You are part of our family and my children love their Aunty Wendy. Your knowledge and talent with food is truly passionate. Thank you. I love ya!

PENGUIN BOOKS: Thank you to Andrea Magyar and the entire team for the opportunity to write *Gastro Grilling*. I am looking forward to future projects together.

STEPHEN MURDOCH: Stephen, what can I say; you are one amazing publicist. You're a movable feast in the promotional world. Thanks for all your support and for getting me some truly amazing press.

DUFF DIXON AND ONTARIO GAS BBQ: Thanks for all your support over the years, Duff. Ontario Gas BBQ is the world's largest BBQ store and you definitely know how to make things sizzle.
bbqs.com

RALPH JAMES, MY AWESOME AGENT: You bring the sizzle to my rockin' barbeque world. Thanks for all your support and encouragement. May our fires continue to burn hot!
theagencygroup.com

MIKE MCCOLL, PHOTOGRAPHER: Once again your photography is amazing. Thanks so much for all your hard work on *Gastro Grilling* and thanks to your photo assistant Lee Waddington.
photoswithsauce.com

MIA BACHMAIER, PRINCIPAL FOOD STYLIST: Thank you for all your hard work on *Gastro Grilling*. Your artistry with the food styling makes the recipes look so delicious, you could eat the pages! Thank you as well to your entire team of chefs, Logan Prong, Tara Grobb and Patrick Engel. Great job!

BLUE GOOSE ORGANICS: To my good, healthy and organic friends at Blue Goose Organics, you guys make me believe that we can make a difference in food, for our children, for the future and for today. Tasty deliciousness that's good for you – AMAZING! I look forward to creating more great products with you and your awesome team! **bluegooseorganics.com**

LABATT CANADA: Charlie and Briar, the yin to my yang, for what would a hot meal off the grill be without ice cold beer right out of the cooler! I love all beer and you guys have a portfolio that pairs perfectly with my culinary style — thanks, and of course cheers!

JIM BEAM: As anyone and everyone who knows me will tell you, I love bourbon, and the folks at Jim Beam make some of the finest anywhere on the planet and they serve it the world over. Thanks, Dorene, for working with us as we rushed to get this book out the door, and I am greatly looking forward to our project together in 2014!

BLACK ANGUS FINE MEATS & GAME: Thank you for your amazing support! Your beef and game are farm-to-table delicious. Cooking is made easy when you have the best quality. All the best! **blackangusmeat.com**

TABASCO®: Thank you for all your great support! I do love my Tabasco! It's my secret ingredient! **tabascosauce.ca**

BRAZILIAN FIRE & ICE: Thank you Maxine for your wonderful grilling stones. The 100% Canadian soapstone grilling stones truly are wonderful. They heat evenly and as a grill accessory they make it fun, easy and absolutely delicious. **brazilianice.com**

CREEKSIDE ESTATE WINERY: Andrew, I remember when Greg first told me about investing in the wine biz, I was left thinking he might just be crazier than I am! From what I hear, things are coming along very nicely, and from what I have tasted, I would say very nicely indeed!

TO THE WORLD OF BBQ: BBQ chefs, fanatics, grill meisters and smoke masters, thank you all for your continued support. Thanks for your passion for the world of smoke and barbeque. You fuel my fire. You are all my inspiration. Keep it sticky and always make it delicious!

INDEX

ABOUT THE AUTHOR

Ted Reader is an award-winning celebrity chef and food entertainer with a legendary passion for the open flame. He is the author of over a dozen bestselling cookbooks, a celebrity spokesperson and culinary consultant for several large food companies and retailers, and the proprietor of a popular line of sauces and seasonings called *Ted's World Famous BBQ*. Ted is a regular guest on TV and radio and has been profiled in a variety of magazines, including *GQ*.

Photo courtesy of Adrian Fiebig